Climb Every Mountain

HELP US KEEP THIS GUIDE UP TO DATE

Every effort has been made by the authors and editors to make this guide as accurate and useful as possible. However, many things can change after a guide is published.

We would love to hear from you concerning your experiences with this guide and how you feel it could be improved and kept up to date. While we may not be able to respond to all comments and suggestions, we'll take them to heart, and we'll also make certain to share them with the authors. Please send your comments and suggestions to the following email address: editorial@GlobePequot.com.

Thanks for your input!

Climb Every Mountain

46 of the Northeast's 111 Hikes over 4,000 Feet

Michele Hernandez Bayliss
and Dean J. Ouellette

FALCONGUIDES

ESSEX, CONNECTICUT

FALCONGUIDES®

An imprint of Globe Pequot, the trade division of
The Rowman & Littlefield Publishing Group, Inc.
4501 Forbes Blvd., Ste. 200
Lanham, MD 20706
www.rowman.com

Falcon and FalconGuides are registered trademarks and Make Adventure Your Story is a trademark of The Rowman & Littlefield Publishing Group, Inc.

Distributed by NATIONAL BOOK NETWORK

British Library Cataloguing in Publication Information available

Library of Congress Cataloging-in-Publication Data
Names: Bayliss, Michele Hernandez, author. | Ouellette, Dean J., author.
Title: Climb every mountain : 46 of the Northeast's 111 hikes over 4,000 feet / Michele
   Hernandez Bayliss and Dean J. Ouellette.
Description: Essex, Connecticut : FalconGuides, [2023] | Summary: "A guide for adventurers-from the
   freshly booted novice to the grizzled mountaineer-to the Northeast's iconic mountains that top out at over
   4,000 feet"— Provided by publisher.
Identifiers: LCCN 2022041691 (print) | LCCN 2022041692 (ebook) | ISBN 9781493070718 (paperback)
   | ISBN 9781493070725 (epub)
Subjects: LCSH: Hiking—New England—Guidebooks. | Hiking—New York (State)—Guidebooks. |
   Mountaineering—New England—Guidbooks. | Mountaineering—New York (State)—Guidebooks. |
   Trails—New England—Guidebooks. | Trails—New York (State)—Guidebooks. | New England—
   Guidebooks. | New York (State)—Guidebooks.
Classification: LCC GV199.42.N38 B38 2023 (print) | LCC GV199.42.N38 (ebook) |
   DDC 796.510974—dc23/eng/20220929
LC record available at https://lccn.loc.gov/2022041691
LC ebook record available at https://lccn.loc.gov/2022041692

∞™ The paper used in this publication meets the minimum requirements of American National Standard for Information Sciences—Permanence of Paper for Printed Library Materials, ANSI/NISO Z39.48-1992.

To my husband, Bruce, who endured my long absences and supported my outdoor explorations; to my children, Alexia and Ian, who cheered me on and often accompanied me; to my longstanding hiking partner, Dean; and to my canine companion, German shepherd and hiker extraordinaire, Argos, who protected me on many solo hikes. Deep thanks to some of my other dedicated and hardcore hiking partners, especially Donna Dearborn, Joyce Mailman, and Heather Shepard.

—Michele Bayliss

To my kids, Alexis and Matthew—completing their 46er journey with them was one of my most precious accomplishments. To Michele for providing the "drive" early in our hiking partnership that transformed me from an "If I have time to hike" hiker to "I will find the time to hike" hiker. Peak bagging isn't so bad after all. And, of course, to Heather, my forever partner. We always find joy with each other, no matter where our adventures take us.

—Dean Ouellette

Contents

CANADA

UNITED STATES

North Troy

Colebrook

11

Lake
Champlain

2

VERMONT

89

91

87

9

21

Morrisville

Stowe

2

93

3

19

91

Montpelier

302

7

Bristol

22

302

23-42

89

Granville

Moosilauke

93

Hancock

Fairlee

NEW YORK

91

Plymouth

93

3

Lake
Winnepesaukee

GREEN MOUNTAIN
NATIONAL FOREST

1-16

4

20

4

4

Ludlow

Ascutney

89

Tilton

87

9

7

91

Concord

4

5

Jamaica

NEW HAMPSHIRE

Manchester

GREEN MOUNTAIN
NATIONAL FOREST

Keene

202

93

Wilton

90

Williamstown

88

91

202

495

Albany

5

190

290

90

87

90

7

Lee

MASSACHUSETTS

18

9

90

Holyoke

90

395

495

17

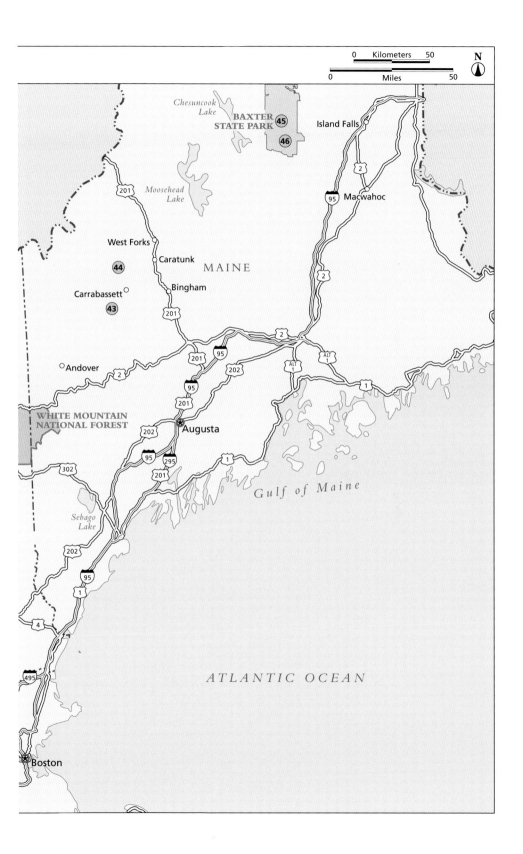

Acknowledgments

We couldn't have completed this project without the help, encouragement, and expertise of all the amazing folks at FalconGuides including editorial director David Legere, senior production editor Meredith Dias, copy editor extraordinaire Paulette Baker, layout artist Melissa Evarts, proofreader Kris Patenaude, and the entire production team. We give deep thanks for believing in our project, for your time and care in producing a definitive guide, and for making us look good with awesome graphics and layout. Honored to work with the "A-team."

Meet Your Guides

Michele

Although I attended Dartmouth College, which has the oldest and probably best outing club in the country, I didn't take advantage of the world-class hiking right in my backyard in New Hampshire. It really wasn't until my 40s, when I moved to Weybridge, Vermont, a town of 800 near Middlebury (home of Middlebury College), that I got the hiking bug when my neighbor Dean invited me to hike with his kids. By day, I am president of Top Tier Admissions, a company dedicated to helping students earn admission to college. When I'm not working, I'm training or hiking. Once I realized you could earn patches for different hiking lists, it was GAME ON. For the next ten years, I (along with Dean) knocked off a bunch of hiking lists, and my confidence and wilderness experience grew exponentially. By the writing of this book, I have completed the 46 high peaks in New York's Adirondack Mountains (my assigned number is #7146, meaning 7,145 people completed the challenge before me); the 48 peaks in New Hampshire's White Mountains (regular and winter); the Northeast 111 (all the high peaks in Vermont, New York, New Hampshire, and Maine over 4,000 feet (my assigned completion number is #706); and the Northeast 111 (winter—my assigned completion number is #82). Along the way, I realized there was also a patch for hiking one of the 4,000-footers every calendar day (the "4K a day" grid). I started filling in holes so I could hike all 366 days (including leap years) of the year. By May 3, 2022, I had earned my number, #30, for completing this hiking challenge. Though I've hiked in the Austrian, Italian, and French Alps, the Dolomites, and the Pyrenees, some of the gnarliest hiking I've done has been right here in the United States' Northeast. Many of the hikes we describe are difficult, especially in winter, but they are all doable if you have the knowledge, dedication, and mindset to take on challenges. My hope is that this guide encourages aspiring hikers to build their stamina, set goals, and hit the trails with a safety-first mentality.

Dean

I am a native Vermonter and have lived here my entire life. Electrician by trade, I have been working for Middlebury College for the past twenty-two years, the last nine as their Energy and Technology Manager. Hiking and backpacking have been my passion since I was a teenager in the Boy Scouts. I thru-hiked Vermont's Long Trail after college, then started hiking in New York and New Hampshire in my early 20s. When my kids got to a good hiking age, they had my enthusiasm and desire to hit the trail as well, so I took them as often as I could. I have hiked on and around Mount Hood in Oregon, in the Great Smoky Mountains, the Austrian and Italian Alps, the Dolomites, the Grand Canyon, and Yosemite National Park. Like Michele, I have several

Michele and Dean in the Pyrenees Michele Hernandez Bayliss

patches—Adirondack Mountain Club (ADK) 46er, Northeast 111, New Hampshire 48—all of which were earned in winter. I'm currently (albeit slowly) working on an ADK Grid (hiking all forty-six mountains in every month of the year). Three years ago, I met someone who shared my love of hiking/backpacking and adventure. Would you believe that we met on Mount Abraham in Vermont and two years later I was asking her to marry me on top of that very same mountain? Heather and I plan to honeymoon, where else, on a thru-hike of the John Muir Trail in California.

Introduction

State/Region Overview

The Northeast 111 challenge covers a huge area across four states and various wilderness preserves. We give you all the key information you need for these hikes including the additional four peaks that were later found to be slightly under 4,000 feet, though you still have to hike them to finish the NE 111 challenge. A bit of background about the various hiker lists and corresponding patches you can earn from completing them is in order, as many New England hikers are obsessed with these lists.

In our home state of Vermont, there are five "high peaks" (defined as peaks over 4,000 feet). Ninety minutes from our base near Middlebury, Vermont, lie the Adirondack Mountains in New York State, a rugged set of mountains nestled in a huge 6-million-acre wilderness. There are forty-six high peaks over 4,000 feet of elevation in the Adirondack High Peak region, and if you hike all forty-six of them, you can apply to become an ADK 46er. At that point, you get to put a number after your name.

If you hike them all in winter, you get to put a "W" after your number on the official roster (Dean and I are #7146W and #7145W) and you get another patch, actually a blue-and-white "rocker" sticker that curves under the 46er patch and says "winter."

Grace Hudowalski was one of the original founders of the Adirondack 46ers and the first woman to climb all forty-six peaks. The official emblem was designed in 1948, with the winter rocker patch not being added until fall of 1991. In the "old" days, the trailless peaks had glass canisters (later, metal) on every summit, and you had to add your name to the notebook as "proof" that you made it. By 1961, every summit had an official canister. By the time we joined the group, they had done away with the canister system, yielding to an honor system. There are stories about winter hikers making it to a remote peak only to find the canister buried so deep that they were unable to locate it and therefore could not "count" the peak. Some climbers spent hours trying to shovel away enough snow to unearth the canister. So . . . maybe the honor system is okay after all. In honor of Grace, the peak previously known as East Dix was renamed Grace Peak in 2014.

Three to four hours to the east of us (in New Hampshire) lie the White Mountains and the majestic Presidential Range (home of Mount Washington, featuring the worst weather on the planet), which constitute part of the forty-eight New Hampshire peaks over 4,000 feet. There are a few outliers, like Mount Cabot and Mount Waumbek to the north, Mount Moosilauke to the southwest, to Whiteface and Passaconaway in the southeast.

If you hike them all, you become an AMC Four Thousand Footer Club member (you also get an AMC 4,000 patch). The Four Thousand Footer Club of New

Hampshire was founded in 1957, a decade after the Adirondack 46ers, to introduce hikers to the lesser-known peaks of the White Mountains.

To our north, there are fourteen high peaks in the state of Maine. If you hike all the high peaks in Vermont, New Hampshire, and Maine, you get a patch for the New England 67. And if you add New York (the Adirondacks) to New England and venture south to climb the two 4,000-plus-foot peaks in the Catskills (New York), you earn the mother of all patches, the Northeast 111 (well, there are actually 115 peaks, but the club is called the Northeast 111, since some peaks were added after the 111 designation, when more accurate surveys were done).

New Hampshire added two peaks (Galehead, Bondcliff) and changed Wildcat E to Wildcat D; Maine added Spaulding and Redington. Those four additional peaks technically make it the New England 115, but we will use the official name, the Northeast 111. Four Adirondack peaks are actually *under* 4,000 feet—Couchsachraga, Nye, Blake, and Cliff—but you still have to hike them. Many hikers have shed tears upon hearing that news, because Couchsachraga is quite a haul to get to on a three-peak day; Blake is notoriously remote and difficult as well. Over a period of five years, we chipped away at the Northeast 111, earning our patch with completion number #705 (Dean) and #706 (Michele).

Different clubs run each list. The Appalachian Mountain Club (AMC) Four Thousand Footer Club recognizes the White Mountain Four Thousand Footers (the forty-eight White Mountain peaks), the New England Four Thousand Footers (those plus the fourteen in Maine), the New England Hundred Highest (the one hundred highest peaks in Vermont, New Hampshire, and Maine), and the Northeast 111 Club (the sixty-seven in Maine, New Hampshire, and Vermont plus the Adirondacks and the two in the Catskills). The Adirondack Mountain clubs runs the ADK 46er lists. A hiking diehard named "Hiker Ed" (I am not kidding) runs the "grid" lists, which we will touch upon below.

One of the toughest patches to earn is the Winter Northeast 111—doing all 115 Northeast peaks between December 21 (actually, the solstice) and March 21 (the vernal equinox). My number for the NE Winter 111 is #82; Dean's is #83. Only a handful of women are on that list, as winter is a whole different ball game.

Some might say, "But 4,000 feet doesn't sound very high." I used to live out West and have climbed 12,000- to 14,000-foot peaks in Colorado, Oregon, Wyoming, and British Columbia. Sure, the peaks are higher, but your initial altitude is high too, so the elevation gain isn't necessarily as great. Not to mention that many western trails were designed for horse and buggy and tend to be wider, less steep (often a *lot* less steep), and more switchback-y (meaning the trail avoids steep inclines by curving back and forth as it rises rather than simply pointing straight up the side of the mountain)—a concept all but unknown to the early Adirondack trail builders.

In contrast, the Adirondacks are gnarly due to brutally steep trails, nary a switchback in sight, very few flat sections that last more than a few feet, mud (often incredible amounts of mud), bugs, man-eating spruce traps in winter (the hole created around a spruce tree that can swallow you whole into a vortex of snow), rugged (and often unmarked) trails, and herd paths. New Hampshire's Presidential Range has some of the worst and most dangerous weather on the planet (why many Mount Rainer climbers train in the Presidentials in the winter), and Maine is just, well, Maine. Out of the weeks we spent tackling some of the most remote mountains of the group, we rarely saw another human being (only on Mount Speck, the most southerly); most often we were the only winter hikers on the mountain. Our Maine refrain was "Where is everyone?"

Another challenge involves doing any major list in a "single season." For the normal patch, you just have to hike all the mountains in a group over time; for example, it might take you eight winters to hike the forty-six peaks in the Adirondacks. But there are those crazy people (see "gridders," or "gridiots," as they are sometimes lovingly referred to) who hike all forty-six ADK or all AMC 4,000-footers in *a single winter season* (which is crazy and takes a lot of dedication). Dean and his fiancée, Heather, did what is known as an ADK Single Season Winter 46er (ADK SSW) during the winter of 2020. Not only that, they added the optional forty-seventh peak, MacNaughton.

The other major type of list is an iteration of the "grid"—basically, the grid part means doing all mountains in a certain region in *every month* of the year. For the ADK grid, that means hiking all forty-six mountains in every calendar month (46 × 12 = 552 hikes). Dean is currently working on this ADK grid, which is much less common than the White Mountain grid, which entails hiking all forty-eight peaks in every month (48 × 12 = 576 hikes). Although I've no interest in doing either of those grids (mostly because there are some mountains I truly don't love, and the thought of doing them ten more times makes me want to cry, and it's supposed to be *fun*), when my hiking buddy Donna introduced me to the "4K every day" grid list, it sounded enticing. This list entails hiking *any* of the 115 peaks in the Northeast 111 *every calendar day*. The rule is, you can only count one peak at a time, and you can't camp unless you are at the trailhead; every hike has to start from the trailhead and be done as a day hike.

On the bright side, you can hike the same mountain all 365 (or 366) days if you want. There are no rules as to which ones, so if you lived near Mount Washington, you could hike it every day *over time*—not in one year—as long as you climbed a high peak January 1, 2, 3, and so on, for every single day of the year. When the pandemic started in March 2020, I was at 38 percent of the "4K a day." I completed this challenge in May 2022, earning my "4K a day" number: #30.

Some of the major hiking lists are listed below so you can get an idea of how many people are tackling each challenge and how many challenges there are. In addition, there are dozens of Facebook groups dedicated to the 4,000-footer list, aspiring gridders, ADK hikers, and the like. The hiking community is supportive and thousands strong, and I love reading about everyone's adventures.

Note: The AMC/New England list was last updated in April 2022.

AMC 4,000-footers regular season:	16,729
AMC 4,000-footers winter:	1,020
AMC 4,000-footers: four-season:	46
NE 4,000-footers (67—VT, NH, ME):	4,091
NE 4,000-footers winter: (67—VT, NH, ME):	220
NE Hundred Highest:	1,164
NE Hundred Highest winter:	129
NE 111:	1,147
NE 111 winter:	107

Note: The grid list was up to date as of November 2022.

White Mountain/NH Grid (48 x 12):	132
NE 4,000 footers (67 x 12 –VT, NH, ME):	4
NE Hundred Highest (100 x 12):	1
NE 111 (111 x 12):	1
ADK 46 (46 x 12):	26
4,000 footer every day (366):	30

In addition, sixty-five people have "traced" every section of marked trail in the White Mountains, and ten people (including some couples) have completed the New Hampshire 500 highest peaks. Interestingly, dogs can also complete the list—as of August 1, 2022, 419 dogs have summited all forty-eight New Hampshire High Peaks.

Weather

The weather in the Northeast corridor, where all these hikes take place, varies wildy from one season to another. These ranges are very spread out, but in general there are four seasons, which we'll define more by the actual weather than the strict "official" cutoff of the equinoxes and solstices. The joke in the Northeast is that "spring" typically doesn't truly arrive until well into April/May.

Spring

Late March to mid-June is probably the most unpleasent time to hike, and many trails are closed. One issue is winter's melting snow, which doesn't disappear fully until as late as June/July. But with the typical rains of spring, the remaining snow shrinks to an awful "monorail" of rotten snow and ice that makes the trails often very challenging, as well as downright unpleasant. Add the emergence of blackflies and copious mud, and you have the perfect storm of the least desirable hiking season.

Summer

Mid-June to late August is the most popular time to hike, and for good reason. At some point the blackflies disappear (though mosquitoes can always be a problem), the sun dries out the trails, and hikers can enjoy amazing views and warm weather. The biggest issue for summer is dehydration. Water on the trail can be scarce (and you have to filter it or treat it with tablets), so you have to carry more than you think you'll need. I found that salt/electrolyte tabs help a ton for those who have trouble dealing with heat. In fact, they saved my life. I am a die-hard winter hiker, but I hate hot weather. I sweat so much that I lose too many electrolytes and have trouble staying hydrated. Now I carry things like V-8 juice, chicken or veggie bouillion, and water with electrolyte powder to maintain my salt and electrolytes. A hat to block the sun is also very helpful, as are DEET-filled bug repellent and plenty of additional warm gear. Keep in mind that you can experience frigid weather in these mountains even in August. We have experienced a drop from 80°F in the valley (in Gorham, New Hampshire, where we started) to a violent hail storm with 50 mile-per-hour winds on top of Mount Adams a few hours later. The moral of the story is: Always, always carry rain gear, along with extra warm layers such as a down jacket, warm vest, mid-layer fleece, or a combination thereof (we cover winter gear in appendix B) even on a warm summer day. You will never regret it. In June 2022, a freak summer storm brought snow and ice to the Presidentials, and an experienced hiker died of hypothermia while attempting a Presidential traverse. Be prepared! It can make the difference between life and death.

Fall

Late August/early September to mid-December weather can range from beautiful fall foliage and clear skies to frigid rain/hail and ice. Check both local and mountain weather forecasts before you hike. From mid-September onward we carry microspikes (Hillsound and Kathoola both make these), which are mini-crampons designed for thin ice over rock/dirt. In winter, when the ice gets thicker, you occassionally need real 8- or 10-point crampons, which are much more aggressive. Fall is one of the most quintessentially New England hiking experiences, and trails are less crowded after Labor Day. It's our second favorite season besides winter, and the foliage and cooler weather make this a terrific time to tackle mountains.

Winter

Mid-December to late March, mountain temperatures often plunge to below zero. You must carry a lot of extra gear, insulated water bottles so your liquid doesn't freeze, and speciality equipment like proper snowshoes, microspikes, or sometimes crampons. We cover winter gear in appendix B, but we recommend carrying extra warm clothing, extra hats/mittens, and an emergency locator beacon. Certain areas, like the Presidential Range in New Hampshire, are known for some of the worst weather in the entire world, rivaling polar regions and Mount Everest, according to the Mount

Washington Weather Observatory (mountwashington.org) where you can track the higher summits forecast. Many books have been written about the deaths that have occurred in these mountains. If there is one safety factor we can emphasize, it's checking the weather and checking it again, especially in winter but truly year-round. Most rescues take a long time, and you cannot count on rescuers reaching you in time when temperatures are as extreme as they often are in winter. We will describe some of our winter hikes to make this evident, but keep in mind that there are rescues almost every few days in these mountains. Be prepared, and don't go above tree line if the winds are over 50 miles per hour or the predicted temps are below minus 20°F.

Flora and Fauna

The most salient feature of the mountain environment in the Northeast is the presence of rare alpine vegetation on many peaks. In fact, some popular mountains, like Mount Marcy in the Adirondacks and Mount Abraham in Vermont, have summit stewards in the summer to remind hikers not to trample the alpine vegetation. Always be careful as you approach any summit to stay on the path (sometimes ropes are set up to facilitate this) so you can help maintain this fragile environment.

Since these hikes span four states, you will find all sorts of amazing trees from birch to pines, spruce traps up high in winter (where snow gathers around pine trees), tons of grouse and jays, hawks, eagles, deer, and the occasional moose. We have been lucky enough to come across moose a few times, twice in Maine and once in New Hampshire on the way to Zealand Hut. Be respectful of wildlife, and remember—you do not want to tangle with an aggressive bull moose.

Don't feed the animals, and guard your packs against aggressive pine martins, which may gnaw through your pack to get to food (one gnawed through my rubber microspikes on a winter camping trip, rendering them useless). In spring and summer, keep an eye out for blueberries and raspberries along the trail and Indian cucumbers, which you can pull up and eat. Though there are always interesting mushrooms, I don't know enough to pick out which ones are edible. In short, be respectful of the environment, don't agitate or feed animals, and pick up after yourself—leave no trace! That includes packing out toilet paper/wipes so we can preserve our beautiful wilderness areas.

Wilderness Restrictions/Regulations

The mountains that make up the Northeast 111 extend over four states and hundreds of miles. Even within the Adirondack Park, different sections have different wilderness/camping restrictions and regulations. We list specifics under each hike, but be sure to check specific guidelines for each area, which can differ from one mountain to the next.

Before You Hit the Trail

This book covers forty-six of the iconic high peaks (over 4,000 feet) spanning wilderness areas in New York, Vermont, New Hampshire, and Maine. The challenge of a region this large is that the wilderness areas are very spread out, from Baxter State Park in Maine, to the White Mountains of New Hampshire, to the Catskills and Adirondack Park in New York State, to disparate areas of Vermont and Maine.

We give you all the key information you need for these hikes, plus a complete list of all the hikes with shorter descriptions should you take on the challenge of completing the Northeast 111.

Each hike begins with a brief description, including highlights. This introduction is followed by informative specs.

Start: This is the starting location for the hike.

Distance: The distance specified in each description is listed as a round-trip from the trailhead to the end of the route and back. When car spots are possible, we mention that in the description.

Hike lengths have been estimated as closely as possible using GPS. Most hikers today use apps like Strava, All Trails, or their own GPS units, so we wanted to be forward-looking and provide GPS coordinates. When we refer to a stated distance from an actual sign, we reference it directly.

Because earlier guidebooks often have incorrect mileage and even mileage signs can be out of date, we use GPS coordinates. As a recommendation, we'd rely more on the hiking time than the mileage, as a mountain mile can often take way longer than a normal mile due to rough terrain, elevation gain, and obstacles like mud and rocks. Hikers often joke about an "Adirondack mile," which is a lot longer than you might think. For these mountains, the standard time calculation is 2 miles per hour plus 30 minutes for every 1,000 feet of elevation. If you are doing an 8-mile hike with 2,000 feet of elevation gain, you should allow at least 5 hours.

Summit elevation: Elevation of the actual summit as what is on the official entry sheet to becoming a Northeast 111er.

4,000-footers rank of the 115: In order from tallest to shortest.

Elevation gain: Elevation is generally the most important factor in determining a hike's difficulty. Most of the time, the trailhead lies at the low point and the end lies at the highest point, although many hikes feature ups and downs on bumpy ridges, and some hikes include an out-and-back to another mountain that makes the elevation gain greater. All the hikes we describe generally have between 2,200 and 5,500 feet of elevation gain, though in theory you can hike Mount Abraham in Vermont the "easy" way from the gap road (1,600 feet) rather than from the Battell Trail (2,500 feet). Because most of the Northeast is close to sea level, it's not the total altitude that makes these hikes hard but the elevation gain, pure and simple. Even the "easy" hikes have significant gain, so it's important to set a moderate uphill pace and not start out too fast. Mount Washington is the highest peak in the Northeast, with an elevation of 6,288 feet. Even hikers who are sensitive to altitude will most likely not notice the high elevation, as the effects of altitude sickness tend to occur at altitudes over 12,000 feet. As with the mileage, GPS is used to determine the elevation gain for each hike.

Difficulty: Assessing a hike's difficulty is very subjective. The elevation, elevation change, and length all play a role, as do trail conditions, weather, and the hiker's physical condition. For us, elevation gain and hours required were the most significant variables in establishing levels of difficulty. Keep in mind that even so-called "easy" hikes in this book are still hard, since all these hikes are considered "high peaks" and all involve a significant amount of elevation gain. The main differences are that some of these hikes are lower mileage and some are all-day treks, especially in winter, when the winter trailhead can be farther way.

The book's chapters are broken up into regions, and each region, as best we could, lists the hikes in order from easiest to hardest. This is subjective and, as noted earlier, many factors are at play, depending on the day.

Hiking time: The average time required to complete the hike.

Trails used: The trails used for the hike to help keep you on track. We use trail names found on popular hiking apps, which may differ slightly from other guidebooks but will makes sense when reading this guide.

Nearest town: The nearest town is the closest city or town to the hike's trailhead that has at least minimal visitor services. The listed town will usually have gas, food, and limited lodging available. In small towns and villages, the hours these services are available may be limited.

Views: The quality of what you'll see along the hike as well as the summit.

Water sources: Where you're likely to find water during the hike.

Canine compatibility: This section describes whether dogs are allowed on the trail. Generally, even where allowed, dogs need to be leashed. In the Adirondacks, dogs are not permitted in any area run by the AMR (Adirondack Mountain Reserve) or the Ausable Club, so check local regulations before bringing your dog. Some regions, like the northern Presidentials, are so rocky that they are tough on dogs' paw pads. Others are simply impossible for dogs; for example, climbing or descending the Saddleback cliffs. Please be courteous and pick up after your dog.

Special considerations: Here is where unique elements of the trail or trailhead that require extra preparation will be listed. This might include water availability, dangerous weather, sun exposure, or dangerous water crossings. Any parking fees will also be noted here.

Finding the trailhead: This section provides detailed directions to the trailhead. With a basic current state highway map or GPS unit, you can easily locate the starting point from the directions. In general, the nearest town is used as the starting point.

Most of this guide's hikes have trailheads that can be reached by a normal car. Except in wet or snowy weather, only a very few usually require four-wheel drive. Rain or snow can temporarily make some roads impassable. Before venturing onto unmaintained dirt roads, you should check with park or forest headquarters. On less-traveled back roads, especially in Maine, you should carry basic emergency equipment such as a shovel, chains, water, a spare tire, a jack, blankets, and some extra food and clothing. Make sure your vehicle is in good operating condition with a full tank of gas.

Theft and vandalism occasionally occur at trailheads. Try not to leave valuables in your car at all; if you must, lock them out of sight in the trunk. We have never had our car broken into, but we have seen cars with smashed windows, so don't leave anything in clear view.

The Hike: All the hikes selected for this guide can be done by people in good physical condition. A little scrambling may be necessary for a few of the hikes, but none require any rock-climbing skills (though the Saddleback cliffs are close). Several hikes in this guide follow designated "herd" paths rather than trails. Always bring a real map and study the trail before you go, as there are rescues almost every day of the year. You should have an experienced hiker, along with a compass, maps, and a GPS unit, with your group before attempting those hikes, at least until you have a few under your belt.

The trails are often marked with rock cairns or blazes. Most of the time the paths are very obvious and easy to follow, but the marks help when the trails are faint or little-used. Cairns are piles of rock built along the route. Tree blazes are painted markings on trees, usually at shoulder or head height. Blazes can be especially useful when a forest trail is obscured by snow. Be sure not to add your own blazes or cairns—they can confuse the route. Leave such markings to the official trail workers. Sometimes, especially in the Adirondacks, small plastic markers are nailed to trees to mark the route.

Possible backcountry campsites are often suggested in the descriptions. Many others are usually available. In the national forests, there are usually few restrictions in selecting a campsite, provided that it is well away from the trail or any water source. Most of the state and national parks require that certain backcountry campsites be used. State parks charge a small fee; national parks sometimes do.

After reading the descriptions, pick the hikes that catch your fancy. There is no shame in turning back before the summit. As we said, many of these hikes are arduous, and it's better to return safe and unharmed than to have search-and-rescue teams spend time and money looking for you. We read the rescue reports and can assure you that hikers get lost or injured and rescued almost every day of the year. Don't be one of those hikers.

Miles and Directions: To help you stay on course, a detailed route finder sets forth mileages between significant landmarks along the trail. Though previous guidebooks used the "old" mileages measured years ago by wheel, we used Gaia GPS software to calculate mileage, so there will be discrepancies from posted signs and mountain guidebooks, although sometimes we mention the "sign mileage" as a waypoint. We find that time is a more helpful variable than mileage (most European trails are marked with time rather than mileage). Most hikers we see on the trail use some kind of GPS tracking, from SPOT devices to Strava, so GPS info is most likely the future of hiking.

Additional Information

Seasons

Every Northeast season has its charms, and we described some of the general seasons above. Naturally, the fall foliage season is incredibly beautiful and one of our favorite times to hike. One thing to keep in mind, though, is ice at high elevations. After September 15, we rarely leave the house without throwing in our Hillsound microspikes, which are like mini-crampons. Though you may not see ice at the trailhead, many peaks cannot be safely ascended in fall/early winter without microspikes. Winter is our favorite season to hike—no mud, no bugs, fewer people. Though it can be easy when trails are packed out from large groups with snowshoes, it can also be brutal when trail breaking is involved. A hike that might take 5 hours with broken-out trails can take 10 or more when the trail needs to be broken out. We cover winter layering techniques and equipment in appendix B, so don't hike in winter without educating yourself.

Spring may be the worst season to hike in New England, with blackflies, mud, leftover rotting snow, and closed trails. By May/June, the worst is usually over and you can get out on the trail again. Many hikers love July and August hiking. For me, it's too hot; I don't do well in heat/humidity. Summer also brings crowds and inexperienced hikers, who venture out without taking the proper safety precautions. In any case, that won't be you, since you will read in depth about hiking conditions and equipment in this guide.

Fees and Permits

Typically most Northeast hikes do not require permits, but since these hikes span four states and several different parks, rules can change. Parking fees are noted in the "Special considerations" category. Bring cash, as credit cards are not accepted at most locations.

Maps

The maps in this guide are as accurate and current as possible. When used in conjunction with the hike description, you should have little trouble following the route.

GPS (Global Positioning System) units, particularly those with installed maps, can be very useful for route finding when used in conjunction with paper maps. However, anyone entering the backcountry should have at least basic knowledge in using a paper map and compass. Batteries die and GPS units get dropped; it's best not to be completely dependent on them. A GPS unit with maps installed can be particularly helpful on off-trail hikes and herd paths.

USGS quads can usually be purchased at outdoor shops or ordered directly from USGS at store.usgs.gov or from online companies such as mytopo.com or topozone .com. To order from USGS, know the state, the number desired of each map, the exact map name as listed in the hike heading, and the scale.

Cell Service

From our experience, there is very little cell service, if any, on many of these hikes, especially in the Adirondacks. The White Mountains have better cell service, but don't count on it. We highly recommend carrying a special device like an emergency locator beacon (I carry the ACR ResQlink 400 PLB) or a SPOT locater. Don't count on cell service anywhere in the mountains, and keep in mind that phone batteries die quickly in the cold.

MAP LEGEND

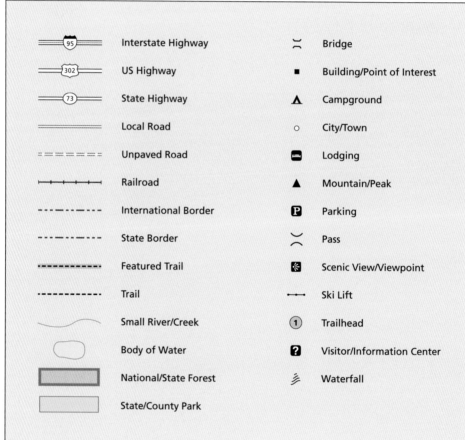

══95══	Interstate Highway	⌣̈	Bridge
══302══	US Highway	▪	Building/Point of Interest
══73══	State Highway	⚊	Campground
════	Local Road	○	City/Town
═ ═ ═ ═	Unpaved Road	▭	Lodging
├─┼─┼─┤	Railroad	▲	Mountain/Peak
─ ─ ·· ─ ─	International Border	🅿	Parking
─ ─ · ─ · ─	State Border	⌣	Pass
▬▬▬▬▬▬	Featured Trail	🏞	Scenic View/Viewpoint
─ ─ ─ ─ ─	Trail	•─→	Ski Lift
⌇	Small River/Creek	①	Trailhead
⬭	Body of Water	❓	Visitor/Information Center
▭	National/State Forest	〰	Waterfall
▭	State/County Park		

New York: Adirondacks

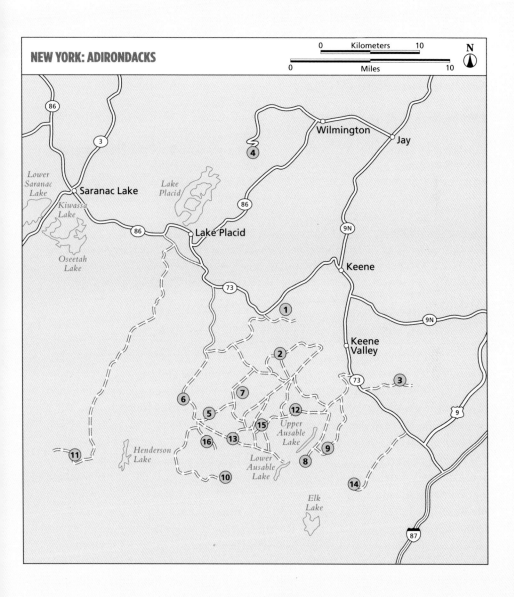

NEW YORK: ADIRONDACKS

1 Cascade and Porter

This is usually considered the "easiest" of the Adirondack 46 because it's shorter. Cascade has one of the most open summits of the range, with views to two-thirds of all the high peaks plus Lake Champlain to the east. Although I'm not the fastest hiker, I typically do both Cascade and Porter in 5 hours.

Start: Cascade Trailhead on NY 73
Distance: 5.7 miles out and back
Summit elevation: Cascade: 4,098 feet;
Porter: 4,059 feet
4,000-footers rank of the 115: Cascade: 83;
Porter: 90
Elevation gain: 2,268 feet
Difficulty: Moderate
Hiking time: 4.5-6 hours

Trails used: Cascade Mountain Trail, Porter Ridge Trail
Nearest town: Lake Placid, Keene
Views: Excellent
Water sources: A few at the beginning of the hike
Canine compatibility: Good. Ensure dogs are leashed above tree line.
Special considerations: Extremely busy trailhead with limited parking. Use caution.

Finding the trailhead: From the village of Lake Placid and the intersection of NY 73 and NY 86, travel east on NY 73 for 7.6 miles, where there are several small parking spaces on the side of the road. From the south and the village of Keene, you'll head east on NY 73 for 6.7 miles, passing the beautiful Cascade Lakes before coming to the parking areas. GPS (parking lot): N44°13'7.99" / W73°53'15.13"

The Hike

If you can, hike on a weekday, as this trail is super popular and parking can be tight. The trail descends to the trail register right from the highway guardrail and then climbs fairly gently (by Adirondack standards) on the Cascade Mountain Trail. After the first mile, the trail gets steeper and ascends a series of neat cliffs, each of which provides worthwhile views. The best view is just under 2 miles, on the highest ledge. On the bright side, there are short flat sections between some of the steeper parts so you can catch your breath. That top ledge means you are near the junction where you continue straight to Cascade or turn right to Porter Mountain. Depending on the weather, you can choose which to do first. Since weather usually gets worse later in the day, we typically head straight toward Cascade through the short and flat tunnel section that deposits you at the base of the final climb. If the wind is blowing or the weather is worsening, you will want to layer up here in the trees before you head out on the final short section up to the summit. Follow the blazes toward the right to a ladder that helps you ascend the final pitch until you break out onto the summit. Enjoy the tremendous views in every direction (I love the view from here of Algonquin, Iroquois, and Wright).

My daughter, Alexia, on the summit of Cascade with amazing views behind
MICHELE HERNANDEZ BAYLISS

When you've had your fill, descend carefully back to the ladder, follow the blazes, and head toward the small opening in the trees (in winter or poor visibility, you will want to take note of this opening when you ascend so you can find it again). Back at the junction, it's about a 30-minute hike to reach Porter. This section can be very muddy or icy, so it takes longer than you might think. Though you might see a big rock on the left and think that's the summit, it's not. Keep descending and you will reach a final "up" section to a flattish rock, which marks the summit. If you have any doubt, continue a few feet down the trail and you'll see the sign for Blueberry Ledge Trail—another route to reach Porter, though much longer. There are views to be had from this rock as well, and it's much more protected than Cascade. The return hike is fairly standard, and you can typically complete these two high peaks in under 6 hours.

DID YOU KNOW?

Porter Mountain is named for Dr. Noah Porter, president of Yale University for fifteen years in the late 1800s. He made the first recorded ascent of Porter Mountain, in 1875.

Miles and Directions

- **0.0** Start from the parking lot. Head downhill and sign the register.
- **1.8** Viewpoint toward Lake Placid.
- **2.0** Junction with Porter Ridge Trail; continue straight.
- **2.2** Follow painted blazes on the open rocks and rock cairns above tree line to the summit of Cascade Mountain. Retrace your steps off the summit.

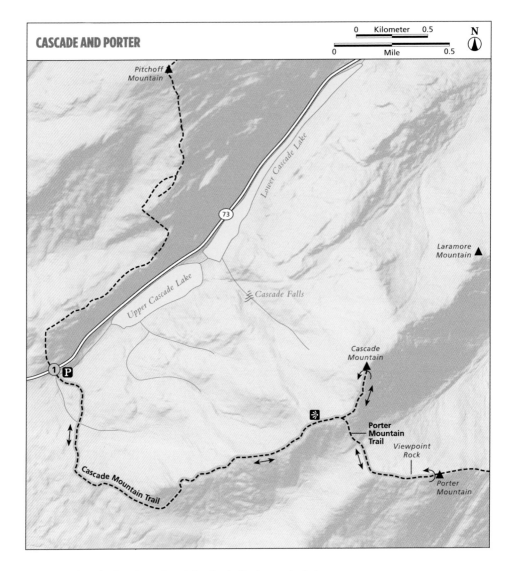

2.5   Back at the junction, take a left to begin the journey to Porter.

2.9   Turn around and soak up the views at Viewpoint Rock.

3.1   Arrive at Porter Mountain summit. Turn around and retrace your steps.

3.7   Back at the junction, turn to the left and head downhill.

5.7   Arrive back at the parking lot.

Option

There is a trail reroute in progress that will make this hike several miles longer but will allow for more (and safer) parking for hikers near the Mount Van Hoevenberg ski area. As of this writing, the trail has yet to be completed.

2 Big Slide

This is a perfect fall hike, with amazing foliage and incredible views into the John Brooks Valley and the Great Range from a unique vantage point.

Start: Garden parking lot
Distance: 7.0 miles out and back
Summit elevation: 4,240 feet
4,000-footers rank of the 115: 62 (tied)
Elevation gain: 3,212 feet
Difficulty: Easy
Hiking time: 6–8 hours
Trails used: The Brothers Trail
Nearest town: Keene Valley
Views: Excellent

Water sources: One small stream crossing at the beginning of the hike; limited reliability after that
Canine compatibility: Very good
Special considerations: The Garden parking lot is small and fills up fast in summer. There is a nominal charge to park here, and an attendant is usually on duty during busy times of the year. The road leading up to the lot is very narrow, so drive cautiously.

Finding the trailhead: From the NY Thruway (I-87), take exit 30 for Lake Placid/Keene Valley and head north on US 9 toward NY 73. Reach an intersection with NY 73 at 2.2 miles; continue on NY 73, passing Round Pond parking for Dix Mountain at 5.2 miles and parking for Giant Mountain at 6.1 miles. At 7.6 miles, the Ausable Club Road and parking will be on your left after heading down a very steep grade—slow down for hikers crossing. Continue on NY 73 until you reach the center of Keene Valley and Adirondack Road, on your left at 10.6 miles. From the north and the town of Keene, travel south on NY 73, passing the intersection with NY 9N at 1.9 miles. Enter the town of Keene Valley and reach Adirondack Road on your right at 4.9 miles. From Adirondack Road, travel up the street for 0.6 mile and bear right onto Interbrook Road. Continue to the end in another 0.9 mile. GPS (garden parking lot): N44°11'19.93" / W73°48'57.80"

The Hike

Though once we tacked this onto our return hike of Saddleback via the Orebed Trail by climbing up the very steep Big Slide Trail, most people do this one as an out-and-back from the Garden parking lot via the "The Brothers," a set of three subpeaks on the way to Big Slide. If you don't like out-and-backs, you can loop down to Johns Brooks Valley and hike out that way. This is a fantastic fall foliage hike, as you get incredible views into Johns Brooks Valley and the Great Range from each Brother. For those who just want views and don't want to peak-bag, you can reach Brother #1 and Brother #2 in under 2 miles from the trailhead, though be forewarned—there is quite an elevation gain and some fun cliffs to scramble up. In winter these cliffs can be super icy and often require crampons to descend. (One winter, I tried to descend in microspikes, but after I fell twice and almost cracked my skull, I put on my crampons and was glad I did.)

Emily and Geoff peeking through a snow window en route to Big Slide DEAN J. OUELLETTE

After a lot of climbing, you reach a great lookout from the first Brother, which is perched 1,437 feet above the parking lot. The trail ducks in and out of the woods for the remainder of the hike. On the bright side, most of the elevation is done early on, so it's a bit less strenuous to get to the second and third Brothers. Stop at each to enjoy the incredible views of the Great Range. I love how the trail darts in and out of the woods—the second half of the ascent has less elevation gain than the first half, so this part seems more pleasant. The elevation from the third Brother is 3,681 feet, and if you look straight ahead, that "shark fin" mountain you are staring at is the actual Big Slide summit. There are even some, gasp, flat sections before more climbing to reach the junction of the Big Slide Trail, just under 4 miles from the Garden. The final 0.3-mile section from the junction is straight up 270 feet (complete with some steep ladders) to the small summit of Big Slide, which is just a large rock ledge. I always forget how steep this pitch is, but it's over quickly. You can then either make a loop

DID YOU KNOW?

From the summit, you can see not only Upper and Lower Wolfjaw, Armstrong, Gothics, Saddleback, Basin, and Marcy but also, if you look east, you can see all the way to Camel's Hump and Mansfield in Vermont.

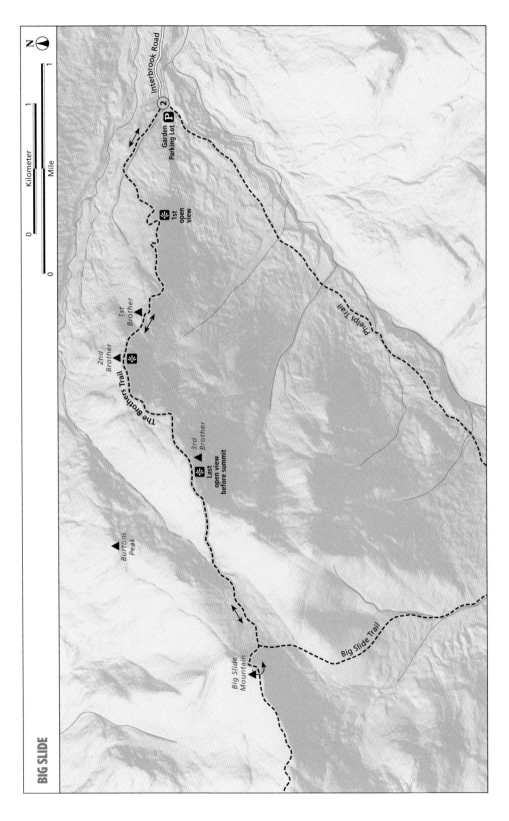

BIG SLIDE

Interbrook Road

Garden
Parking Lot

1st open
view

1st
Brother

2nd
Brother

The Brothers Trail

3rd
Brother

Last open view
before summit

Burtons
Peak

Big Slide
Mountain

Big Slide Trail

Phelps Trail

N

Kilometer

Mile

by heading down the Big Slide Trail to the John Brooks Valley and back (longer) or simply head back down the way you came, descending all the Brothers and the final descent back to the Garden. Allow 6–8 hours round-trip, depending on how much time you spend admiring the views.

Miles and Directions

0.0 Start from the trail register and head northwest.

0.8 First open view.

1.4 First Brother.

1.6 Second Brother.

2.3 3rd Brother and last good view until the summit.

3.3 Take a right at the Big Slide Trail junction.

3.5 Big Slide summit.

3.7 Turn left onto the Brothers Trail.

6.1 Last open view before heading down.

7.0 Arrive back at the Garden parking lot.

Option

Make a loop hike by heading down the Big Slide Trail, turning left on the Phelps Trail. Distance: 8.7 miles; elevation gain: 3,139 feet.

3 Giant and Rocky Peak Ridge

Giant Mountain towers over Keene Valley and practically beckons you to hike to its open summit. From the top, you have incredible views of almost the entire Adirondack Park.

Start: Roadside parking for Round Pond Trailhead
Distance: 7.4 miles out and back
Summit elevation: Giant: 4,627 feet; Rocky Peak Ridge: 4,420 feet
4,000-footers rank of the 115: Giant: 28; Rocky Peak Ridge: 42
Elevation gain: 4,386 feet
Difficulty: Moderate
Hiking time: 7-9 hours

Trails used: Ridge Trail, Roaring Brook Trail, East Trail
Nearest town: Keene Valley
Views: Excellent
Water sources: At the beginning and again at the Washbowl
Canine compatibility: Good
Special considerations: Lots of sun exposure on the ridge, so plan accordingly.

Finding the trailhead: From the NY Thruway (I-87), take exit 30 to NY 9 in North Hudson. Drive north for 2.3 miles and then merge with NY 73W, heading toward Keene. The parking lot will be on your left in 3.8 miles. GPS (NY 73, Giant Wilderness parking): N44°8'18.16" / W73°44'37.32"

The Hike

This is one of the most popular hikes in the Adirondacks, so arrive early to park. Most hikers ascend via the Ridge Trail, an unrelentingly steep ascent of 3,000 feet. There are almost no flat sections. Despite its steepness, I love the Ridge Trail; several exciting rock ledges offer amazing views and also make for good rest stops. In winter, you often need full crampons here due to the thick ice and the steepness. In fact, this is the mountain they often use for ADK Winter Mountaineering School. In summer, bring way more water than you think you'll need; it gets hot, and the climb is arduous. This trail is very straightforward and marked with blazes. You hit a gentle flat section at the Washbowl (stop to enjoy the views of Chapel Pond below), but then truly it's up, up, and up. I love the near vertical, cliffy climb (again, often requires crampons) and all the ledges as you get higher and higher. Each ledge has spectacular views right into the heart of the Adirondacks as you stare at the Dix Range and also the Great Range, MacIntyre Range, and Big Slide. Just when you think you are

DID YOU KNOW?

Giant Peak was the first recorded ascent of any peak in the Adirondacks (1797) when Charles Broadhead and his survey party marked it "Giant-of-the-Valley."

View from Rocky Peak back toward Giant summit MICHELE HERNANDEZ BAYLISS

there, you still have more to go. This is a very long ascent despite the relatively "low" mileage. There are a few last chute-like climbs right before the summit when you finally reach the junction sign to Rocky Peak. The final section to the Giant summit is fairly quick and easy, especially after all the climbs you have already done. You bear left at the top of the summit rock and break out onto a spacious ledge with views for days into the entire high peaks' wilderness.

It's easy to see why this is a popular hike, though many mistake the short distance for easy. Heading back to the junction, you bear left and head down very steeply toward Rocky Peak. Check how much water you have, as you have to reclimb this section before the descent. This section from the junction is very steep and has some tricky spots for winter that often require an ice ax or rope when icy. Once you reach the col, you have a slightly easier climb up toward Rocky Peak. The ascent to Rocky is more straightforward, with a super-fun rock scramble near the top. Rocky is a bald peak with awesome views and is usually less crowded. Looking back toward Giant, you can see how much you have to climb to regain the altitude you lost earlier. That last climb back up to the junction below Giant is tough, but then you have all downhill back to your car. Although this hike is under 8 miles, it often takes 7–9 hours, so underestimate at your own risk.

Miles and Directions

0.0 Start from the roadside parking and head east.

0.5 View of Chapel Pond.

0.6 Junction with the Washbowl Trail; bear right across the log bridge.

0.9 Junction with the Nubble Trail on the left; continue straight.

GIANT AND ROCKY PEAK RIDGE

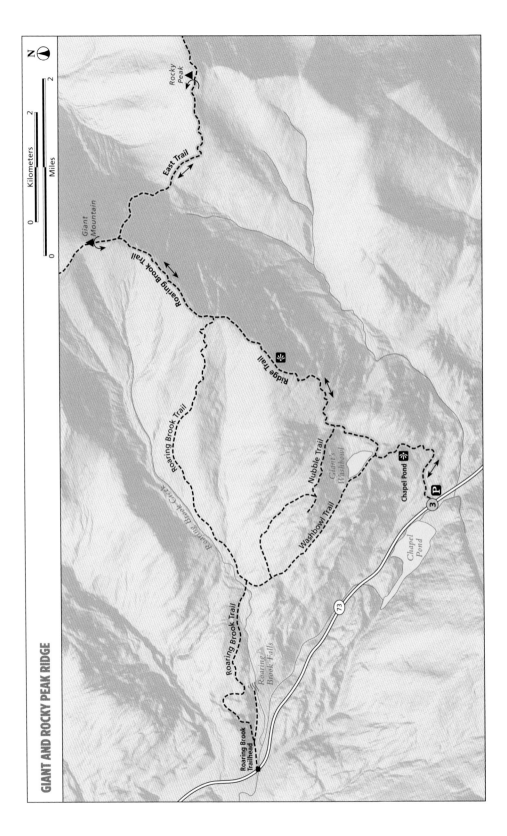

Gorgeous view toward Chapel Pond as you climb Ridge Trail, with Great Range views to the upper right MICHELE HERNANDEZ BAYLISS

1.5 Begin the open views of the ridge.

1.9 Roaring Brook Trail junction; bear right and continue uphill.

2.6 East Trail to Rocky Peak comes in from the right; continue up the hill.

2.7 Arrive at Giant Mountain summit. Turn around and continue your trip.

2.8 At the Rocky Peak junction; turn left and follow the trail downhill.

3.8 Arrive at the open Rocky Peak Ridge summit.

4.8 Back at the Roaring Brook junction, turn left.

5.5 The Roaring Brook Trail goes right; bear left on the Ridge Trail and continue down.

6.5 The Nubble Trail enters from the right; continue straight.

6.8 At the Washbowl, cross the bridge and stay left to continue to the road.

7.4 Arrive back at the road.

Option

Make a loop of this hike with a car shuttle. Head down the Roaring Brook Trail to the Roaring Brook Trailhead and pass beautiful Roaring Brook Falls. Distance: 8.1 miles; elevation gain: 4,402 feet. GPS (Roaring Brook Trailhead): N44°9'1.49" / W73°46'2.08"

4 Whiteface and Esther

Though Mount Esther is nothing to write home about, the trail to Whiteface from the Esther junction is one of the most scenic climbs in the Adirondacks, and Whiteface itself features a super cool summit complete with tower/observation deck. In summer you can drive right up to the summit.

Start: Atmospheric Science Research Center (ASRC) Road
Distance: 9.3 miles out and back
Summit elevation: Whiteface: 4,867 feet; Esther: 4,240 feet
4,000-footers rank of the 115: Whiteface: 14; Esther: 62 (tied)
Elevation gain: 3,607 feet
Difficulty: Moderate
Hiking time: 7–8 hours

Trails used: Marble Mountain Trail, Wilmington Trail, Esther Herd Path
Nearest town: Wilmington
Views: Excellent
Water sources: Not many; a small stream after the junction with the Esther Herd Path is unreliable.
Canine compatibility: Good
Special considerations: Above tree line; plan accordingly.

Finding the trailhead: From Lake Placid, take NY 86 east toward Wilmington for 12.1 miles to the junction with NY 431. From I-87 take exit 34 and head south on NY 9N for 16.6 miles to the town of Jay. At the intersection go right on NY 86 for 5.1 miles to the intersection with NY 431. Drive west on NY 431 toward Whiteface Mountain for 2.3 miles. Marble Mountain Road is on your left. Travel down the road for 0.6 mile; the small lot will be on your right. There's enough room for maybe 10 cars. GPS (parking lot): N44°23'39.67" / W73°51'27.80"

The Hike

Though this hike never takes us that long, I am not a fan of starting a straight-up climb from the get-go. On the bright side, the majority of the tough elevation is done in the first 2 miles.

You start on the Atmospheric Science Research Center (ASRC) Road and head basically straight up an old ski path to Marble Mountain, where you bear right and then up a super-steep ramp until you hit the Esther junction at 2.2 miles. Though it's a herd path, it's clearly marked by a sign and a cairn—the herd path only goes up a total of about 350 feet. Although you may not notice, in the first 10 minutes you cross a small subpeak called Lookout Mountain, which provides good views toward Esther. *Caution:* In winter the herd path can get tricky as you approach the summit, and it takes some care to find the route. We fell into body-size spruce traps one winter that made it nearly impossible to reach the summit. There is one steep section to navigate with some scrambling before you reach the small summit of Esther. From the summit, you can see over to Whiteface.

My hiking buddy and friend Donna Dearborn and her two intrepid dogs, Eva and Ella, on the summit of Whiteface MICHELE HERNANDEZ BAYLISS

Hiking back to the junction, the best is yet to come. I love the section on the Wilmington Trail. It's almost flat, a nice change, until you arrive at the huge rock wall. This is a good place to layer up if it's super windy. If you're only headed to Whiteface (skipping Esther), it's about 3 hours to reach the summit from the ASRC. The last section to the summit is exciting. Note that in winter, the one section that requires climbing up from the road onto the final ascent can be very icy and often requires crampons. Several hikers have fallen here and broken limbs, so wear microspikes or crampons on this short section over the highway that leads directly to the summit. From here to the summit takes only about 15 minutes but is memorable because of the extreme exposure and incredible views.

The summit itself features views toward almost every Adirondack high peak. Because the auto road leads right to the summit, it is often crowded in summer, but in winter you are likely to have the peak all to yourself. We usually do Esther on the

DID YOU KNOW?

Whiteface Mountain hosted the alpine events of the 1980 Winter Olympics. The downhill skiing events took place at the old ski resort.

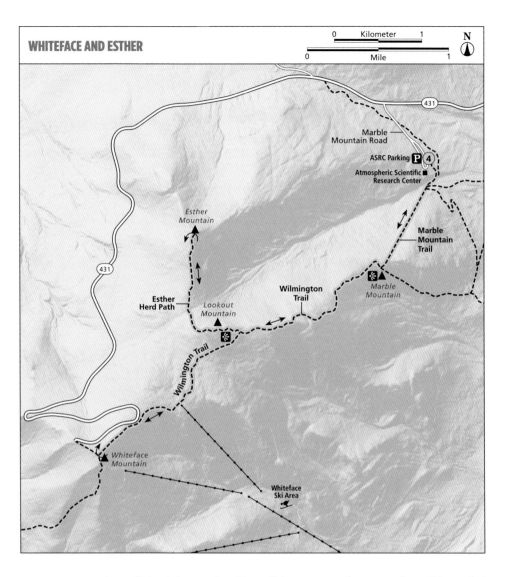

0   Kilometer   1

0   Mile   1

N

431

Marble
Mountain Road

ASRC Parking 🅿 4

Atmospheric Scientific ■
Research Center

Esther
Mountain

Marble
Mountain
Trail

431

Wilmington
Trail

Marble
Mountain

Esther
Herd Path

Lookout
Mountain

Wilmington Trail

Whiteface
Mountain

Whiteface
Ski Area

way up, so the walk back is very fast. If conditions are good, you can butt slide or sled down from the Esther junction. In summer you'll have to suffer the rocky descent and hope your knees survive.

We usually complete both peaks in about 7 hours, but due to the steep ascent, we'd allow 7–8 hours total.

Miles and Directions

0.0   Start from the small parking lot and head due east down the hill. Quickly come to a service road, which you'll follow.

0.1   Continue following the road as it bears to the right.

0.2 At the end of the road, continue into the woods and uphill.

0.9 Arrive at Marble Mountain lookout. Turn right and join the Wilmington Trail that comes in from the left.

2.2 Take a right at the Esther Herd Path junction.

2.4   Cross over Lookout Mountain.

3.2 Arrive at Esther Mountain; turn around and retrace your steps.

4.2 At the junction, take a right and continue on the Wilmington Trail.

5.3 You'll see a gigantic wall on your right. Continue up and this wall becomes Whiteface Mountain Road. Stay to the left of the road and make your way up the rocky ridge.

5.7 Arrive at the developed Whiteface Mountain summit. Retrace your steps down the ridge.

6.0 At the road, bear right and down the rocks.

7.1 At the Esther Herd Path junction, continue straight.

8.4 At Marble Mountain, bear left at the Wilmington–Marble Mountain Trail junction.

9.3 Arrive back at the parking lot.

5 Mount Colden

This is one of our very favorite peaks in the entire Adirondacks. Colden not only provides 360-degree views of much of the Adirondack high peaks and wilderness but also is on the easier side of Adirondack hikes for such an incredible view and beautiful trail.

Start: High Peaks Information Center (HPIC) parking lot
Distance: 12.2 miles out and back
Summit elevation: 4,714 feet
4,000-footers rank of the 115: 25
Elevation gain: 2,930 feet
Difficulty: Difficult
Hiking time: 7–8 hours
Trails used: Van Hoevenberg Trail, Avalanche Pass Trail, Lake Arnold Trail, L. Morgan Porter Trail

Nearest town: Lake Placid
Views: Splendid, at both the false and true summits
Water sources: Several water sources on the entire hike except for the top of the mountain
Canine compatibility: Very good
Special considerations: Weekend summertime parking is very busy, and securing a spot will require an early start. There is a fee for parking in this lot.

Finding the trailhead: Travel on NY 73 east 1.6 miles from the Lake Placid Olympic Ski Jumping Complex. Or, from the town of Keene, drive 10.9 miles west on NY 73 toward Lake Placid. Turn south onto Adirondack Loj Road and travel 4.7 miles to the end, where there is a payment collection station. Pay a fee and park in one of several lots. GPS (parking lot): N44°10'58.32" / W73°57'46.78"

The Hike

You can hike Mount Colden either as a loop (in which case we'd recommend counterclockwise) or the easier way, which we describe here, as it has 500 fewer feet of gain.

Park in the HPIC lot and head toward the trail head at the far end of the lot, following the Van Hoevenberg Trail toward Marcy Dam. When the trail forks, take a sharp left to stay on the Van Ho until Marcy Dam (45 minutes). Now that the bridge is out, you have to swing left to cross and then right to the "old" bridge. On a clear day, you can see Colden beckoning along with Algonquin and Phelps. Continue to the trail register and sign in (the DEC interior outpost is about 50 yards to the left of the trail register if you need help).

Continuing on the Van Ho, you will hit the Avalanche Pass junction in roughly 100 yards. Follow the signs to Avalanche Pass Trail, marked with yellow markers (though you will *not* go the entire route to Avalanche Pass), where you head up for the next 1.1 miles until you reach another junction. Here is where we recommend heading left to Lake Arnold, following the blue markers. You continue with some

View of Algonquin, Wright, and Iroquois from the summit of Mount Colden
MICHELE HERNANDEZ BAYLISS

gentle sections and then steep climbing until the junction to Indian Falls. The section from the start of the Lake Arnold Trail can take over 1 hour due to the elevation gain and rougher terrain, but you can take a breather when you finally reach the junction on the right side to the L. Morgan Porter Trail to Colden.

Though I usually don't find climbing easy, I love the final climb to the summit. The trail is beautiful in all seasons and actually features many switchbacks to make the ascent a bit less of a "huffer." In winter you can butt slide down some of the steeper sections, but mind the sharp curves. Somewhere in the middle section, on a flat, the trail can be hard to find. You may be tempted to go left, but to stay on the trail, head toward the right to pick it up again. Almost every time we ascend Colden, we see hikers celebrating the peak on the bald area you come out on, the subsummit. But all you have to do is look to the south to see the actual peak looming ahead of you.

The short downhill and steep ascent only takes 20 minutes as you climb past a large boulder and angle up toward the right. Continue a bit farther to tag the actual summit, which is to the left of the trail, and then walk another minute or so to the large boulder with amazing views down toward Avalanche Pass and Algonquin, Wright, and Iroquois.

I love the summit of Colden in all seasons. If you are lucky, you may witness hikers/climbers emerging near that rock up the "trap dike" route to Colden, which is definitely more of a climbing route than a hiking route.

If you want a challenge, continue over the summit and descend the *very* steep, nearly 2,000-foot drop to get down to Avalanche Pass. The out-and-back typically

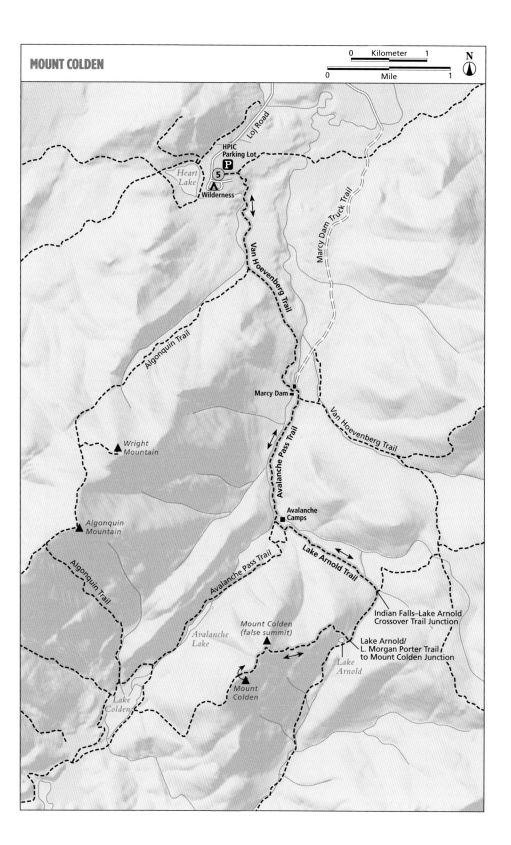

MOUNT COLDEN

0 ... Kilometer ... 1
0 ... Mile ... 1

N

Loj Road

HPIC
Parking Lot

P
5

Heart
Lake

Wilderness

Van Hoevenberg Trail

Marcy Dam Truck Trail

Algonquin Trail

Marcy Dam

Van Hoevenberg Trail

Wright
Mountain

Avalanche Pass Trail

Algonquin
Mountain

Avalanche Camps

Algonquin Trail

Lake Arnold Trail

Avalanche Pass Trail

Indian Falls–Lake Arnold
Crossover Trail Junction

Mount Colden
(false summit)

Avalanche
Lake

Lake Arnold/
L. Morgan Porter Trail
to Mount Colden Junction

Lake
Arnold

Mount
Colden

Lake
Colden

The very steep/rocky back-side section climbing up to Mount Colden from Avalanche Lake
MICHELE HERNANDEZ BAYLISS

takes us under 8 hours, while the loop takes more like 10–11. It's not recommended in icy/snowing conditions; the back side is super steep with some exposed sections that could lead to a fall. The hike back to the HPIC is often faster, since you can make up some time on the downhill sections.

Miles and Directions

0.0 Start from the parking lot and head west after signing the trail register.

1.0 At the Van Hoevenberg-Algonquin Trail junction, turn left and continue on the well-worn path.

2.2 Arrive at Marcy Dam. Turn sharply left to follow the pond outlet and reach a footbridge crossing the stream; turn right after the crossing.

2.4 Come to the Van Hoevenberg-Avalanche Pass Trail junction; bear right here on the Avalanche Pass Trail.

3.5 Avalanche Camps-Lake Arnold Trail junction. Head left at this intersection in the small grassy area.

4.5 The Indian Falls-Lake Arnold Crossover Trail junction is on your left, across the flowing stream.

5.0 At the Lake Arnold-L. Morgan Porter Trail to Mount Colden junction, turn right; you'll see campsites to your right in 100 feet.

5.8 Colden false summit and first great view. The trail takes an extreme left turn down a steep section and can be easy to miss in inclement weather.

6.1 Reach the summit with a short 50-foot spur trail on your left. Turn around and retrace your steps downhill.

7.2 At Lake Arnold, turn left.

8.7 Arriving at Avalanche Camps, bear right and head toward Marcy Dam.

10.0 Reach Marcy Dam.

11.2 With only 1.0 mile to go, turn right at the Algonquin junction.

12.2 Arrive back at the HPIC parking lot.

Option

From the junction with the Lake Arnold Trail at mile 3.5, take the Avalanche Pass Trail to Avalanche Lake, where you can walk across the "Hitch-up Matildas" then continue to Lake Colden and work yourself around the east side of the lake. Not quite halfway around the lake, take the Mount Colden Trail to the top. Return via Lake Arnold for a nice loop. Distance: 13.0 miles; elevation gain: 3,456 feet.

6 Wright, Algonquin, and Iroquois

Algonquin is the second-highest peak in the Adirondacks and one of the most spectacular, with a 360-degree view of almost every high peak in the park.

Start: High Peaks Information Center (HPIC) parking lot
Distance: 10.1 miles out and back
Summit elevation: Wright: 4,580 feet; Algonquin: 5,114 feet; Iroquois: 4,840 feet
4,000-footers rank of the 115: Wright: 33; Algonquin: 9; Iroquois: 16 (tied)
Elevation gain: 4,300 feet
Difficulty: Strenuous
Hiking time: 8–11 hours
Trails used: Van Hoevenberg Trail, Algonquin Trail, Wright Peak Spur, Iroquois Herd Path

Nearest town: Lake Placid
Views: Superior
Water sources: Fill up at MacIntyre Falls; not much after that.
Canine compatibility: Okay; be sure to keep them close in the alpine zone and off the vegetation.
Special considerations: Weekend summertime parking is very busy, and securing a spot will require an early start. There is a fee to park in this lot. A lot of this hike is above tree line with no shade; plan accordingly.

Finding the trailhead: Travel on NY 73 east for 1.6 miles from the Lake Placid Olympic Ski Jumping Complex. Or, from the town of Keene, travel west 10.9 miles on NY 73 toward Lake Placid. Turn south onto Adirondack Loj Road and travel 4.7 miles to the end, where there is a payment collection station. Pay a fee and park in one of several lots. GPS (parking lot): N44°10'58.32" / W73°57'46.78"

The Hike

Like many hikes in the Adirondacks, this one starts at the HPIC, where you pick up the Van Hoevenberg Trail toward Marcy Dam. Less than 1 mile in, you reach the junction to Marcy Dam; continue *straight* toward Algonquin, avoiding all the side ski trails. When you cross the Whales Tail Ski Trail, bear right to stay on the trail. The grade is gradual at first, with some steep sections mixed with short flats in between as you head up toward the junction to Wright Mountain. We usually save Wright for last and head up the very steep next section of trail until you break out of tree line into the arctic zone. At this point, make sure you have good enough visibility to find the entrance back to tree line—many a hiker has gotten lost on the way down. Cairns

DID YOU KNOW?

These mountains are part of the MacIntyre Range, the spelling of which matches the USGS topographic map, but the man the mountains were named for is spelled "McIntyre," for Archibald McIntyre, who worked in the Tahawus Ironworks.

View from the wide-open summit of Algonquin toward the slides on Mount Colden
Michele Hernandez Bayliss

and yellow blazes mark the rocky above–tree line route, but they can be hard to see in fog, rain, or swirling snow. The trail winds up to the right and then back to the left as you scramble up rocks and break out onto the incredible summit of Algonquin—an impressive open peak with tremendous views right into the flank of Colden (see picture), the trap dike, Lake Colden, the Flowed Lands, and almost every peak in the park.

Hikers trying not to face-plant as they descend the very steep final section between Wright and Algonquin
Michele Hernandez Bayliss

If you have the energy, head down the steep back side of Algonquin toward Boundary (a subpeak) and eventually Iroquois. At the bottom of the steep descent, you'll see the junction on the left-hand side that would descend to Lake Colden. The herd path to Iroquois is straight ahead. This section can be very closed in during summer with heavy mud (I almost lost my hiking boot here due to a mud flat) and tough to find in winter. It's a short climb to Boundary Peak, which you go up and over to continue on to Iroquois. There is a very steep final ascent to Iroquois, but if you bear a bit to the right, you can skip the rock climb and take the slightly easier route. The view from Iroquois toward Marshall is impressive, not to mention the intimidating view of the mountain you just climbed.

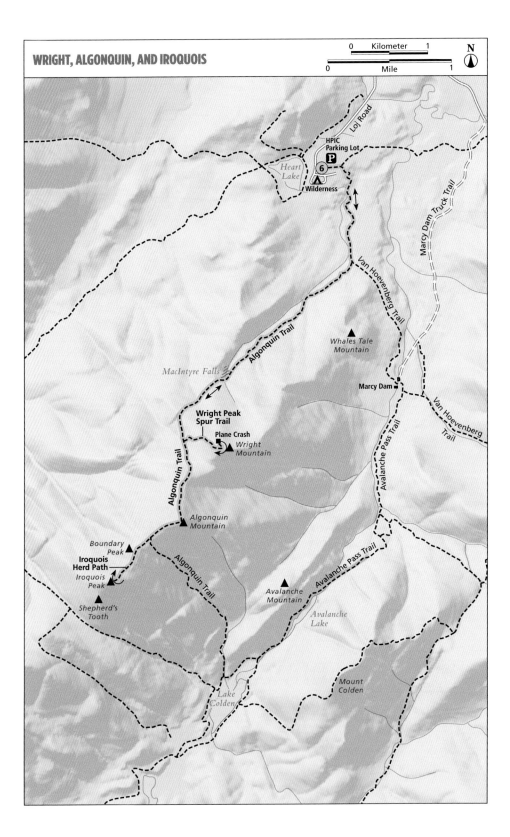

0   Kilometer   1

0   Mile   1

N

Loj Road

HPIC
Parking Lot

P

6

Wilderness

*Heart
Lake*

Marcy Dam Truck Trail

Van Hoevenberg Trail

Algonquin Trail

▲
*Whales Tale
Mountain*

Marcy Dam ■

Van Hoevenberg
Trail

MacIntyre Falls

**Wright Peak
Spur Trail**

Plane Crash
▲
*Wright
Mountain*

Avalanche Pass Trail

Algonquin Trail

▲
*Algonquin
Mountain*

*Boundary
Peak* ▲

**Iroquois
Herd Path**
*Iroquois
Peak* ▲

Algonquin Trail

Avalanche Pass Trail

▲
*Avalanche
Mountain*

*Shepherd's
Tooth*

*Avalanche
Lake*

*Lake
Colden*

*Mount
Colden*

It may look impossible, but typically we reascend in less than 20 minutes. We take in the views one more time before the steep descent off the cone back to tree line.

Head back down the very steep section to the Wright junction. It's about a 15-minute steep climb to a rock scramble that takes you above tree line and in 0.4 mile to the summit on an open/rocky ascent. This section is not only steep but also often very windy. There have been many accidents here in winter due to ice, so watch your footing. The view from Wright is likewise spectacular—you stare right into the side of Algonquin and have views toward Colden and dozens of other peaks. If you have the time, follow over the summit a bit toward the north to reach the bronze plaque that honors the airman who died in a US Air Force plane crash just behind the summit in 1962. Descending back to the junction, the final hike out typically takes under 2 hours reach the HPIC.

In winter we have done this hike in 9 hours. With stops for views, 9–11 hours would take into account all three peaks in the Macs.

Miles and Directions

0.0 Start from the HPIC parking lot. Sign the hiker register and head east.

1.0 Van Hoevenberg trail junction; stay straight on the Algonquin Trail.

2.5 Arrive at MacIntyre Falls and cross the stream to continue.

3.1 Junction with the Wright Peak Spur Trail; stay straight on the Algonquin Trail.

3.6 Above tree line, follow rock cairns and yellow paint blazes to the Algonquin summit. Cross the top and head down the other side toward Iroquois.

4.1 At tree line, this is a tricky spot; turn right through the trees and follow the Iroquois Herd Path.

4.3 Cross over Boundary Peak, continuing to follow rock cairns.

4.7 There is no sign, but a large rock marks the open summit of Iroquois. Turn around and retrace your steps.

5.6 Arrive back at the Algonquin summit.

6.2 Back at the junction with the Wright Peak Spur Trail, turn right and head up the trail.

6.6 Follow large rock cairns to the Wright Peak summit. Turn around and make your way back down.

7.0 Turn right onto the Algonquin Trail and follow it down the hill.

9.2 Back at the junction with the Van Hoevenberg Trail. Stay straight to get back to the parking lot.

10.1 Arrive back at the HPIC parking lot.

Option

Forgo Wright and Iroquois Peaks and head down toward Lake Colden and Avalanche Lake with the "Hitch-up Matildas." Travel past Marcy Dam for a loop hike. Distance: 11.1 miles; elevation gain: 3,712 feet.

7 Tabletop and Phelps

Phelps is one of the easiest peaks to reach in the Adirondacks and has the "money" view of Marcy, the highest peak in New York State. Tabletop is easy to tack on and features decent views as well.

Start: High Peaks Information Center (HPIC) parking lot
Distance: 12.1 miles out and back
Summit elevation: Tabletop: 4,427 feet; Phelps: 4,161 feet
4,000-footers rank of the 115: Tabletop: 40; Phelps: 72
Elevation gain: 3,841 feet
Difficulty: Moderate
Hiking time: 8-10 hours

Trails used: Van Hoevenberg Trail, Phelps Mountain Trail, Tabletop Herd Path
Nearest town: Lake Placid
Water sources: Several water sources available on this hike
Canine compatibility: Good
Special considerations: Weekend summertime parking is very busy, and securing a spot will require an early start. There is a fee to park in this lot.

Finding the trailhead: Travel east on NY 73 for 1.6 miles from the Lake Placid Olympic Ski Jumping Complex. Or, from the town of Keene, travel west for 10.9 miles on NY 73 toward Lake Placid. Turn south onto Adirondack Loj Road and continue 4.7 miles to the end, where there is a payment collection station. Pay a fee and park in one of several lots. GPS (parking lot): N44°10'58.32" / W73°57'46.78"

The Hike

If you are just starting out, you can certainly break this hike into two separate hikes; but since the trailheads are fairly close to each other, climbing both in one day is completely doable. You begin at the HPIC and head out on the Van Hoevenberg Trail toward Marcy. In 45 minutes to an hour, you arrive at Marcy Dam (remember to bear *left* at 1 mile in to head toward Marcy Dam rather than straight to Algonquin), where a ton of trails branch out; keep left to follow the Van Ho toward Marcy. As you head up the trail, you will see the left-hand exit to the trail up Phelps, a little over 1 mile past Marcy Dam, though typically we like to continue on the very steep uphill section to Tabletop first, since it's the farther of the two.

DID YOU KNOW?

Phelps Mountain is named for "old mountain" Phelps, who designed the Marcy Trail and guided hikers up Marcy. It is said that he actually never climbed Phelps himself, but the mountain bears his name.

Girls' hike with my dear friends Shelly and Leslie on the summit ledge of Phelps, with Mount Marcy behind us REBECCA KINKEAD

Continuing up the Van Ho, you will climb some steep sections followed by some more moderate sections for roughly 45 minutes until you reach the turnoff to the herd path for Tabletop. Though maps label this climb a 0.5-mile herd path, GPS confirms that it's a bit longer. This summit is less exciting than Phelps, as it is treed, but you can walk past the closed-in summit to a small ledge to get a few views before heading back down to the junction.

After heading downhill from the Tabletop junction to the Phelps junction (just over 1 mile), head up the marked climb that alternates gentle sections with some steep and rocky sections until a nice rock lookout, where it seems you have arrived. This is *not* the summit (I know this because I once guided a friend up and we stopped here—big mistake). Continue toward the right (there is also a "back" way you can arrive at Phelps, but the ledges are more spectacular) and wind around some very scenic ledges with amazing views before the slight uphill to the actual summit, a large rock outcropping with spectacular views right to Marcy and the Dix Range. This is

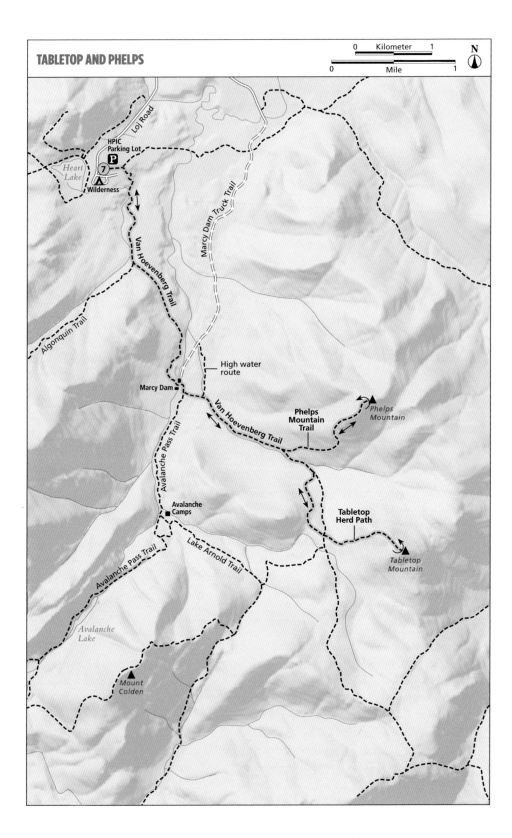

TABLETOP AND PHELPS

Loj Road

HPIC
Parking Lot

Heart
Lake

7

Wilderness

Van Hoevenberg Trail

Marcy Dam Truck Trail

Algonquin Trail

High water
route

Marcy Dam

Van Hoevenberg Trail

Phelps
Mountain
Trail

Phelps
Mountain

Avalanche Pass Trail

Tabletop
Herd Path

Tabletop
Mountain

Avalanche
Camps

Lake Arnold Trail

Avalanche Pass Trail

Avalanche
Lake

Mount
Colden

0   Kilometer   1

0   Mile   1

N

one of our favorite peaks. Combined with Tabletop, it's longer, but you get the satisfaction of knocking off two peaks in a day. Together we'd allow 8–10 hours, but a lot of the mileage is fairly easy with the up and back to Marcy Dam.

Miles and Directions

0.0   Start from the parking lot. Sign the trail register and head west.

1.0   Van Hoevenberg–Algonquin Trail junction; turn left and continue on the well-worn path.

2.2   Arrive at Marcy Dam. Turn sharply left to follow the pond outlet and reach a footbridge crossing the stream; turn right after the crossing.

2.4   Come to the Van Hoevenberg–Avalanche Pass Trail junction; bear left here on the Van Hoevenberg Trail.

3.3   The trail up to Phelps comes in from your left; continue straight on the Van Hoevenberg Trail.

3.6   Cross the bridge over Phelps Brook.

4.3   Turn left onto the trail to Tabletop and make your way up this narrow herd path.

5.0   Arrive at the Tabletop summit; turn around and retrace your steps.

5.7   Back at the Van Hoevenberg Trail, turn right and make your way downhill.

6.4   Cross the bridge back over Phelps Brook.

6.7   Turn sharply right and start up the Phelps Mountain Trail.

7.8   Arrive at the summit of Phelps Mountain; turn around and retrace your steps.

8.9   Reach the intersection with the Van Hoevenberg Trail; bear right.

9.7   Back near the dam, the Avalanche Pass Trail reenters from your left.

9.9   Arrive back at Marcy Dam.

11.1   With only 1 mile to go, turn right at the Algonquin Trail junction.

12.1   Arrive back at the HPIC parking lot.

Option

For a change of pace, try parking at South Meadows Road and following the old truck trail to the high-water route then the Van Hoevenberg. Distance: 12.8 miles; elevation gain: 3,896 feet. GPS (South Meadows parking lot): N44°11'28.67" / W73°56'10.58"

8 Colvin and Blake

Colvin is one of the most spectacular summits in the Adirondacks. Because you are slightly lower in elevation and in the middle of taller mountains, you can enjoy unforgettable views of Sawteeth and Pyramid/Gothics/Armstrong, plus Nippletop and Dial, Ausable Lake, and Giant.

Start: Ausable Club parking lot
Distance: 14.0 miles out and back
Summit elevation: Colvin: 4,057 feet; Blake: 3,960 feet
4,000-footers rank of the 115: Colvin: 91; Blake: 112 (tied)
Elevation gain: 4,097 feet
Difficulty: Difficult
Hiking time: 9–13 hours
Trails used: Ausable Club Road, Lake Road, Gill Brook Trail, Colvin Trail, Blake Trail
Nearest town: Keene Valley
Views: Okay; great at the top of Colvin
Water sources: Several water sources on the hike up toward Colvin

Canine compatibility: Dogs are not allowed on Adirondack Mountain Reserve (AMR) property, which this track crosses.
Special considerations: Parking is free as of publication, but a permit is required ahead of time (purchase online at hikeamr.org), and there is an attendant on duty during the summer months. This approach crosses private Ausable Club property, so be respectful of their property. Move out of the way of all vehicular traffic, as Lake Road can be busy with buses transporting guests to the Ausable Lakes (no bus rides for hikers).

Finding the trailhead: From the NY Thruway (I-87), take exit 30 for Lake Placid/Keene Valley and head north on US 9 toward NY 73, reaching an intersection with NY 73 at 2.2 miles. Continue on NY 73, passing Round Pond parking for Dix Mountain at 5.2 miles and parking for Giant Mountain at 6.1 miles. At 7.6 miles, the Ausable Club Road and parking will be on your left after heading down a very steep grade; slow down. From the north and the town of Keene, travel south on NY 73, continuing past the intersection with NY 9N at 1.9 miles, passing through the town of Keene Valley at 4.9, until finally arriving at the road and parking lot on your right at 8 miles. GPS (parking lot): N44°8'58.94" / W73°46'4.05"

The Hike

Do not underestimate this hike. By itself, Mount Colvin would be an easy out-and-back of about 7 hours with minimum stress, but at some point peak-baggers have to tackle the "evil brother" Blake, which is a killer. One day you will have already done Blake and then enjoy just doing Colvin, but together, this is a 14-mile day that takes 9–13 hours, with some near-technical scrambles, scary ladders, and lots of total elevation gain (over 4,000 feet).

From the St. Huberts parking area, follow the golf club road, make a left onto Lake Road, pass the tennis courts, and arrive at the AMR gate and register. I love the

Michele on Indian Head Cliff en route to Mount Colvin PUANANI PERDUE

gentle warm-up hike up Lake Road. You pass the Leach Trail on the left and continue a little over an hour until you reach the sign for Gill Brook/Colvin/Indian Head on the left. This trail is very gentle and winds around the brook before climbing until you arrive at a small junction with the other trail from Lake Road you could have taken. Follow the blue trail until the Indian Head junction, a worthy detour on its own, but not combined with Colvin and Blake unless you are a true masochist. Continue climbing until the sign for Elk Pass (which you would take to Nippletop and Dial), where you bear right toward Colvin. Now the real climbing starts, although there are some nice switchbacks and it is scenic. There is one dicey section with a ladder to help you scramble (often there is a rope left here to help you, but don't count on it). Just when you think you can't climb anymore, you come out right below the summit to Colvin, where you step out onto a rock and marvel at the views. There is another ledge on the right (careful in winter) from which you can see Blake, Allen, the Great Range, and Upper Ausable Lake. Don't linger—you have to get moving to do the out-and-back to Blake.

Although the first 10 minutes toward Blake seems deceptively easy and flat, it soon drops down, down, down. And that's before you hit the down ladders, where you go down, down, down again. In winter this section can be quite scary. After you pass the junction for the Elk Lake–Marcy Trail (the famous "elevator" descent), you have a very steep climb up, up, and up to Blake. The actual summit is up to the left, where you can see the "Colvin and Ridge to Pinnacle" sign, but it is wooded with

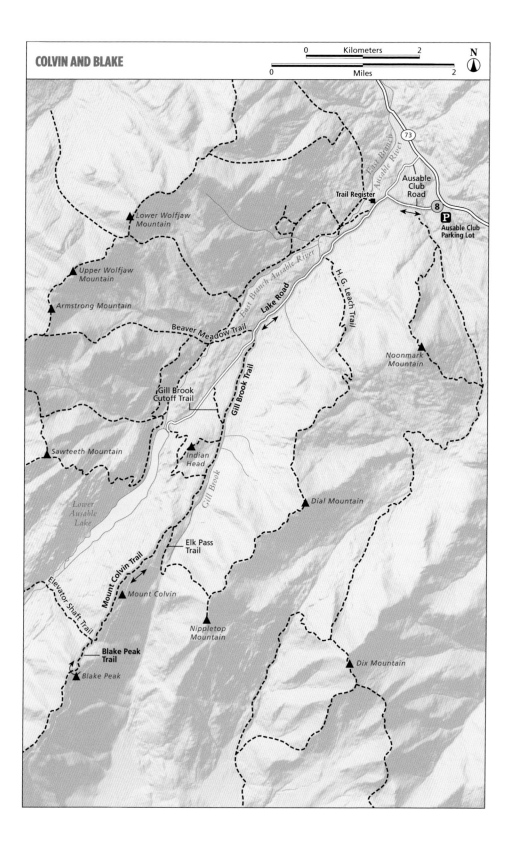

0   Kilometers   2

0   Miles   2

N

73

East Branch Ausable River

Ausable Club Road

Trail Register

8

P
Ausable Club
Parking Lot

Lower Wolfjaw
Mountain

Upper Wolfjaw
Mountain

Armstrong Mountain

East Branch Ausable River

Lake Road

Beaver Meadow Trail

H. G. Leach Trail

Noonmark
Mountain

Gill Brook
Cutoff Trail

Gill Brook Trail

Sawteeth Mountain

Indian
Head

Gill Brook

Dial Mountain

Lower
Ausable
Lake

Elk Pass
Trail

Mount Colvin Trail

Elevator Shaft Trail

Mount Colvin

Nippletop
Mountain

Dix Mountain

Blake Peak
Trail

Blake Peak

no views. I recommend doing it once and then doing Colvin "a la carte." In any case, you now have to go back down and then ascend the ladders and then reclimb Colvin (shouldn't it count twice?). The out-and-back can take a good 3 hours; though if conditions are not too icy or muddy, 2.5 is possible. Once you check out the view from Colvin again, head down the way you came, being careful to bear left at the Nippletop junction back toward the Lake Road. The descent usually takes us a bit less time, but the entire hike is a doozy thanks to Blake.

Miles and Directions

0.0 Start at the parking lot and head west up the road, away from NY 73.

0.6 Turn left onto Lake Road.

0.8 Sign in at the trail register.

1.5 Pass the H. G. Leach Trail to the Dial Mountain junction.

2.7 Pass the Beaver Meadow Trail on your right; in 70 yards turn left onto the Gill Brook Trail.

3.7 Pass the Gill Brook Cutoff Trail on your right.

3.8 The Indian Head Trail junction will be on your right; continue straight.

4.3 Fish Hawk Cliff Trail junction, also on your right; continue straight.

4.9 At the junction with the Elk Pass Trail, turn right and head uphill.

5.8 An opening on your right signifies the Mount Colvin summit. Continue south on the ridge.

6.5 At the bottom of the col is the junction with Elevator Shaft Trail (no outlet to Lake Road). Follow the path uphill.

7.0 Reach a rock and sign indicating that you've reached the summit of Blake Peak. Turn around here to head back.

8.2 Return to the Colvin summit. The trail here goes down and to the right.

10.3 Junction with the Gill Brook Cutoff Trail on your left; continue straight.

11.3 Once you reach Lake Road, turn right and follow it to the end.

13.2 Sign out at the trail register.

14.0 Arrive back at the parking lot.

Option

On your way out, take the Gill Brook Cutoff Trail for a change of scenery. Distance and elevation gain are unchanged.

9 Nippletop and Dial

On a clear day the view from Nippletop Mountain is amazing: Due west, you stare right at Sawteeth, Gothics, Armstrong, and the Wolfjaws; to the southeast you see the Dix Range. As a bonus, the ridge walk to Dial is amazing.

Start: Ausable Club parking lot
Distance: 13.4-mile loop
Summit elevation: Nippletop: 4,620 feet; Dial: 4,020 feet
4,000-footers rank of the 115: Nippletop: 29; Dial: 102
Elevation gain: 4,294 feet
Difficulty: Difficult
Hiking time: 9.5-10 hours
Trails used: Ausable Club Road, Lake Road, Gill Brook Trail, Elk Pass Trail, H. G. Leach Trail
Nearest town: Keene Valley
Views: Good from the summit of each mountain and the old burn area

Water sources: Several water sources on the hike up toward Nippletop; none on the ridge
Canine compatibility: Dogs are not allowed on Adirondack Mountain Reserve (AMR) property, which this track crosses.
Special considerations: Parking is free as of publication, but a permit is required ahead of time (purchase online at hikeamr.org), and there is an attendant on duty during the summer months. This approach crosses private Ausable Club property, so be respectful of their property. Move out of the way of all vehicular traffic, as Lake Road can be busy with buses transporting guests to the Ausable Lakes (no bus rides for hikers).

Finding the trailhead: From the NY Thruway (I-87), take exit 30 for Lake Placid/Keene Valley and head north on US 9 toward NY 73, reaching an intersection with NY 73 at 2.2 miles. Continue on NY 73, passing Round Pond parking for Dix Mountain at 5.2 miles and parking for Giant Mountain at 6.1 miles. At 7.6 miles, the Ausable Club Road and parking will be on your left after heading down a very steep grade; slow down. From the north and the town of Keene, travel south on NY 73, continuing past the intersection with NY 9N at 1.9 miles, passing through the town of Keene Valley at 4.9 miles, until finally arriving at the road and parking lot on your right at 8 miles. GPS (parking lot): N44°8'58.94" / W73°46'4.05"

The Hike

Like many hikes in this region, you park via lottery in the Ausable Club lot and head up about 0.5 mile on the golf course road before turning left just before the club building to the AMR gate, marked by the Ranger Hut, where you sign in. It's about a 20-minute walk to get to the AMR gate from the parking lot. From the gate, you follow the gently graded Lake Road as it gains about 500 feet of elevation. You will pass the Henry Leach Trail on your left early on (where this loop ends up many hours later) before arriving at the Gill Brook Trail. I much prefer doing this loop counter-clockwise—once you are done with the Elk Pass climb, the rest of the day is easier and you are heading *toward* your car not away from it.

A deer on the side of the trail up Nippletop DEAN J. OUELLETTE

This trail winds around Gill Brook and heads toward the junction to Colvin and Blake. Since this is a longish loop, we would skip Indian Head and Fish Hawk Cliffs (though they make for a great day hike with awesome views) and bear left toward Nippletop via Elk Pass. There is a nice flat section with a few beaver ponds, and if the day is clear you can see that it's going to be a climb to reach Nippletop. I have to admit, I love the short/steep climbs. From the base of the Elk Pass Trail after the ponds, it's close to 2,000 feet of up as you go up an elevator shaft–like section. Take your time;

DID YOU KNOW?
At 4,620 feet, Nippletop is "lucky 13" in the Adirondacks height rating.

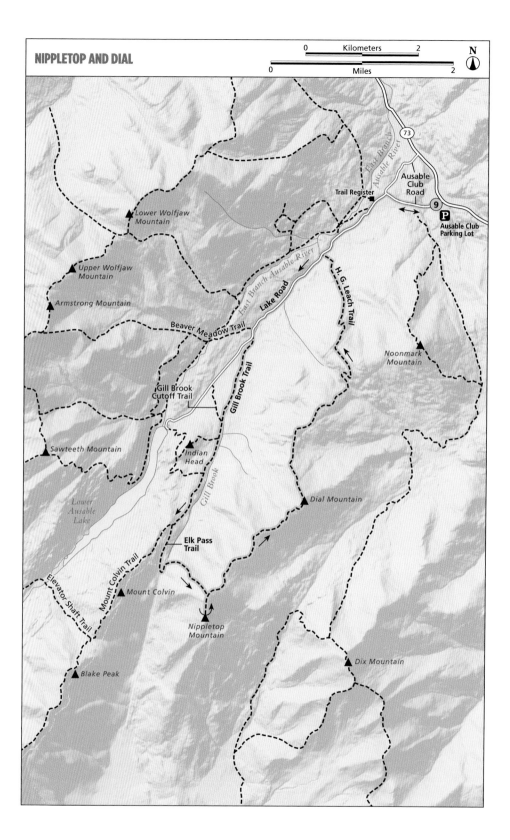

0 Kilometers 2

0 Miles 2

N

First Branch Ausable River

73

Ausable Club Road

Trail Register

9

Ausable Club Parking Lot

Lower Wolfjaw Mountain

Upper Wolfjaw Mountain

Armstrong Mountain

Beaver Meadow Trail

East Branch Ausable River

Lake Road

H. G. Leach Trail

Noonmark Mountain

Gill Brook Cutoff Trail

Gill Brook Trail

Sawteeth Mountain

Indian Head

Gill Brook

Dial Mountain

Lower Ausable Lake

Elk Pass Trail

Mount Colvin Trail

Elevator Shaft Trail

Mount Colvin

Nippletop Mountain

Dix Mountain

Blake Peak

this is the major climb of the day. Though it can be faster or slower depending on conditions, it will take you about 1.5 hours to gain the ridge. At this point, you are just shy of the summit, toward the right. Explore the summit area for views southeast toward the Dix Range. From the parking lot to the summit takes 3–3.5 hours.

I love the descent back to the ridge junction and the trip to Dial. Because Nippletop is quite a bit higher, the ridge is mostly straight with a bit of downhill as you slowly lose elevation and head toward Dial Mountain on a trail that follows the ridge to the summit of Dial. After Nippletop, this summit may seem far less exciting. The Henry Leach Trail winds downward (one more "bump" to get up Bear Den, a subpeak) at a fairly easy grade, where it's 2 hours to return to the Lake Road junction you passed hours before. As you approach the "burn" area (the shoulder of Noonmark, which had a major fire years ago), you have to will your legs to do one more uphill to regain a bit of elevation before it is all downhill. Because you did the loop counterclockwise, every step from Nippletop onward brings you closer to your parked vehicle. The Henry Leach Trail dumps you fairly close (20- to 25-minute walk) to the AMR gate, and then it's just the final return to the golf club road to loop back. Although I'm usually tired by then, I try to focus on the spectacular views of Giant Mountain to the left and glance back to gaze upon the Great Range.

Miles and Directions

0.0 Start at the parking lot and head west up the road, away from NY 73

0.6 Turn left onto Lake Road.

0.8 Sign the trail register.

1.5 Pass the H. G. Leach Trail to the Dial Mountain junction.

2.7 Pass the Beaver Meadow Trail on your right; in 70 yards turn left onto the Gill Brook Trail.

3.7 Pass the Gill Brook Cutoff Trail on your right.

3.8 Indian Head Trail junction is on your right; continue straight.

4.3 Fish Hawk Cliff Trail junction, also on your right; continue straight.

4.9 Junction with the Elk Pass Trail; turn left and continue.

5.5 Pass between two ponds at Elk Pass; turn sharply left and pass a few campsites, continuing uphill.

6.2 T junction into the H. G. Leach Trail; turn right and head for the summit.

6.4 Nippletop Mountain summit; turn around here.

6.6 The Elk Pass Trail is on your left, continue straight onto the ridge.

8.2 Scoot out onto the rock at the Dial Mountain summit; bear right in the woods to continue.

9.4 Cross over the Bear Den Mountain summit.

10.1 Old burn area viewpoint.

11.9 Turn right at Lake Road and follow it to the end.

12.6 Sign out at the trail register.

13.4 Arrive back at the parking lot.

10 Allen Mountain

Given its length and difficulty, many wonder why anyone would hike Allen at all. If you want to become a 46er, you have to tackle it. As a bonus, you can get some nice views from the summit, although in my three ascents, I saw nothing.

Start: Mount Adams/Allen Mountain Trailhead
Distance: 18.0 miles out and back
Summit elevation: 4,340 feet
4,000-footers rank of the 115: 51
Elevation gain: 3,693 feet
Difficulty: Difficult
Hiking time: 10–14 hours
Trails used: East River Trail, Allen Mountain Herd Path
Nearest town: Newcomb
Views: Good

Water sources: Several along the way, so no issues finding water
Canine compatibility: Fair (long distance); may need to be careful with dogs if the water crossing is high at the Opalescent River. Bridges have been erected and washed away in this location.
Special considerations: Crossing the Opalescent (and Skylight Brook) can be dangerous during high water.

Finding the trailhead: From the NY Thruway (I-87), take exit 29 for North Hudson and head west on Blue Ridge Road for 17.5 miles. Turn right onto Tahawus Road. If coming from the west, take NY 28N and travel east 2.8 miles from the Newcomb post office and turn left onto CR 75. In 0.4 mile merge with Blue Ridge Road; continue east 0.9 mile and turn left onto Tahawus Road. Travel on Tahawus Road and in 0.5 mile bear left, staying on Tahawus Road. Travel another 5.9 miles and take a sharp left turn onto Upper Works Road. In 2 miles you will see trailhead parking for the Santanoni Range on your left. In 2.8 miles you will pass the old McIntyre Furnace, on your right; in another 0.2 mile, the trailhead parking will be on your right as well. GPS (parking lot): N44°4'52.15" / W74°3'18.29"

The Hike

Not to discourage anyone, but Allen Mountain earns its moniker—"bane of the 46ers"—for good reason. It's the longest hike of the Adirondack 46 peaks; much of it's on herd paths; the final ascent up the Allen slide is brutal in any season; and it's a treed summit, as you can see from the photo. But let's focus on the positive: this area of the Adirondacks tends to be less trafficked; there are, for a change, several near-flat sections that provide respite; and I have heard of the views that can be had from Allen, although I have never seen them myself.

From the trailhead in Newcomb, follow the trail to the first water crossing of the Hudson River within a few short minutes. A half mile into the hike you reach the bypass around Lake Jimmy, curving left around the water. A few minutes later you'll see some small cabins and the trail to Adams on the left (a cool fire tower hike), which we always joke about "running up," as if you'd have enough energy on an Allen hike.

Treed summit of Allen, a site for sore eyes MICHELE HERNANDEZ BAYLISS

You follow state trails, old foot trails, and even some old logging/gravel roads along the way until you reach the Opalescent River at the 4-mile mark.

Around the 2- to 2.5-hour mark, you arrive at the junction to Marcy the long way via Flowed Lands, as you can see on the sign. You want to bear right onto the official "herd path," which is well marked and easy to find. You cross a logging road and follow the arrows until you arrive at an internal register. Continuing, you have mostly woods until you cross Lower Twin Brook and finally reach the High Peaks Wilderness. Now the trail heads down a bit as you approach the Skylight Brook basin and then Skylight Brook. From the brook, you climb almost 1 mile until you reach a small waterfall, which marks the beginning of the super steep climb.

Now the fun begins. Although this is a trail of sorts, it's mostly a slide and has a ton of obstacles, "red slime" on the rocks, which makes the footing very slick, and brutally steep sections. It's one of the hardest climbs in the Adirondacks, 1.5 miles nearly straight up. Near the top, you traverse to the left on a shelf—taking care not to tumble to your death—and enter the woods for the final (and, you guessed it) uphill section until you reach the Allen Mountain sign. If it's clear, you can see Nippletop, the Dixes, Panther Gorge, and much of the Great Range from the lookout past the summit. The climb of the slide takes typically 1.5–2 hours up, 1 hour down. The down is terrifying in parts, especially if it is wet. I actually prefer this hike in winter, when we can butt slide down several super steep sections. Take care—you are basically 9 long miles from civilization, and rescue would not be fast. Don't be afraid to crabwalk down steep sections, and use all the trees and branches you can.

Once you return to the base, you have 15–20 minutes to Skylight Brook before the long hike out. This section features some uphill sections you might not have

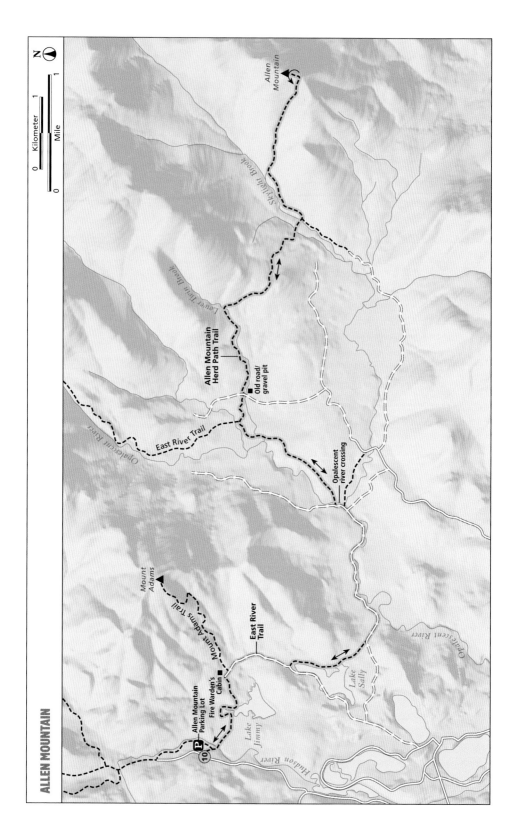

ALLEN MOUNTAIN

noticed on the approach, but your legs will remind you on the return. In winter, this hike took us 14.5 hours, which is not unusual when trail breaking is involved. The fastest I've done it is 11 hours. In short, depending on the conditions, hikers should allow between 10 and 14 hours but understand that it could take longer. Super-fast hikers have done it in 8–9 hours (you can backcountry ski parts of the trail), but that would not be me.

Miles and Directions

0.0   Start from the trailhead parking lot.

0.1   Cross the Hudson River on a fun suspension bridge.

0.5   Travel around Lake Jimmy on the left.

0.7   Once around Lake Jimmy, the trail becomes an old woods road.

1.0   Pass the Mount Adams fire warden cabin.

1.1   The Mount Adams Trail is on your left, but continue on the road.

1.7   Turn left off the old woods road and follow the marked path. You'll see Lake Sally on your right.

2.5   The trail comes to another old woods road; turn left on this road and head east.

4.0   Turn right off the road onto the marked path; you're at the Opalescent River crossing.

5.2   Once across the river, continue on the marked path till you reach the East River Trail–Allen Mountain Herd Path junction. Bear right to follow the unmarked herd path.

5.5   Arrive at yet another old log road; turn left and follow this road for 100 yards to an old gravel pit on your right. Head east into the gravel pit; the herd path continues on the other side.

6.3   Cross Lower Twin Brook and continue following the path.

7.5   Cross Skylight Brook with caution and continue. Now the climbing begins.

8.9   Reach the height of land after a steep climb; turn left to make your way to the summit.

9.0   Allen Mountain summit with lookouts just past the top and to the east. Turn around and retrace your steps. You've got a long walk out.

18.0   Arrive back at the parking lot.

11 Santanoni, Panther, and Couchsachraga

There are not many hikes where you can reach three peaks in one day and make a loop hike of it. Bonus: You get to hike in one of the most remote areas of the park.

Start: Bradley Pond Trailhead parking lot
Distance: 15.1-mile loop
Summit elevation: Santanoni: 4,607 feet; Panther: 4,442 feet; Couchsachraga: 3,820 feet
4,000-footers rank of the 115: Santanoni: 31; Panther: 38; Couchsachraga: 115
Elevation gain: 4,813 feet
Difficulty: Strenuous
Hiking time: 12–14 hours

Trails used: Bradley Pond Trail, forest road, herd paths, Santanoni Express Trail
Nearest town: Newcomb
Views: Excellent
Water sources: Several water sources on the hike up toward the ridge
Canine compatibility: Okay
Special considerations: This is a very long and often wet hike. Be prepared!

Finding the trailhead: From the NY Thruway (I-87), take exit 29 for North Hudson and head west on Blue Ridge Road for 17.5 miles. Turn right onto Tahawus Road. If coming from the west, take NY 28N east for 2.8 miles from the Newcomb post office and turn left onto CR 75. In 0.4 mile merge with Blue Ridge Road; continue east 0.9 mile and turn left onto Tahawus Road. Travel on Tahawus Road and in 0.5 mile bear left, staying on Tahawus Road. Continue another 5.9 miles and take a sharp left turn onto Upper Works Road. In 2 miles you will see trailhead parking for the Santanoni Range on your left. GPS (trailhead parking): N44°4'8.77" / W74° 3' 41.97"

The Hike

This hike is never easy; in spring and summer, the trail tends to be super muddy. The so-called Express Trail allows you to make a loop, but it is hardly an express, with some crazy steep downhills and a water crossing near the end that can cause problems in any season.

The trail starts fairly flat as you follow an old logging road. Enjoy it while you can, as there are not many other flat sections. About 1.5 to 2 hours into the hike, you will see the left-hand turn for the unmarked Express Trail, which you can descend later in the day. For now, continue to wind through the woods toward Bradley Pond. The several major bridges and mud crossings you have to navigate make this not as fast as you

DID YOU KNOW?

By itself, Couchsachraga Peak would require 3,800 vertical feet to hike, which is why you might as well do all three peaks. It's one of four peaks that was later determined to be under 4,000 feet, but to be a 46er, you still have to hike it.

View from the summit of Santanoni looking out toward many of the ADK high peaks in the Adirondacks and Bradley Pond below MICHELE HERNANDEZ BAYLISS

might think/hope. The trail heads left from Bradley Pond up Panther Brook. You'll hike alongside a huge rock cliff followed by steep climbing, a flat section, and more steep climbing. Finally, as you head up the last steep staircase-like section, you reach a small clearing called Herald Square. We start by doing Panther Peak so we don't have to retrace our steps, so bear right here and head north for the short 15-minute climb up to Panther Peak. Right before the summit is a rock scramble/small cliff you have to navigate to reach the summit platform. The actual summit is back from the rock, so tag it first and then enjoy the views. You can gaze over toward the small hill (Couchsachraga, or Couch) and wonder how it's actually a 4,000-footer. Heading back to Herald Square, follow the trail away from Panther for another 5 minutes until the bigger clearing called Times Square. If you stay to the right of the giant boulder, you will be on the trail toward Couch. This is not my favorite part of the hike, as you lose a lot of vertical feet (900 or so) here, only to have to reclimb it on the return to Times Square. After descending to a col, you have to cross a gigantic bog before the short climb up to Couch, which is steep for the last 5 minutes or so. Although the summit is treed, you do get some very nice views toward Panther and Santanoni Peaks. On the way back, take time to enjoy the northwesterly viewpoint toward the Seward Range and Cold River Valley before chugging back up to the large boulder in Times Square.

For the final leg, head steeply down behind that boulder toward the final peak. The trail is easy to follow until the open woods, when it can be hard to navigate in winter. You have to make your way up to the ridgeline and then follow it up over a few bumps until you reach the beautiful Santanoni summit. The final ascent here is thrilling and will always hold a special place in my heart—it was my final winter

SANTANONI, PANTHER, AND COUCHSACHRAGA

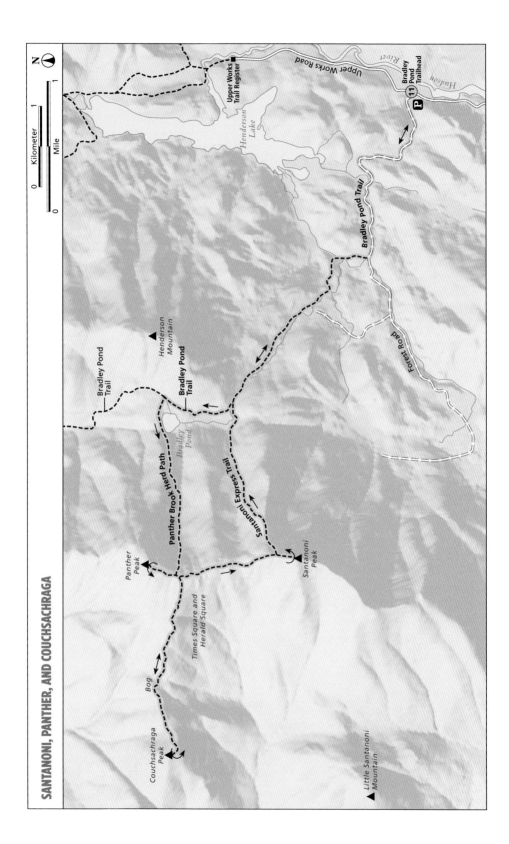

Panther Peak

Bradley Pond Trail

Bradley Pond Trail

Bradley Pond

Panther Brook Herd Path

Santanoni Express Trail

Times Square and Herald Square

Bog

Couchsachraga Peak

Santanoni Peak

Little Santanoni Mountain

Henderson Mountain

Henderson Lake

Upper Works Trail Register

Upper Works Road

Forest Road

Bradley Pond Trail

Bradley Pond Trailhead

Hudson River

P 11

N

0   Kilometer   1

0   Mile   1

Adirondacks peak for my winter 46er patch. If you want to take the "express" trail down, you have to backtrack to the second "hump" and find the entry point. It's super steep at first. You do hit a lovely flat wooded section, but then it's down, down, down, quite steeply for the remainder. When you finally reach the logging road, you have the final slog out. This hike typically takes 12–14 hours to do the loop we

What your tired feet will look like after wading through the "Couch swamp"
MICHELE HERNANDEZ BAYLISS

describe. After completing it, you can vote on whether you think this is harder than doing the three Sewards in a day or not. It's a close race for most difficult Adirondacks hike.

Miles and Directions

0.0 Start from the parking lot and head west on the forest road.

1.8 Turn right off the road and onto the hiking trail.

3.5 A small rock cairn marks the left-hand turn to the Express Trail; stay straight on the Bradley Pond Trail.

4.1 Signs indicate the left-hand turn to the start of the herd path.

5.6 Arrive at Herald Square; turn right, heading north toward Panther Peak.

5.8 Arrive at the Panther Peak summit; retrace your steps to Herald Square.

6.1 Pass straight through Herald Square to arrive at an opening known as Times Square; head west from this point.

7.0 Cross the bog.

7.6 Arrive at Couchsachraga Peak; retrace your steps to Times Square.

8.2 Recross the bog.

9.1 Back at Times Square, bear right around a boulder and head south toward Santanoni Peak.

10.0 The Express Trail heads down on your left on the bump right before the final summit bump.

10.1 Arrive at the summit of Santanoni Peak; retrace your steps toward the Express Trail.

10.2 Bear right down the Express Trail, which can be somewhat hard to find at times.

11.6 Enter back onto the Bradley Pond Trail.

13.3 At the road, turn left.

15.1 Arrive back at the parking lot.

Option

Couldn't find the express route down? Retrace your steps to Bradley Pond and out. Distance: 17.1 miles; elevation gain: 5,213 feet.

12 Sawteeth, Gothics, Armstrong, Upper Wolfjaw, and Lower Wolfjaw

This is one of the most iconic hikes in the Northeast, with tons of elevation gain but also amazing views and a huge sense of accomplishment to knock off five of the 46er peaks in one shot. (Pyramid is a bonus peak that doesn't "count," but, as you can see from the photo, it has the best view in the park.)

Start: Ausable Club parking lot
Distance: 14.4-mile loop
Summit elevation: Sawteeth: 4,100 feet; Gothics: 4,736 feet; Armstrong: 4,400 feet; Upper Wolfjaw: 4,185 feet; Lower Wolfjaw: 4,175 feet
4,000-footers rank of the 115: Sawteeth: 81 (tied); Gothics: 24; Armstrong: 45 (tied); Upper Wolfjaw: 65; Lower Wolfjaw: 68
Elevation gain: 5,337 feet
Difficulty: Strenuous
Hiking time: 10–13 hours
Trails used: Ausable Club Road, Lake Road, A. W. Weld Trail, Sawteeth Trail, State Range Trail, W. A. White Trail, Wedge Brook Trail, West River Trail, River Crossover Trail
Nearest town: Keene Valley

Views: Excellent
Water sources: Several water sources down low; however, once on the ridge, water is extremely scarce.
Canine compatibility: Dogs are not allowed on Adirondack Mountain Reserve (AMR) property, which this track crosses.
Special considerations: Parking is free as of publication, but a permit is required ahead of time (purchase online at hikeamr.org), and there is an attendant on duty during the summer months. This approach crosses private Ausable Club property, so be respectful of their property. Move out of the way of all vehicular traffic, as Lake Road can be busy with buses transporting guests to the Ausable Lakes (no bus rides for hikers).

Finding the trailhead: From the NY Thruway (I-87), take exit 30 for Lake Placid/Keene Valley and head north on US 9 toward NY 73, reaching an intersection with NY 73 at 2.2 miles. Continue on NY 73, passing Round Pond parking for Dix Mountain at 5.2 miles and parking for Giant Mountain at 6.1 miles. At 7.6 miles the Ausable Club Road and parking will be on your left after heading down a very steep grade; slow down. From the north and the town of Keene, travel south on NY 73. Continue past the intersection with NY 9N at 1.9 miles, passing through the town of Keene Valley at 4.9 miles, until finally arriving at the road and parking lot on your right at 8 miles. GPS (parking lot): N44°8'58.94" / W73°46'4.05"

The Hike

From the St. Hubert's parking, follow the golf club road about 0.5 mile toward the Ausable Club and bear left down the hill to the ranger cabin/trail register. Allow your legs to warm up on the relatively gentle upward-sloping Lake Road, which rises about 700 vertical feet. At the final hill crest/height of land before you would descend to lower Ausable Lake, make a sharp right and walk downhill to a bridge that offers

My favorite Adirondack view from the summit of Pyramid Peak; from left to right: Marcy, Basin, Saddleback, west ridge and west peak of Gothics MICHELE HERNANDEZ BAYLISS

picture-perfect views of Indian Head cliffs on the left. Follow the Gothics Trail (the well-built Arthur Weld Trail), but do take a peek over Rainbow Falls on the right; just don't be a dropout (stay back from the ledge)—several people have fallen from here.

Continue winding up and around until you reach a flat section that means you are now on state land. Get ready for the climbing—straight up the Weld Trail until, miraculously, the trail flattens out and you come to the Sawteeth/Gothics col and a fork. Fuel up before starting the 25-minute ascent of Sawteeth, to the left. Although it starts gradually, there are some challenging scrambles, with one particularly tricky spot that involves skirting to the left, pushing off a tree, and powering up a rock face to safety. After a bit more scrambling, turn around and enjoy a very imposing view back toward Pyramid Peak. Once the trail levels off, you have a short flattish section for a few minutes until you arrive at the "summit" on the right-hand side, marked by a rock with one of the best views in the Adirondacks. The only mountain with a better view is the next one you will hit, Pyramid Peak (not an official 46er). Enjoy the views of Marcy, Haystack, Skylight, Basin, Saddleback, and the west ridge and west peak of Gothics.

Back at the col you hit the unrelenting climb to Pyramid as you skirt some cliffs. Cling to the trees and head up several rock faces until you emerge just under the summit rock, to your left, once the climbing ends. Though this peak doesn't "count," do *not* miss the views from the overlook rock on Pyramid—our favorite perch. Though you are staring toward the north into the face of Gothics, which looks terrifying, it actually takes only about 10 minutes to descend the very steep next section of trail to

Looking back to the super-steep cone of Pyramid Peak after having just climbed up toward Gothics MICHELE HERNANDEZ BAYLISS

a col and then another 10–15 minutes to claw your way up Gothics. I love this uphill scramble—once you reach the top, you get to turn around and see just how steep Pyramid is and marvel at how you made it. Before reaching the official summit, you pass the left-hand entrance to the Range Trail, which comes up the west side of the valley (the infamous "cable" section of Gothics), climbs the west ridge of Gothics, and deposits you right on the ridge trail. You still have about 5 minutes straight ahead to reach the actual summit of Gothics, marked with a survey marker on a rock.

Although there are not many ridges in the Adirondacks, you do get to follow a beautiful ridge as you head downhill until you reach the junction with the Beaver Meadow Trail. Many times, we take this trail back and just do Gothics alone or in combination with Sawteeth as a loop. But once you have gained all this elevation, you may want to bag the final three peaks of the day, as the additional gain is nothing like what you have already done. From the col, it's only about 25 minutes to Armstrong Peak, a ledge with an awesome view.

Enjoy the downhill sections on the way to Upper Wolfjaw, where you have to descend an infamous ladder (often snow/ice covered in winter and very treacherous), navigate boulders and obstacles, and then do a short but steep climb to reach Upper Wolfjaw. One more push to descend *very* steeply (where you will hit the junction

DID YOU KNOW?

The section from Lower Wolfjaw to Gothics you traversed is part of the Great Range Traverse—an even harder hike that starts at Rooster Comb; does Lower Wolfjaw, Upper Wolfjaw, and Gothics; but then adds Saddleback, Basin, Haystack, and Marcy for the ultimate challenge. Attempt if you dare!

on the right with the Wedge Brook Trail, on your left to head toward John Brooks Lodge) before the final uphill of the day to regain some elevation to reach the summit of Lower Wolfjaw. Now you head back down to the intersection to catch the Wedge Brook Trail back toward the Ausable Club. This trail is quite gentle and will give you a chance to reflect on the fact that you did one of the hardest hikes in the Adirondacks. Follow the trail back to Lake Road (we'd avoid the other trails that parallel) and head left back toward the gate and the road walk back to your car 10–13 hours later.

Miles and Directions

0.0 Start at the parking lot and head west up the road, away from NY 73.

0.6 Turn left onto Lake Road.

0.8 Sign in at the trail register.

1.5 Pass the H. G. Leach Trail to the Dial Mountain junction.

2.7 Pass the Beaver Meadow Trail on your right; in 70 yards, the Gill Brook Trail is on your left.

3.3 Pass the junction with the Gill Brook Cutoff Trail, on your left.

3.9 Pass the Indian Head Trail junction and the end of Lake Road; drop down and cross the lake outlet on the footbridge.

4.2 The spur trail to Rainbow Falls is on your right.

4.3 View from the top of Rainbow Falls.

5.5 At the T intersection of the Weld and Sawteeth Trails, take a left.

6.0 At the Sawteeth Mountain summit viewing platform, turn around and descend.

6.5 At the junction, continue straight.

6.9 Cross over Pyramid Peak; the summit view is a short hop to the left.

7.2 At the Weld–State Range Trail junction, bear right onto the Gothics ridge.

7.3 Cross over the open summit of Gothics Mountain. Descend the trail.

7.7 Arrive at the Range–Beaver Meadow Trail junction and bear left, continuing on the Range Trail.

8.1 Reach the viewing rock of Armstrong Mountain. Continue on the trail.

8.7 Arrive at the short, 20-yard spur trail on your left to the summit of Upper Wolfjaw.

9.1 Continue and arrive at the Upper Wolfjaw false summit with a large boulder in an open area.

9.4 At the Range–Wolfjaw–W. A. White Trail junction, continue straight on the W. A. White Trail.

9.4 In 150 feet, reach the Wolfjaw Cutoff Trail; turn left and make your way uphill.

9.5 The Wedge Brook Trail comes in from the right; bear left and head uphill.

9.8 Reach the Lower Wolfjaw summit; turn around to retrace.

10.1 Back at the Wedge Brook junction, turn left onto the Wedge Brook Trail.

10.3 At the Wedge Brook–Wolfjaw Notch Cutoff Trail junction, turn left.

11.6 Arrive at the Wedge Brook–West River Trail junction and turn left, crossing a small footbridge.

12.4 At the West River–River Crossover Trail junction, turn right, heading toward the river; cross the footbridge.

12.7 Cross straight through the River Crossover–East River Trail junction, making your way to Lake Road.

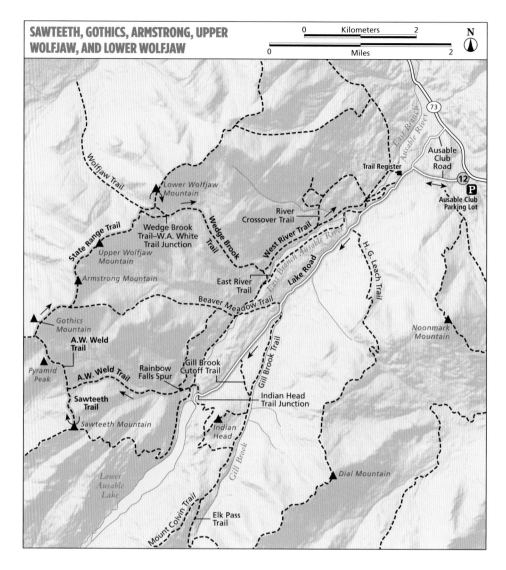

12.8 Turn left onto Lake Road and follow it to the end.

13.6 Sign out at the trail register.

14.4 Arrive back at the parking lot.

Options

If you don't think you have the legs for so much elevation gain in one hike, try breaking it up into two:

1. Do Sawteeth, Gothics, and Armstrong and come out on the Beaver Meadow Trail to Lake Road. Distance: 13.7 miles; elevation gain: 4,393 feet.

2. Upper and Lower Wolfjaw can be tackled as an out-and-back hike on the Wedge Brook Trail. Distance: 11.0 miles; elevation gain: 4,075 feet.

13 Marcy, Skylight, and Gray

While you are tackling the highest mountain in New York State (5,344 feet) and the Adirondacks, you might as well tag two more peaks toward your 46er quest and enjoy the five-star view from Skylight.

Start: High Peaks Information Center (HPIC) parking lot
Distance: 17.2-mile loop
Summit elevation: Marcy: 5,344 feet; Skylight: 4,926 feet; Gray: 4,840 feet
4,000-footers rank of the 115: Marcy: 6; Skylight: 12; Gray: 16 (tied)
Elevation gain: 4,952 feet
Difficulty: Extremely strenuous
Hiking time: 12–14 hours
Trails used: Van Hoevenberg Trail, Avalanche Pass Trail, Lake Arnold Trail, Mount Marcy Trail, Skylight Trail, Gray Herd Path

Views: Excellent
Nearest town: Lake Placid
Water sources: Several water sources on the hike except for the tops of each mountain
Canine compatibility: Maybe; a long day for dogs, and the rock scrambles up Gray can prove difficult.
Special considerations: Weekend summertime parking is very busy, and securing a spot will require an early start. There is a fee for parking in this lot. Extremely long day; plan accordingly.

Finding the trailhead: Travel east on NY 73 for 1.6 miles from the Lake Placid Olympic Ski Jumping Complex. Or, from the town of Keene, travel west 10.9 miles on NY 73 toward Lake Placid. Turn south onto Adirondack Loj Road and travel 4.7 miles to the end, where there is a payment collection station. Pay a fee and park in one of several lots. GPS (parking lot): N44°10'58.32" / W73°57'46.78"

The Hike

Like many hikes in this area, you begin at the HPIC and head out on the Van Hoevenberg Trail toward Mount Marcy. In 45 minutes to 1 hour, you arrive at Marcy Dam, where a ton of trails branch out. After enjoying the views of Mount Colden and Wright Peak, keep left to follow the Van Ho toward Phelps and Tabletop. As you head up the trail, you will see the left-hand exit to the trail up Phelps; continue straight until you reach the Tabletop junction, on the left. Soon after, you can detour for the scenic side trip to Indian Falls.

Stay on the Van Ho and continue the climb to Marcy. When you break out from the trees and get near the cone, you are treated to some amazing views of the open approach if it's clear. In good weather, this part of the hike is my favorite. In foggy or snowy weather, however, many have gotten hopelessly lost as the trail winds around above tree line. The ascent is fairly mild here compared to what you have already done, and when you reach the summit (stop to read the plaque), you can see almost

Our fearless crew (Melissa and Heather) near the summit of Mount Marcy, with Haystack and Little Haystack behind us DEAN J. OUELLETTE

every mountain in the Adirondacks (forty-three of the other forty-five peaks). I love the view toward Skylight and Haystack/Little Haystack and the Macs.

If you are continuing (as opposed to an out-and-back), you descend steeply on the southwest side toward Skylight. This section can be very icy in winter, so watch your step. It's less than 1 mile to the Four Corners, but it goes by quickly (unless you lose the trail in winter, as we did; in which case it can take 2 hours). It's exciting to reach Four Corners—four trails converge here, and the left-hand route takes you down Panther Gorge, a wild and less-trafficked area. From here it's a straight shot up a short steep section to reach Skylight, one of our favorite peaks due to its large bald summit and wide-angle views. Enjoy the views back to Marcy, Gray, and also to Allen, the Santanonis, the Sewards, Haystack, and more.

The trip back to Four Corners is quick, so now you just have one more peak—if you have the energy. You head left as you skirt Lake Tear of the Clouds; right at the end of the lake is a small cairn that marks the herd path to Gray. Although the path is short, it's quite steep, and this one always seems to drag on. You have to drop down to a rock and then up again to reach the true summit, from which you can usually see over to Marcy. Head back down to Lake Tear and continue away from Four Corners

DID YOU KNOW?

Lake Tear of the Clouds is the highest water source that serves as the origin point of the mighty Hudson River.

to the Feldspar Lean-to in under 1.5 miles down a quite steep but beautiful trail. Although normally you have all downhill to look forward to, the section that always kills me is regaining the height of land late in the day as you head back up toward Lake Arnold and Mount Colden. This section is also swampy, with boardwalks, and can be tough when it's very muddy. Take your time—once you head up this section, it really is downhill the rest of the way back to Marcy Dam and the final 2-plus miles back to the HPIC. This hike is *long*. If you do all three peaks, it's typically takes 12–14 hours. Bring a lot of water or a pump, as there is nothing easy about doing all three of these in one day.

Miles and Directions

0.0 Start from the parking lot and head west after signing the trail register.

1.0 At the junction of the Van Hoevenberg and Algonquin Trails, turn left and continue on the well-worn path.

2.2 Arrive at Marcy Dam and turn sharply left to follow the pond outlet and reach a footbridge crossing the stream; turn right after the crossing.

2.4 Come to the Van Hoevenberg-Avalanche Pass Trail junction; bear left on the Van Hoevenberg Trail.

3.3 The trail to go up Phelps comes in from your left; continue straight on the Van Hoevenberg Trail.

3.6 Cross the bridge over Phelps Brook.

4.3 The trail to Tabletop is on your left; continue straight.

4.4 The spur to Indian Falls takes off to your right; the Lake Arnold Crossover Trail heads off to the right within 100 yards.

6.0 The Hopkins Trail comes in from your left; bear right to continue on the Van Hoevenberg Trail.

6.4 Beautiful view of Mount Marcy on your right.

6.6 The Phelps Trail intersects the Van Hoevenberg Trail and the beginning of travel above tree line; bear right and continue up.

7.1 Arrive at the summit of Mount Marcy; continue down the other side.

7.4 You're back into the trees just after Schofield Cobble (a rocky knob).

7.8 Arrive at the Four Corners junction; continue straight.

8.3 Arrive at the above-tree line summit of Skylight; turn around retrace your steps.

8.8 Back at Four Corners, turn left on the Mount Marcy Trail.

9.1 Turn right at a rock cairn to head up Gray Peak.

9.4 Arrive at the Mount Gray summit; retrace your path back down.

9.7 At the junction, turn right and head downhill.

10.9 At the Lake Arnold–Mount Marcy Trail junction, turn right. After 60 yards, the Feldspar Lean-to spur will be on your left; continue on the Lake Arnold Trail.

12.3 The Lake Arnold–L. Morgan Porter Trail to the Mount Colden junction is on your left; continue straight.

12.8 The Indian Falls–Lake Arnold Crossover Trail junction is on your right across the flowing stream.

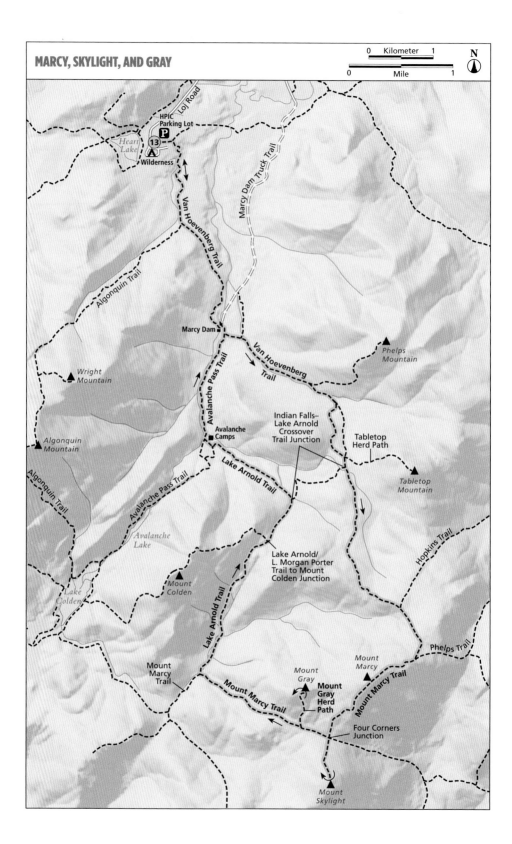

0   Kilometer   1

0   Mile   1

N

HPIC
Parking Lot

LOJ Road

Heart
Lake

P

13

Wilderness

Marcy Dam Truck Trail

Van Hoevenberg Trail

Algonquin Trail

Marcy Dam

Van Hoevenberg
Trail

Phelps
Mountain

Wright
Mountain

Avalanche Pass Trail

Avalanche
Camps

Indian Falls–
Lake Arnold
Crossover
Trail Junction

Tabletop
Herd Path

Algonquin
Mountain

Lake Arnold Trail

Tabletop
Mountain

Algonquin Trail

Avalanche Pass Trail

Avalanche
Lake

Lake Arnold/
L. Morgan Porter
Trail to Mount
Colden Junction

Hopkins Trail

Lake
Colden

Mount
Colden

Lake Arnold Trail

Phelps Trail

Mount
Marcy
Trail

Mount
Gray

Mount
Marcy

Mount Marcy Trail

Mount Marcy Trail

Mount
Gray
Herd
Path

Four Corners
Junction

Mount
Skylight

Michele, Heather, and Dean atop Mount Marcy on Heather's ADK 46er finish hike. MICHELE HERNANDEZ BAYLISS

13.8 Arrive at Avalanche Camps; bear right and head toward Marcy Dam on the Avalanche Pass Trail.

14.8 Back near the dam, the Van Hoevenberg Trail reenters from the right.

15.0 Arrive back at Marcy Dam.

16.2 With only 1 mile to go, turn right at the Algonquin junction.

17.2 Arrive back at the HPIC parking lot.

Option

From the Lake Arnold Trail junction, continue down the Mount Marcy Trail to Lake Colden. Work around the lake and on to Avalanche Lake, where you can walk across the "Hitch-up Matildas" then down to Avalanche Camps. Distance: 18.8 miles; elevation gain: 5,152 feet.

14 Dix Range (Macomb, South Dix, Grace, Hough, Dix)

Where else can you nail five peaks in one day without adding more mileage than hiking just one of the mountains as an out-and-back in the range? Did we mention the killer views from every peak?

Start: Elk Lake Trailhead on Elk Lake Road
Distance: 17.5 miles point to point (from overflow lot) with car shuttle
Summit elevation: Macomb: 4,405 feet; South Dix: 4,060 feet; Grace: 4,012 feet; Hough: 4,400 feet; Dix: 4,857 feet
4,000-footers rank: Macomb: 43; South Dix: 88 (tied); Grace: 104; Hough: 45 (tied); Dix: 15
Elevation gain: 5,138 feet
Difficulty: Extremely strenuous
Hiking time: 11–14 hours
Trails used: Elk Lake Trailhead, Hunter's Pass Trail, unmaintained herd paths, NY 73 trail, Round Pond lot
Nearest town: Keene Valley

Views: Excellent
Water sources: None once up at elevation. Fill up before leaving the Hunter's Pass Trail going toward the Macomb slide and then again at the Bouquet River Lean-to once you've done all five mountains.
Canine compatibility: Okay; a few rock scrambles toward the top of Dix could be difficult.
Special considerations: The Hunter's Pass Trail crosses private land, so mind your manners and adhere to the proper trail. No camping while on private land. The Elk Lake Trailhead access and access to the Hunter's Pass Trail are closed in the fall during big game season. Check for actual hunting season dates, which can change from year to year.

Finding the trailhead: From the NY Thruway (I-87), take exit 29 for North Hudson and head west on Blue Ridge Road for 4 miles. Turn right onto Elk Lake Road and at 2.8 miles you will see a parking lot on your left. This lot is an overflow lot in summer and the main parking lot during winter. There is an open gate after this lot (this gate will be closed in winter). Continue down the road 0.5 mile to Clear Pond and drive past an open gate (this gate will also be closed in winter). Continue for 2 miles and you'll see trailhead signs and a small parking lot on your right. Do not park off the road; stay in the lot. If the lot is full, drive back past Clear Pond to the overflow lot. *Warning:* Your car will be towed if it's not in one of these lots. GPS (summer lot): N44°1'14.73" / W73°49'39.64"; (overflow lot): N43°59'15.23" / W73°49'51.14"
   Round Pond Trailhead: From the NY Thruway (I-87), take exit 30 to US 9 in North Hudson. Drive north for 2.3 miles and then merge with NY 73, going west toward Keene. In 3 miles the parking lot will be on your left. GPS (NY 73, Round Pond): N44°7'55.18" / W73°43'55.04"

The Hike

The five-mountain Dix Range is one of the most notorious hikes in the Adirondacks. In part that's because of the remoteness and the long mileage. We usually drop a car on NY 73 near Keene Valley to leave all our options open (one route off Dix heads to NY 73 while the other loops back to Elk Lake, where we start)—important in winter, when these trails are not always broken out. Out of the forty-six Adirondack peaks,

Spectacular view from a rocky ledge past the Grace summit looking out toward Hough/Pough and Mount Dix on the right MICHELE HERNANDEZ BAYLISS

twenty are "untrailed," meaning there are no signs/markers. Instead, you must follow the "herd paths," which in summer are fairly easy to make out, although many hikers get lost trying to follow these routes, even during summer.

The flat hike to the Macomb slide is quick and easy until the climbing begins. The route follows a slide (Adirondack code for "a heap of rubble that heads straight up the side of a mountain where a bunch of rocks once slid down"). Near the top of the slide, you exit the slide itself to enter the woods where, heartbreakingly, you still have more to ascend before reaching the actual summit. From here you descend steeply and then have a fairly easy approach to South Dix, which has a beautiful and open summit. From South Dix out and back to Grace takes just over 1 hour, with a bit of up and down but nothing too intimidating, although it is a herd path and can be hard to follow in winter. We recommend continuing a few feet past the Grace summit to the incredible rock ledge just beyond, from which we took the chapter photo of Hough and Dix. Returning to South Dix, assess the time and weather to see if you

The Macomb Slide on approach to Macomb
Michele Hernandez Bayliss

are up for the major challenge of the next two peaks. As you head down the flank of South Dix toward Pough (a subpeak) and Hough, the work begins. The 1.8-mile stretch from South Dix to Hough and then to Dix may be the hardest section in the Adirondacks, and with deep snow and herd paths, you might face the impossible twin task of trail finding and trail breaking.

This section in summer typically takes us 2–3 hours, but one winter it took us 6.5 hours. Finally you reach the rock scramble, which is right before the actual intersection with the Beckhorn Trail, which approaches from the left. At this juncture you can either continue over the summit and descend toward Round Pond (if you left a car on NY 73) or return via the Beckhorn Trail (about the same distance). The Beckhorn Trail is a tough one with some intimidating rock ledges, so if it's wet, you may opt to head back toward Round Pound by climbing over Dix near Hunter's Pass and then taking a right toward Round Pond.

After the first super steep 1-mile staircase-like section, the going gets easier. The next signpost is the lean-to that marks the 4-mile point and a long walk out. This challenging five-summit hike is challenging in any season but features some of the most remote and beautiful trails in the Adirondack wilderness. Allow 11–14 hours.

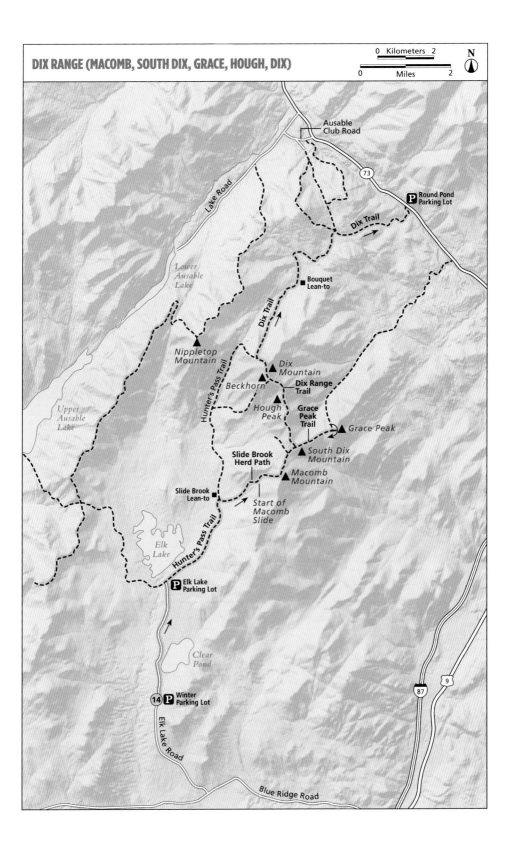

0   Kilometers   2

0   Miles   2

N

Ausable
Club Road

73

Round Pond
Parking Lot

Dix Trail

Lake Road

Lower
Ausable
Lake

Bouquet
Lean-to

Dix Trail

Nippletop
Mountain

Dix
Mountain

Beckhorn

Dix Range
Trail

Hough
Peak

Grace
Peak
Trail

Grace Peak

Upper
Ausable
Lake

Hunter's Pass Trail

Slide Brook
Herd Path

South Dix
Mountain

Macomb
Mountain

Slide Brook
Lean-to

Start of
Macomb
Slide

Elk
Lake

Hunter's Pass Trail

Elk Lake
Parking Lot

Clear
Pond

14   Winter
Parking Lot

Elk Lake Road

87   9

Blue Ridge Road

Miles and Directions

0.0 Start at the overflow/winter lot and head north on the gravel road.

0.5 Clear Pond will be on your right, a caretaker house and outbuildings on your left.

2.5 The summer lot and trailhead are on your right. The Elk Lake–Marcy Trail is right before this on your left (this trail goes into Panther Gorge). Turn right through the parking lot and follow the Hunter's Pass Trail.

4.8 Come to the Slide Brook crossing/Slide Brook Lean-to and turn right to summit Macomb Mountain up the Macomb slide.

5.1 Start of the Macomb slide.

6.2 Arrive at the Macomb summit.

6.8 The herd path to the left heads down Lillian Brook and connects with the Hunter's Pass Trail.

7.0 Head up the rock scramble to the summit of South Dix. Continue east down the herd path.

7.9 Just before you start to climb, a trail comes in from the left; continue straight.

8.0 Arrive at the rocky summit of Grace Mountain. Turn around and retrace your steps.

9.0 At South Dix, 40 yards to the west is a herd path heading north toward Hough; take this path.

9.5 Another herd path heading down Lillian Brook comes in from the left; continue straight.

9.8 Pass over the pointy Hough summit.

10.7 Arrive at the boulder that is the Beckhorn. Around to the west and down is the Beckhorn Trail. Continue north on the ridge to Dix.

10.8 Dix Mountain summit. Continue north and down the trail.

11.3 At this junction, bear right. (The trail on the left is the Hunter's Pass Trail, which will lead you back to Elk Lake.)

13.2 Cross the stream and arrive at the Bouquet Lean-to.

15.3 Reach the four-way junction with the Felder-Adler and Old Dix Trails. Bear right at this junction.

16.6 Come to Round Pond and follow the trail around to the left.

17.5 Arrive at NY 73 and reach the Round Pond Trailhead in a few hundred feet.

Options

1. Elk Lake summer lot to Macomb via slide to South Dix to Grace to South Dix to Lillian Brook herd path to the Elk Lake parking lot. Distance: 11.3 miles; elevation gain: 3,200 feet.

2. Elk Lake summer lot to Hough via the Lillian Brook herd path to Dix to the Beckhorn Trail to the Elk Lake parking lot. Distance: 12 miles; elevation gain: 3,400 feet.

3. Round Pond parking to Dix summit as an out-and-back. Distance: 13.6 miles; elevation gain: 3,200 feet.

15 Haystack, Basin, and Saddleback

This hike features what is generally considered the most challenging section of the entire Adirondacks, the infamous Saddleback cliffs, plus you get three mountains in less mileage (but more elevation) than just doing an out-and-back to Haystack.

Start: Garden parking lot
Distance: 17.0-mile loop
Summit elevation: Haystack: 4,960 feet; Basin: 4,827 feet; Saddleback: 4,515 feet
4,000-footers rank of the 115: Haystack: 11; Basin: 19; Saddleback: 35
Elevation gain: 5,079 feet
Difficulty: Extremely strenuous
Hiking time: 10-13 hours
Trails used: Phelps Trail, State Range Trail, Orebed Brook Trail, Woodsfall Trail
Nearest town: Keene Valley
Views: Excellent

Water sources: Several water sources on the hike up toward the ridge. John's Brook Lodge has an outside faucet in the summertime.
Canine compatibility: Not good; the Saddleback cliffs will prove an extreme challenge unless you can carry your dog up a 100-foot cliff.
Special considerations: The Garden parking lot is small and fills up fast in summer. There is a nominal charge to park here, and an attendant is usually on duty during busy times of the year. The road leading up to the lot is very narrow, so drive cautiously.

Finding the trailhead: From the NY Thruway (I-87), take exit 30 for Lake Placid/Keene Valley and head north on US 9 toward NY 73, reaching an intersection with NY 73 at 2.2 miles. Continue on NY 73, passing Round Pond parking for Dix Mountain at 5.2 miles and parking for Giant Mountain at 6.1 miles. At 7.6 miles, the Ausable Club Road and parking will be on your left after heading down a very steep grade; slow down for hikers crossing. Continue on NY 73 until you reach the center of Keene Valley and Adirondack Road, on your left at 10.6 miles. From the north and the town of Keene, travel south on NY 73, continuing past the intersection with NY 9N at 1.9 miles. Enter the town of Keene Valley and Adirondack Road on your right at 4.9 miles. From Adirondack Road, travel 0.6 mile and bear right onto Interbrook Road. Travel to the end in another 0.9 mile. GPS (parking lot): N44°11'19.93" / W73°48'57.80"

The Hike

This hike is super challenging in terms of sheer length, elevation gain, and technical difficulty. Do not bring a dog—the cliffs are no joke. We always start with Haystack and do a counterclockwise loop over Basin and Saddleback. Starting at the Garden Trailhead, follow the yellow DEC markers on the Phelps Trail to Johns Brooks Lodge. This section is quite easy, and you should make it in 1.5 hours or less. The signs here are confusing, but you want to head straight (not left) on the Phelps Trail toward Marcy. It usually takes 45 minutes to reach the Bushnell Falls Lean-to, where you want to head left toward Slant Rock, crossing over Johns Brook. Although you cover a lot of mileage from the Garden to Slant Rock, much of it is fairly flat. The climb starts after Slant Rock. Pay attention—the trail markers are now the red DEC markers. Otherwise, you would be heading to Marcy on the Hopkins Trail.

An hour later you'll hit the junction for the Shorey Shortcut just pass Slant Rock. (FYI, it's not really a shortcut, and many hikers have cursed its rough, steep-up/steep-down terrain.) We recommend continuing on the red trail for the steep ascent toward Haystack. I prefer this route; it is more direct, plus you get the best view in the entire park—the view from the height of land (Horse Head Hill) toward Little Haystack and Haystack. This subpeak is more challenging than Haystack, as you scramble up the large rock face then follow the blazes carefully down the steep back side rather than going right down the cliff. In winter, this section often requires crampons/ice axes. Once you get down, it's a fun and relatively easy ascent up Haystack except for

Heather braving the ladder section on the way up Basin MICHELE HERNANDEZ BAYLISS

Sunrise view from Haystack with the lumpy outline of Basin Michele Hernandez Bayliss

one cliff-like crack that will get your heart pumping. Take time to enjoy what is our favorite summit of all, as it's less hiked than Marcy and more remote. Little Haystack looks scary from here, but the reclimb is easier than the descent. Once at the junction, head down the very steep trail toward Basin. For those who want to split up this hike, the Sno-Bird tentsite is beautiful; at over 4,000 feet, it's the highest campsite in the Adirondacks.

Now comes a very tough uphill to Basin. Ladders, scary slabs, and tough footing make this a challenge in any season. The view from Basin is also one of the best viewpoints in the park. Continuing past the summit, you start the brutally steep descent to the col between Saddleback and Basin. From the viewpoint you can see the cliffs up ahead, although it takes about an hour to reach them. My daughter burst into tears the first time she got to this point. The cliffs are scary if you are not a climber. I'm 5-foot-5 and typically need a boost up the first section; then it's manageable if you follow the yellow blazes and the main crack. There are two tough spots for short people, so this hike is best done as an experienced group; turning around would require a brutal reclimbing of Basin and a lot of extra mileage. Once on top of Saddleback, the bulk of the work is done and you wind your way down to the Orebed Trail (awesome butt-sliding in winter). Take a moment to check out the "cable" section of Gothics, which departs from the col you will walk right by at the base of Saddleback. That was one of my favorite routes up the west face of Gothics. Continue down the steep ladder section and head back to Johns Brooks Lodge and then to the Garden. This hike

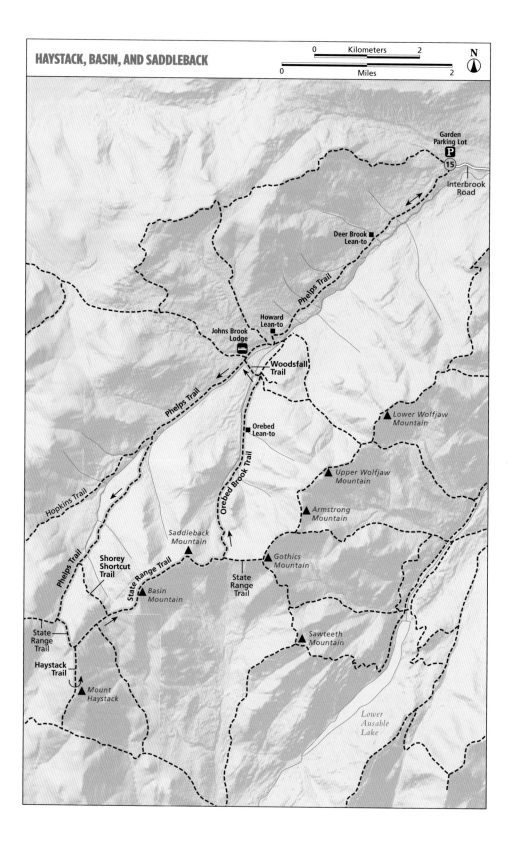

0   Kilometers   2

0   Miles   2

N

Garden
Parking Lot
P
15
Interbrook
Road

Deer Brook
Lean-to

Phelps Trail

Howard
Lean-to
Johns Brook
Lodge

Woodsfall
Trail

Phelps Trail

Lower Wolfjaw
Mountain

Orebed
Lean-to

Upper Wolfjaw
Mountain

Orebed Brook Trail

Armstrong
Mountain

Hopkins Trail

Phelps Trail

Saddleback
Mountain

Gothics
Mountain

Shorey
Shortcut
Trail

State Range Trail

State
Range
Trail

Basin
Mountain

State
Range
Trail

Sawteeth
Mountain

Haystack
Trail

Mount
Haystack

Lower
Ausable
Lake

can take anywhere from 10 to 13 hours (accounting for time to appreciate the views and navigate the challenging sections), so bring enough food/water.

Miles and Directions

0.0 Start from the parking lot; head west and sign the trail register.

1.2 Pass the path to the Deer Brook Lean-to, on your right.

2.9 The Howard Lean-to is on your left; bear slightly right and go downhill.

3.0 At the junction, the ranger cabin is to your left 60 yards. Turn right and follow the brook.

3.4 At Johns Brook Lodge, continue straight through the grassy lawn.

4.8 At the Phelps Trail–Hopkins Trail junction, Bushnell Falls is a sharp left and down a steep path. The lean-to is on the right. Continue straight and cross the brook.

5.1 Pass Bushnell Falls Lean-to #2.

6.4 Cross the brook and arrive at Slant Rock; go around to the left and continue on the trail. The Lean-to will be on your right through the woods.

6.5 The lower part of Shorey Shortcut Trail comes in from the left.

7.2 At the Phelps Trail–State Range Trail junction, go left.

7.6 Cross over the bare rock of Horse Head Hill summit.

7.7 At the State Range Trail–Haystack Trail junction, take a right and rock-scramble up the hill.

7.8 Cross the bare summit of Little Haystack. Drop down the back side and follow painted blazes and rock cairns.

8.2 At the top of Haystack, turn around and go back down the hill.

8.7 Back at the trail junction, turn right and go downhill.

9.0 The State Range Trail–Haystack Brook Trail junction comes in from the right. Sno-Bird tentsite is across the stream 50 yards and to the right.

9.2 The upper part of the Shorey Shortcut Trail enters from the left. Continue up the hill.

9.5 Viewpoint looking back at Haystack.

9.8 Cross over the open Basin summit and continue.

10.5 Arrive at Saddleback summit after scaling the steep cliffs. Continue on the path through the woods.

11.0 Arrive at the State Range Trail–Orebed Brook Trail junction and turn left, going downhill.

12.5 Pass by the Orebed Lean-to, on your right.

13.2 At the four-way intersection, turn left and take the Woodsfall Trail.

13.5 After crossing a footbridge over the brook at Johns Brook Lodge, turn right and continue following the brook downstream.

13.9 Turn left at the junction near the ranger cabin and follow the trail uphill.

17.0 Arrive back at the Garden parking lot.

16 Redfield and Cliff

You have to climb these peaks to be a 46er. It's a good test of endurance, and Redfield is actually one of my favorite mountains, especially in winter.

Start: High Peaks Information Center (HPIC) parking lot
Distance: 18.2 miles out and back
Summit elevation: Redfield: 4,606 feet; Cliff: 3,960 feet
4,000-footers rank of the 115: Redfield: 32; Cliff: 112 (tied)
Elevation gain: 4,800 feet
Difficulty: Extremely strenuous
Hiking time: 12-14 hours
Trails used: Van Hoevenberg Trail, Avalanche Pass Trail, Lake Arnold Trail, Mount Marcy Trail, Cliff and Redfield Herd Paths

Views: Average
Nearest town: Lake Placid
Water sources: Several water sources on the hike except for the top of each mountain
Canine compatibility: Maybe; long day for dogs, and the rock scrambles up Cliff can prove very difficult.
Special considerations: Weekend summertime parking is very busy, and securing a spot will require an early start. There is a fee for parking in this lot. Extremely long day; plan accordingly.

Finding the trailhead: From the Lake Placid Olympic Ski Jumping Complex, travel east on NY 73 for 1.6 miles. Or, from the town of Keene, travel west 10.9 miles on NY 73 toward Lake Placid. Turn south onto Adirondack Loj Road and travel 4.7 miles to the end, where there is a payment collection station. Pay a fee and park in one of several lots. GPS (parking lot): N44°10'58.32" / W73°57'46.78"

The Hike

This hike clocks in at over 18 miles whether you start from Upper Works or from the HPIC, so prepare yourself. When the trail is broken, I find winter easier; but if you have to break trail as we did on Redfield, it can be a serious undertaking.

This hike from the HPIC starts out exactly the same as heading to Colden via the Van Hoevenberg Trail toward Marcy Dam. Continue on the Van Ho to the Avalanche Pass junction, where you at first follow the yellow markers for just over 1 mile until the Lake Arnold junction, at which point you bear left and follow the blue markers up and up until you reach the height of land for the Colden turnoff (the L. Morgan Porter Trail).

DID YOU KNOW?

Cliff Mountain is one of four Adirondack mountains that was later found to be under 4,000 feet. You shouldn't have to climb it to become a 46er, but you do—so suck it up.

Summer view of the waterfall just before the Uphill Lean-to
MICHELE HERNANDEZ BAYLISS

Now you head down through many planks and bogs, following the trail—be careful not to bear right toward the campsite, as we did on our first try. You will reach the Feldspar Lean-to first, but continue on until you reach the Uphill Lean-to. To make this hike easier, you can camp at either of these two sites, which would make good bases for not just Cliff and Redfield but also Skylight, Gray, and Marcy.

But no rest for the weary. Right behind Uphill Lean-to you'll find the path to the junction for Cliff and Redfield. Since we like Redfield more, we usually do Cliff first, toward the right a few feet into the path, where there is a small rock pile to indicate the turnoff. Though the map and guidebooks say Cliff's herd path is only 0.5 mile,

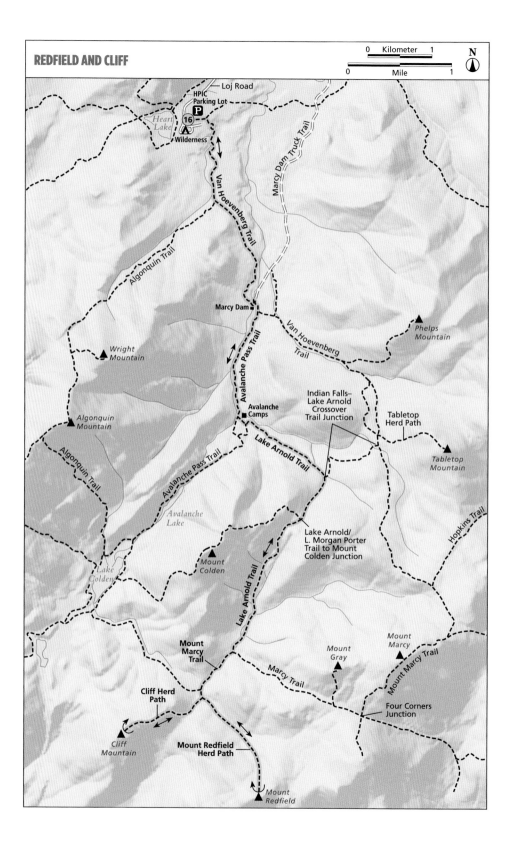

0   Kilometer   1

0   Mile   1

N

Loj Road

HPIC
Parking Lot

P

Heart
Lake

16

A

Wilderness

Marcy Dam Truck Trail

Van Hoevenberg Trail

Algonquin Trail

Marcy Dam

Van Hoevenberg
Trail

Phelps
Mountain

Wright
Mountain

Avalanche Pass Trail

Indian Falls–
Lake Arnold
Crossover
Trail Junction

Tabletop
Herd Path

Algonquin
Mountain

Avalanche
Camps

Lake Arnold Trail

Tabletop
Mountain

Algonquin Trail

Avalanche Pass Trail

Avalanche
Lake

Lake Arnold/
L. Morgan Porter
Trail to Mount
Colden Junction

Hopkins Trail

Lake
Colden

Mount
Colden

Lake Arnold Trail

Mount
Marcy
Trail

Mount
Gray

Mount
Marcy

Mount Marcy Trail

Cliff Herd
Path

Marcy Trail

Four Corners
Junction

Cliff
Mountain

Mount Redfield
Herd Path

Mount
Redfield

GPS shows it as 0.9 mile, which is more like it. With all the mud, the famous "cliff" (very icy/snowy in winter, can require crampons), and the false summit, it takes about 1 hour up and 1 hour down. Just be sure you see the summit sign so that you don't get that close and miss the summit itself or you can't count it. Take care going down the steep cliffy part. We usually downclimb, but there are roots and trees you can use for help.

Back to the junction, head left this time, up Redfield. I like this path much better in winter, without the rocks and roots. It's fairly gradual (by Adirondack standards) until near the top, where it gets steeper. The top section is gorgeous, with views of Allen, Marcy, Skylight, and other peaks. The final push to the summit seems to take longer than it should—but, again, this path takes about 2–2.5 hours round-trip on easier terrain. Although treed, a cool boulder behind the summit provides very nice views toward Allen.

If only you could call it quits here (well, you can if you are camping); but for the rest of us, it's the late-day elevation gain back to the height of land by the Colden turnoff and the easy but long hike out. This hike is never easy. You want to grab both peaks, because orphaning one only saves you a mile or two; it's way better to climb both while you are here. On the return you can loop around Avalanche Lake; just keep in mind that it will add both mileage and time, although it is more scenic.

It's not unusual for this hike to take 12–14 hours, as the terrain is challenging, especially the climb to Cliff Mountain.

Miles and Directions

0.0   Start from the parking lot and head west after signing the trail register.

1.0   At the junction of the Van Hoevenberg Trail with the Algonquin Trail, turn left and continue on the well-worn path.

2.2   Arrive at Marcy Dam; turn sharply left to follow the pond outlet and reach a footbridge crossing the stream. Turn right after the crossing.

2.4   Come to the Van Hoevenberg-Avalanche Pass Trail junction; bear right here on the Avalanche Pass Trail.

3.5   Avalanche Camps-Lake Arnold Trail junction. Head left at this intersection in the small grassy area.

4.5   The Indian Falls-Lake Arnold Crossover Trail junction is on your left, across the flowing stream.

5.0   At the Lake Arnold-L. Morgan Porter Trail to Mount Colden junction, continue straight.

6.4   At the Feldspar Lean-to-Mount Marcy Trail junction, turn right and mostly follow the river.

7.0   Cross a stream; the herd path to Cliff and Redfield is on your left. A few steps farther, and a short trail on your right leads to the Uphill Lean-to.

7.1   Reach a split in the trail with a small rock cairn. Bear right to go to Cliff.

7.7   After the steepest of climbs over bare rock, arrive at a height of land known as the Cliff false summit. Continue following the path or you'll miss the real summit.

8.0   At Cliff summit, retrace your steps.

View of Allen Mountain from the summit of Mount Redfield
MICHELE HERNANDEZ BAYLISS

8.9   Back at the split in the trail; turn right and mostly follow the stream.

10.1   Redfield summit; retrace your steps.

11.3   At the Uphill Lean-to junction, turn right and recross the stream.

11.8   Arrive at the junction for the Feldspar Lean-to; take the trail left across a small stream.

13.2   At Lake Arnold, continue straight.

14.7   Arrive at Avalanche Camps; bear right and head toward Marcy Dam.

16.0   Reach Marcy Dam.

17.2   With only 1 mile to go, turn right at the Algonquin Trail junction.

18.2   Arrive back at the HPIC parking lot.

Options

1. From the Uphill Lean-to, drop down the Mount Marcy Trail to Lake Colden. Work yourself around the lake and on to Avalanche Lake, where you can walk across the "Hitch-up Matildas" then down to Avalanche Camps. Distance: 18.6 miles; elevation gain: 4,880 feet.

2. From the Upper Works parking lot, take the Calamity Brook Trail to Lake Colden and then the Mount Marcy Trail to the Uphill Lean-to. Distance: 18.5 miles; elevation gain: 4,372 feet. GPS (Upper Works parking lot): N44°5'9.98" / W74°3'20.06"

New York: Catskills

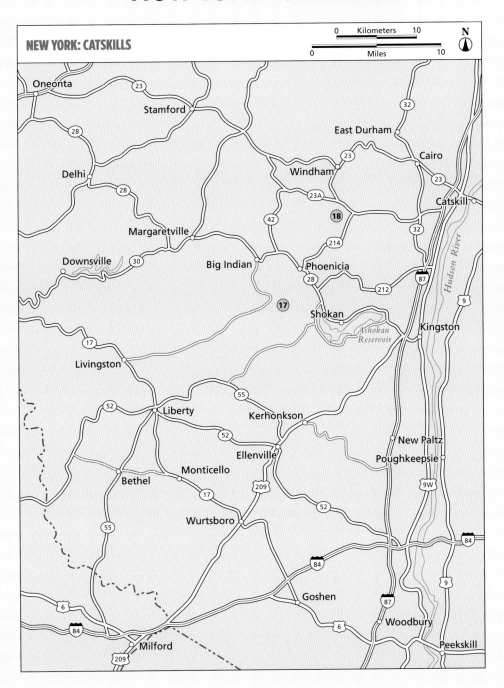

17 Slide Mountain

There are not many "easy" hikes on the way to the Northeast 111, but this one actually is quite easy, so enjoy it. Not to mention you can do both of the required Catskills hikes in one day.

Start: Slide Mountain parking area on CR 47
Distance: 5.2 miles out and back
Summit elevation: 4,180 feet
4,000-footers rank of the 115: 66 (tied)
Elevation gain: 1,738 feet
Difficulty: Easy
Hiking time: About 3 hours

Trails used: Wittenberg–Cornell Slide Trail, Phoenicia East Branch Trail
Nearest town: Phoenicia
Views: Good
Water sources: Cross a river in the beginning; small spring partway on the trail.
Canine compatibility: Very good
Special considerations: None

Finding the trailhead: Take exit 19 off I-87 and travel west on NY 28. Pass the towns of Phoenicia and Shandaken; 31.2 miles from the highway, Oliverea Road (CR 47) will be on your left. Travel on this road for 9.3 miles to the parking area, on your right. GPS (DEC parking lot): N42°0'30.95" / W74°25'39.55"

The Hike

I don't ever find a mountain easy, but, truly, Slide was super easy because you start at a higher elevation than usual and it's not that far up and back. The Department of Environmental Conservation (DEC) parking lot is already at 2,400 feet, so the total climb is under 1,800 feet and very gradual—a nice change of pace. The one thing to note is the large stream crossing right near the beginning; after heavy rains, it can be impassable, so plan accordingly. Follow the path and then bear right on an old carriage road that gently rises. Turn left onto the Wittenberg–Cornell Slide Trail; you then have a few more ups and flats before the final push. Enjoy the great viewpoint on the *left* side of the trail, with views toward Woodland Valley and Giant Ledge, Panther Mountain, and Wittenberg Mountain. The summit (the tallest in the Catskills) is very close and marked by a large rock with a summit plaque.

Because we knew we had to also grab Hunter, we didn't linger too long, although we did stop to read the John Burroughs summit plaque before descending. This hike took us under 3 hours, as the grade is easy.

DID YOU KNOW?

The body of water you have to cross, the "Neversink," comes from the Algonquin word for "mad river," as it can be either an easy crossing or totally impassable.

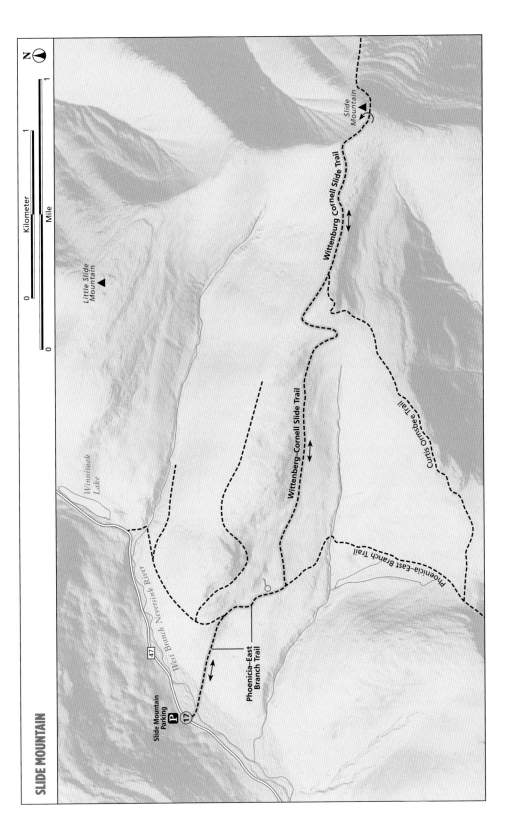

SLIDE MOUNTAIN

N

Kilometer

Mile

Little Slide Mountain

Winnisook Lake

West Branch Neversink River

47

Slide Mountain Parking

P

17

Phoenicia-East Branch Trail

Wittenberg-Cornell Slide Trail

Phoenicia-East Branch Trail

Curtis Ormsbee Trail

Wittenberg Cornell Slide Trail

Slide Mountain

View from summit of Slide Mountain Dean J. Ouellette

Miles and Directions

0.0 Start from the parking lot and head east.

0.4 An old carriage road comes in on your left; bear right.

0.7 Turn left onto the Wittenberg–Cornell Slide Trail.

2.0 The Curtis Ormsbee Trail enters on your right.

2.6 Reach the summit of Slide Mountain; turn around and retrace your steps.

3.2 Stay to the right at the Ormsbee Trail junction.

4.6 At the intersection, turn right.

4.8 Bear left to head toward the parking lot.

5.2 Arrive back at the parking lot.

18 Hunter Mountain

Like Slide, Hunter Mountain is relatively quick and easy and features a super fun fire tower that you can climb for amazing vistas.

Start: Becker Hollow parking lot
Distance: 4.6 miles out and back
Summit elevation: 4,040 feet
4,000-footers rank of the 115: 97 (tied)
Elevation gain: 2,213 feet
Difficulty: Easy
Hiking time: About 4 hours
Trails used: Becker Hollow Trail, Hunter Mountain Trail

Nearest town: Tannersville
Views: Excellent
Water sources: Several water sources on the hike up toward the ridge; nothing on the ridge until Carter Notch
Canine compatibility: Good
Special considerations: None

Finding the trailhead: Take exit 20 off I-87. If coming from the south, turn left onto NY 32 North; immediately after the underpass, turn right to stay on NY 32 North. In 0.25 mile, the intersection with I-87 ramps will be on your right. If traveling from the north on I-87, turn right and drive on NY 32 North. In 5.9 miles, continue straight onto NY 32A. In 1.9 miles, merge with NY 23A West. In 9.2 miles, turn left onto NY 214 South; the parking lot will be on your right in 1.3 miles. GPS (parking lot): N42°10'54.68" / W74°11'48.93"

The Hike

After driving to Hunter, the second-highest mountain in the Catskills, we opted to take the direct Becker Hollow Trail, which is steep but not that bad if you are used to the Adirondack trails. Right near the trailhead, you cross a bridge to a concrete dam in the first 5 minutes; continue about 1.5 miles until you reach the 3,500-foot

Fire tower and clearing in the mist MICHELE HERNANDEZ BAYLISS

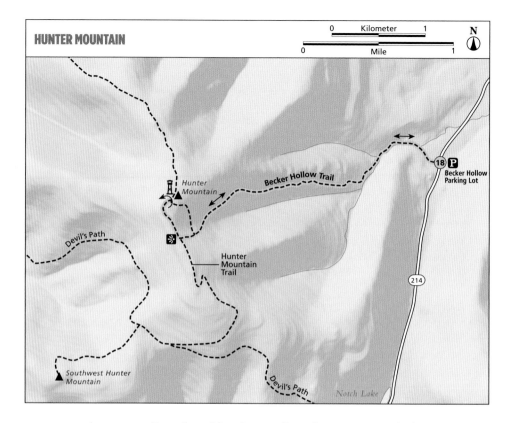

contour mark on a tree. From here it's a short walk to the junction with the Hunter Mountain Trail and 0.3 mile to the summit. This is one to hang out on—it's flat and open and has a super fun fire tower that provides amazing views. It's only 4.6 miles round-trip, so even though it's steep and harder for sure than Slide Mountain, it's still a quick hike with fantastic views. There are many other routes you can take if you want a longer hike, but we were looking for efficiency and speed.

Miles and Directions

- **0.0** Start from the parking lot and head west.
- **2.0** Turn left at the junction with the Hunter Mountain Trail.
- **2.3** Arrive at the summit. Turn around and retrace your steps.
- **2.6** Turn left and head back down the hill.
- **4.6** Arrive back at the parking lot.

Option

Start from the Devil's Path parking area and hike on the Devil's Path. Parking is just another 1.8 miles south of the Hunter Mountain lot. Distance: 7.4 miles; elevation gain: 2,225 feet. GPS: N42°9'25.02" / W74°12'18.61"

Vermont

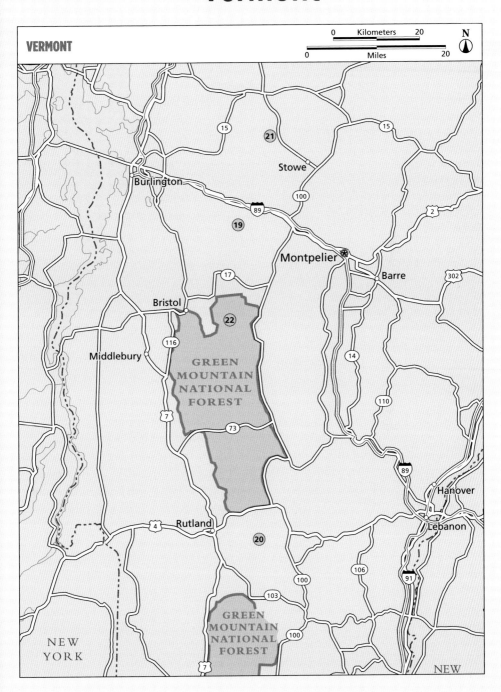

19 Camel's Hump

One of the iconic hikes of Vermont with tremendous views, a fairly short time investment and true alpine conditions. My favorite of the 5 summits of Vermont.

Start: Parking lot at the end of Camel's Hump Road
Distance: 5.1-mile loop
Summit elevation: 4,083 feet
4,000-footers rank of the 115: 85 (tied)
Elevation gain: 2,374 feet
Difficulty: Moderate
Hiking time: 4–5 hours
Trails used: Connector trail from the Burrows Trailhead parking lot, Forest City Trail, Long Trail, Burrows Trail

Nearest town: Huntington (no gas)
Views: Excellent
Water sources: Multiple sources along the way below the Long Trail. Fill up at the Montclair Glen cabin.
Canine compatibility: Good. Please leash dogs above tree line to protect fragile alpine vegetation.
Special considerations: Parking lot fills early in the day. Do not block private driveways.

Finding the trailhead: Travel to Huntington Center. From the north, go south on Main Street 2.6 miles from the Huntington post office. From the south, travel north on Main Street 6.2 miles from VT 17. In the center of town, turn onto Camel's Hump Road and travel 2.7 miles to a small parking lot for the Forest City trailhead; in another 0.7 mile you'll come to the trailhead for the Burrows Trail. GPS (Burrows trailhead): N44°18'17.96" / W72°54'27.56" W; (Forest City trailhead): N44°18'17.96" / W72°54'27.56"

The Hike

Although the Burrows Trail is by far the most direct and shortest route up Camel's Hump, we tend to do a loop hike—it's far more beautiful and less crowded. Either way, you park at the end of Camel's Hump Road. At the register, just over a small footbridge, you bear *right* onto the Connector Trail rather than straight up Burrows. After a short downhill and a scenic bridge crossing, you follow Brush Brook until you hit the Forest City Trail. Keeping left, you continue up a gentle grade until you arrive at the junction with the Long Trail. Once again, you head left and then reach the Camel's Hump summit sign, announcing that you have 1.6 miles to reach the summit. Take care; many miss this left-hand turn and continue straight—but that route will not lead to the summit anytime soon.

The next section is really what makes this hike fun; there are some excellent rock scrambles, one of which involves squeezing through a narrow rock, and then several ledges. Once you complete the first series of climbs, you come to a flat section with fantastic views eastward toward New Hampshire. From these rocks you get an incredible view of the flank of Camel's Hump. Though you may think you are almost there, you still have to ascend some final steep sections in order to reach the rocky section

Summit view looking due west to the Bristol Gap, Lake Champlain, and the Adirondacks in the distance MICHELE HERNANDEZ BAYLISS

below the summit. If the weather is frightening, you can always bail toward the right on the bad-weather bypass. A little farther up, you hit our favorite part of the hike. You follow to the left around the edge of a rocky cliff and then wind your way up and around the left-hand flank, with one final rock scramble to reach the flat section with amazing views to the west that rival the summit, followed by a tunnellike section about 10 minutes below the summit. Head up through the tunnel until you hit the alpine section and continue toward the right-hand side, taking care not to trample the alpine vegetation. This is a dramatic approach to the actual summit; most hikers ascend from the opposite direction.

Enjoy the views in every direction: Burlington to the northwest, the Adirondacks and Lake Champlain to the west, New Hampshire's peaks to the east, and half of Vermont. Traversing the summit, you descend toward the woods and follow an inspiring alpine path through some gorgeous scenery and descend about 15 minutes to the clearing, where four different trails enter. The Monroe Trail is to the right, the Long Trail is straight ahead; you want to take a sharp left and descend the Burrows Trail, the only way to return to your car. The top sections are *very* steep (and often icy in fall/ early winter); bring microspikes if it's cold/icy. Once you get past the steep sections, the rest of the trail is quite gentle and well-traveled. From the clearing, it's a straight 1- to 1.5-hour hike back to the parking lot.

DID YOU KNOW?

A B-24 bomber crashed into the mountain in 1944. You can search for the wreck, but you have to ascend from the other side, as the wreck lies on the Alpine Trail.

CAMEL'S HUMP

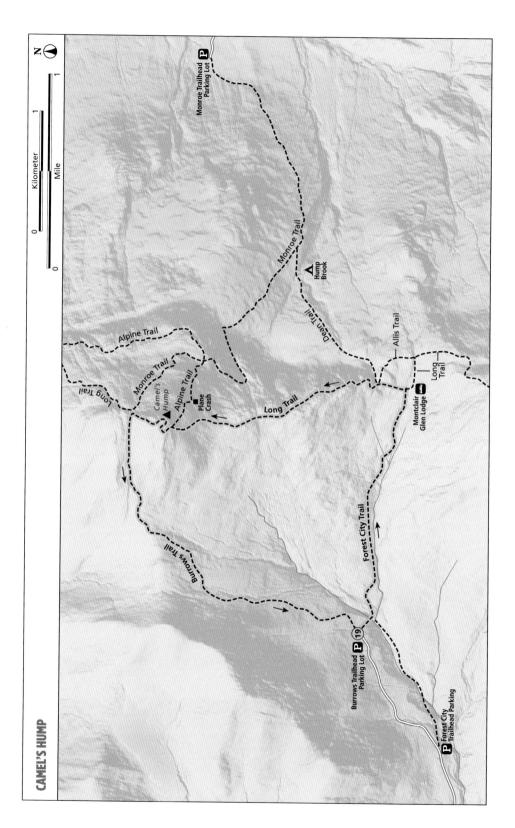

N

Kilometer

Mile

0   1

Monroe Trailhead Parking Lot

Alpine Trail

Monroe Trail

Monroe Trail

Alpine Trail

Long Trail

Camel's Hump

Plane Crash

Alpine Trail

Long Trail

Long Trail

Dean Trail

Hump Brook

Allis Trail

Long Trail

Montclair Glen Lodge

Forest City Trail

Burrows Trail

Burrows Trailhead Parking Lot

19

Forest City Trailhead Parking

View from Camel's Hump summit looking north to Mount Mansfield, Vermont's highest peak, in the distance MICHELE HERNANDEZ BAYLISS

If we just go up and down Burrows, it's typically a 3-hour round-trip; ascending the Forest City Trail/connector/Long Trail takes more like 4–5 hours total for the loop.

Miles and Directions

0.0 Start from the parking lot. Take a right at the trail register, head southeast down the hill, and cross a footbridge over the gorge.

0.2 At the junction with the Forest City Trail, which starts lower on the mountain, turn left.

1.4 Junction with the Long Trail. A right goes a short distance to the Montclair Glen Lodge. Turn left onto the Long Trail.

1.5 At the intersection with Allis and Dean Trails, bear left and continue uphill.

2.8 The Alpine Trail comes in from your right; turn left. From here it begins to be more open, with very short trees.

2.9 Continue climbing, following blazes on rocks and small cairns to reach the Camel's Hump summit. Head north and start down the mountain.

3.1 At the clearing below the summit is the intersection with the Monroe, Long, and Burrows Trails. Turn left and head west to follow the Burrows Trail out.

5.1 Arrive back at the parking lot after an uneventful trek with no turns.

Option

Try going up the eastern side of the mountain on the Monroe Trail—a moderate 6.2-mile out-and-back hike. Easier though a bit longer, it's the route Michele took on her final 366/4K every day challenge so her friends could enjoy an easier hike.

To reach the trailhead: From Main Street in the town of Duxbury, go west on River Road for 5 miles. Turn left onto Camel's Hump Road and travel 3.5 miles to the end of the road. GPS (trailhead parking lot): N44°18'58.33" / W72°50'59.09"

20 Killington Mountain

Though most know this peak as a ski mountain, this southernmost peak in Vermont offers a fantastic viewing platform with 360-degree views of the entire state.

Start: Bucklin Trail parking area
Distance: 7.2 miles out and back
Summit elevation: 4,241 feet
4,000-footers rank of the 115: 61
Elevation gain: 2,467 feet
Difficulty: Easy
Hiking time: 4–5 hours

Trails used: Bucklin Trail, Long Trail/Appalachian Trail
Nearest town: Rutland
Views: Excellent
Water sources: There is a crossing of Brewers Brook at 1.3 miles into the hike.
Canine compatibility: Good
Special considerations: None

Finding the trailhead: From the center of Rutland, where US 4 heads east from US 7, travel east on US 4 through the city of Rutland for 5 miles. Turn right onto Wheelerville Road and continue on this windy dirt road for 4 miles to the Bucklin Trailhead parking lot, on your left. GPS (parking lot): N43°37'10.71" / W72°52'35.62"

The Hike

There are several ways to get up Killington Mountain (including the gondola, but then you can't count the peak as a hike), but we typically take the blue-blazed Bucklin Trail. This hike ascends just over 2,400 feet. The first 2 miles of the trail are mostly flat except for a gentle uphill section that winds up and around a bit before dropping you near the second bridge crossing. You follow Brewer's Brook until the trail makes a sharp turn to the right and starts uphill. Although the trail is relatively short to the summit from here, it is very steep. At the top of the climb, you will reach the junction with both the Long Trail and the Appalachian Trail, which run together here, and then turn right to follow the white blazes for about 5 minutes until you arrive at Cooper Lodge.

I love the final rocky climb to the summit, which only takes about 10–15 minutes but can be hairy in wet or icy weather. Near the top, the trail seems to fork; the better footing is on the right-hand side as you ascend. The trail spits you out right under the summit, where you cross the rocks and observe the tower and the skiway. You can continue up and over the rock if you want to visit the ski area or have lunch in summer. We have been met with ferocious winds in this spot in winter, but in spring, summer, and fall, we usually take a lunch break to enjoy the views of the Green Mountains all the way north to Mount Mansfield, south to Mount Ascutney, northeast to the White Mountains, and west to the Taconics along with Lake Champlain and the Adirondacks.

Michele atop Killington's summit DONNA DEARBORN

Eva, Ella, and Holmes crossing a bridge on the Bucklin Trail DONNA DEARBORN

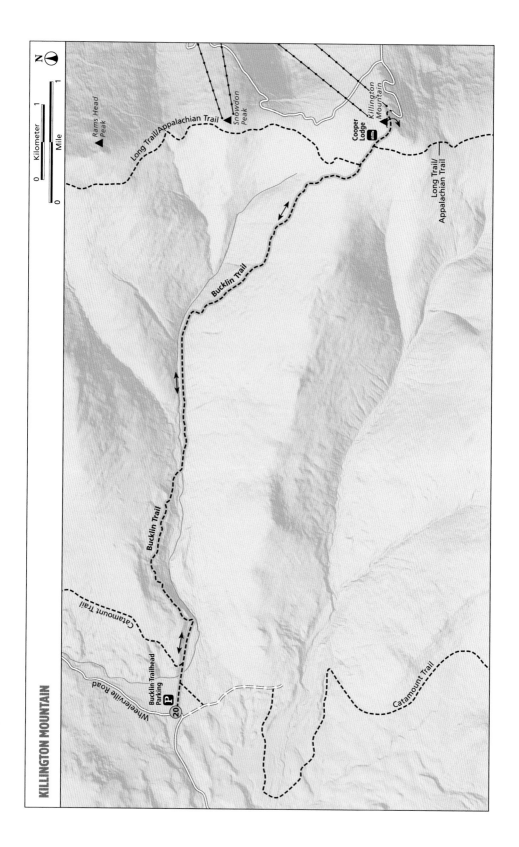

KILLINGTON MOUNTAIN

N

0   Kilometer   1

0   Mile   1

Rams Head
Peak ▲

Long Trail/Appalachian Trail

Snowdon
Peak

Bucklin Trail

Cooper
Lodge

Killington
Mountain

Long Trail/
Appalachian Trail

Bucklin Trail

Catamount Trail

Wheelerville Road

Bucklin Trailhead
Parking

P

20

Catamount Trail

As you might guess, the way down is faster as you descend the steeps and then enjoy the mostly flat final section back to the parking area. This is a great hike if you are pressed for time and need a good workout with a great view in under 5 hours.

Miles and Directions

0.0 Start from the parking lot and head east on the Bucklin Trail.

0.1 Catamount Ski Trail comes in from your right.

0.3 Catamount Ski Trail heads off to the left; stay straight on the Bucklin Trail.

3.3 The Long Trail/Appalachian Trail heads north; continue uphill.

3.5 Reach Cooper Lodge. The Long Trail/Appalachian Trail splits here and goes south; continue up to the summit.

3.6 Reach the Killington Mountain summit; retrace your steps.

3.7 Arrive at Cooper Lodge; continue downhill.

3.9 The Long Trail/Appalachian Trail bears right; continue downhill on the Bucklin Trail.

6.9 Catamount Ski Trail bears right; continue on the Bucklin Trail.

7.1 Catamount Ski Trail comes in from your left; continue the short walk to your car.

7.2 Arrive back at the parking Lot

21 Mount Mansfield

This is simply one of the highlight hikes of Vermont—the trifecta of 360-degree views for days, a true alpine environment, and bragging rights for climbing the highest mountain in Vermont.

Start: Underhill State Park
Distance: 4.4-mile loop (This is one of the few times when the GPS mileage seems too short; allot a bit more time and expect more distance.)
Summit elevation: 4,393 feet
4,000-footers rank of the 115: 47
Elevation gain: 2,517 feet
Difficulty: Easy
Hiking time: 5-6 hours
Trails used: Eagle Cut Trail, CCC Road, Laura Cowles Trail, Long Trail, Sunset Ridge Trail

Nearest town: Underhill
Views: Excellent
Water sources: A small stream crossing at the beginning of the hike
Canine compatibility: Good; dogs must be leashed and current vaccinations shown to enter the park.
Special considerations: Exposure above tree line; travel through fragile alpine vegetation areas. There is a nominal fee for parking.

Finding the trailhead: From the post office in Jericho, travel east on VT 15 for 2.4 miles to the town of Underhill. Turn right onto River Road and travel 2.7 miles to Underhill Center. At a church green, the road changes to Pleasant Valley Road. Follow this road for another mile and turn right onto Mountain Road. Continue on this dirt road for 2.7 miles to the state park. GPS (parking lot): N44°31'46.38" / W72°50'30.50"

The Hike

This is one of our favorite hikes, with a multitude of trails that approach from both the east (where Stowe resort is) and west sides. Luckily, one of the easier routes also happens to be one of the most spectacular. Although most hikers simply go up and down Sunset Ridge, we typically hike up the Laura Cowles Trail from the west side to avoid the crowds and then down the Sunset Ridge Trail.

Park at the upper lot on the right-hand side (first stop at the ranger cabin and pay the day-use fee). The Eagle Cut Trail is right behind that parking lot, so it's easy to find. This is the most direct route over the dirt road, which winds around so that you cross it three times before coming out on the final section of road, where you head left and up a gentle slope for about 15 minutes until you reach the trailhead. At this junction, head *left* toward the Sunset Ridge/Laura Cowles Trail. In short order you reach another junction. As long as it's not raining or very icy, we prefer ascending Laura Cowles, as it's the steeper but more direct route and much less crowded. Our dogs have no problems, although there are a few scrambly sections.

Fragile alpine vegetation on the final leg before Mount Mansfield's summit
MICHELE HERNANDEZ BAYLISS

The first part of the trail is quite mellow; it gets steeper, with some scrambles, but nothing that presents a problem. At one point higher up, it looks as though you might dead-end into a large rock, but the trail takes a sharp right over some rocks and then winds up a few cliff-like sections, some of which have amazing views to the left. Finally you crest, after a short rock scramble, to where the Sunset Ridge Trail comes in on the left. Now you are fairly close to the summit! Follow the trail up and to the left, heading toward "The Chin" area and then through a narrow tunnel section (a sharp turn right would put you on the Long Trail heading south near the boardwalk's wooden planks). The final gentle uphill takes you to the actual summit, which typically is fairly crowded, although there is lots of room to share. Since many hikers ascend from the eastern side, you will see an influx (not to mention those who

DID YOU KNOW?

Mount Mansfield is one of only two places in Vermont where arctic tundra can be found (the other is Camel's Hump). It is by far the larger, roughly 200 acres, so tread carefully!

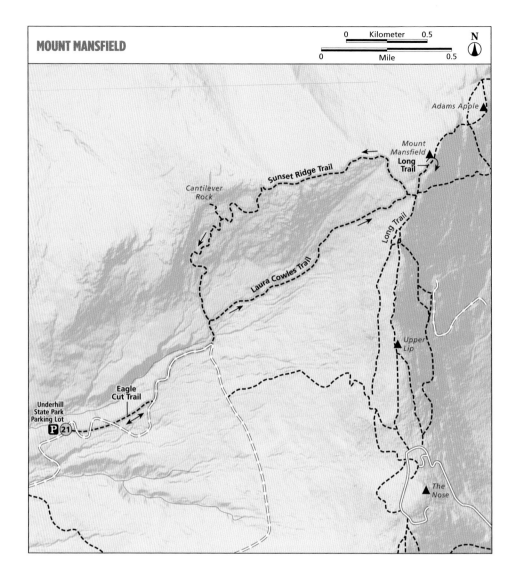

drive up from the east and then walk up from a parking area). Enjoy the views of the resort town of Stowe, the White Mountains in the distance, Burlington up to Canada on a clear day, and the Adirondacks due west.

Taking care not to step on the alpine vegetation, head back to the junction with the Laura Cowles Trail, but this time bear right to follow Sunset Ridge. This trail is super exposed but gorgeous, especially the top part. You follow cairns up and over several boulders and rocks; take care—the rocks can be slippery, and microspikes are often needed here, even in fall. There are several great spots to take a break and look back up to the summit as you descend. About halfway down, you hit some very fun scrambling sections that often involve using your hands to get down. The trail then enters the woods for a relaxing walk back to the intersection with the spur trail to

Cantilever Rock (a worthwhile 0.2-mile detour if you have time), the Laura Cowles intersection, and the final road/woods walk back to your car. Keep your eyes peeled for the right-hand turn back to Eagle Cut; it's easy to miss.

Miles and Directions

0.0 Start from the parking lot and head east onto the Eagle Cut Trail.

0.3 After three road crossings, turn left and follow the road.

0.7 Bear left from the road and follow the hiking path.

0.8 At the split, bear right to follow the Laura Cowles Trail.

1.7 At the junction with the Sunset Ridge Trail, turn right.

1.7+ Gain the ridge and the junction with the Long Trail; turn left and head north.

1.9 Arrive at the Mount Mansfield summit; turn around and retrace your steps.

2.1 Turn right and head down the Sunset Ridge Trail.

3.1 The spur trail to Cantilever Rock is on your right if you'd like to see it.

3.6 The Laura Cowles Trail enters from your left.

3.7 Back onto the CCC road.

4.1 Turn right off the road to follow the Eagle Cut Trail back to the parking lot.

4.4 Arrive back at the parking lot.

Option

For a longer loop hike, follow the CCC road to the end and go up the Maple Ridge Trail. Cross over "The Forehead" and walk the entire ridge on the Long Trail North. Come down the Sunset Ridge Trail. Distance: 7.3 miles; elevation gain: 2,781 feet.

22 Abraham and Ellen

Mount Abraham is the tallest peak in Addison County (where we live) and is our "home" mountain. It offers 360-degree views west to the Adirondacks and east to New Hampshire's peaks. Exciting alpine scrambles provide maximum bang for the buck. Mount Ellen is right down the ridge.

Start: Battell Trailhead parking
Distance: 11.6 miles out and back
Summit elevation: Abraham: 4,006 feet; Ellen: 4,083 feet
4,000-footers rank of the 115: Abraham: 107; Ellen: 85 (tied)
Elevation gain: 3,745 feet
Difficulty: Moderate
Hiking time: 8-9 hours
Trails used: Battell Trail, Long Trail
Nearest town: Bristol

Views: Excellent
Water sources: One good stream crossing; then again at Battell Shelter
Canine compatibility: Good, but dogs must be leashed on the summits, especially Mount Abraham.
Special considerations: A summit steward is on Mount Abraham during the summer months, instructing you on how to conduct yourself in an alpine zone. Basically, stay on the rocks and avoid treading on the alpine vegetation.

Finding the trailhead: In the town of Bristol, at the stoplight intersection, go east on Main Street, following VT 116 North/VT 17 East out of town. Immediately after crossing the second bridge at 1.6 miles, turn right onto Lincoln Road and travel toward the town of Lincoln. Lincoln Road morphs into West River Road. At 3.4 miles turn left onto Quaker Street; you'll see the Lincoln General Store on your right. After 0.7 mile turn right onto Elder Hill Road. Travel on this dirt road for 1.9 miles; it will seem to end, but bear left on this noticeably rougher section for 0.1 mile to the small lot for only a handful of cars. **Warning:** Do *not* just park off the road; stay in the lot. If the lot is full, drive back to where the road is wide again and try to find someplace that will not block traffic. If you can't find a spot, pick a different hike. GPS (parking lot): N44°6'45.42" / W72°57'49.39"

The Hike

Although you can save yourself some elevation by starting from Lincoln Gap, we much prefer the more scenic and less rocky Battell Trail. Don't underestimate this hike. While most hikes we describe have 2,500 feet of gain over many miles, for Abe just by itself, you do 2,500 feet of elevation in just over 3 miles.

The climbing starts right from the parking lot. In fact, the first 30 minutes has more climbing than the second 30 minutes. After winding up and up with only one flat section to catch your breath, you turn left and come to a large rock we like to call "15-minute rock." Continue up to a few hairpin turns and the steepest sections of the whole hike until the trail flattens out through beautiful woods and you arrive at a footbridge and stream. This is "30-minute stream" and a great place to splash water on

Gorgeous fall foliage view of Mount Abraham from the valley below
Michele Hernandez Bayliss

your face and have a snack. After another 10–15 minutes of more gradual climbing, the trail curves right and enters the spruces for the most enjoyable part of the hike, up a rocky stream bed with more gradual grades. At about the 45-minute mark, you come to a small clearing where you can see Abe's summit. As you approach a steep ramp-like section, you crest and follow the trail sharply left until you arrive at the junction where the Lincoln Gap Trail enters from the right. A short stretch brings you to the Battell Shelter, part of the Long Trail. From the junction you follow Vermont's Long Trail up the ridge just under 1 mile to the summit. We call this the "fun" section, as the half-hour hike from the shelter involves some exciting rock scrambles. In fall and spring, be sure to bring microspikes—these rocks are very dangerous if iced over. After one final scramble, you see the summit sign ahead of you and exit to the beautiful open summit. In all seasons, it's worth taking a break on the summit to enjoy the views in every direction: north toward Mount Ellen, east toward the White

DID YOU KNOW?

In 1973 a pilot encountered thick clouds while flying from Twin Mountain, Vermont, to Newburgh, New York, and crashed into the mountain. He survived the plane crash. Mount Abraham used to be called Potato Hill, but was then named in honor of Abraham Lincoln.

Michele's dogs, Holmes and Argos, just before the summit of Mount Abraham in late fall after an unexpected snowfall MICHELE HERNANDEZ BAYLISS

Mountains, west toward the Adirondacks, and south toward Mount Killington and the Long Trail South.

It's a relatively easy 3.2-mile hike to Mount Ellen following a 3,700-foot-high ridge that undulates a bit (you will pass over three minor peaks: Lincoln, Nancy Hanks, and Cutts Peaks) but has such great views of the Sugarbush ski area that you may not notice. It is called the "Monroe Skyline" section of the Long Trail. A few minutes into the hike from Mount Abraham, you can see the remains of a plane crash on the left-hand side. Though Mount Ellen itself is a wooded summit, it's worth continuing an additional 5 minutes to reach the ski lift area of Sugarbush, which has a fantastic viewing platform. Then head back along the ridge to Abe, descend the rocks with care, and just remember when you reach the junction of the Battell and Long Trails to continue *straight* rather than left, which would take you to Lincoln Gap.

You can descend Mount Ellen via the Jerusalem Trail to make a loop, but that involves a longer car shuttle.

Miles and Directions

0.0   Start from the parking lot and head east.
0.4   Pass "15-minute rock."
1.0   Cross "30-minute stream" on a small footbridge.
1.8   The Long Trail enters from your right; continue following the Long Trail North.

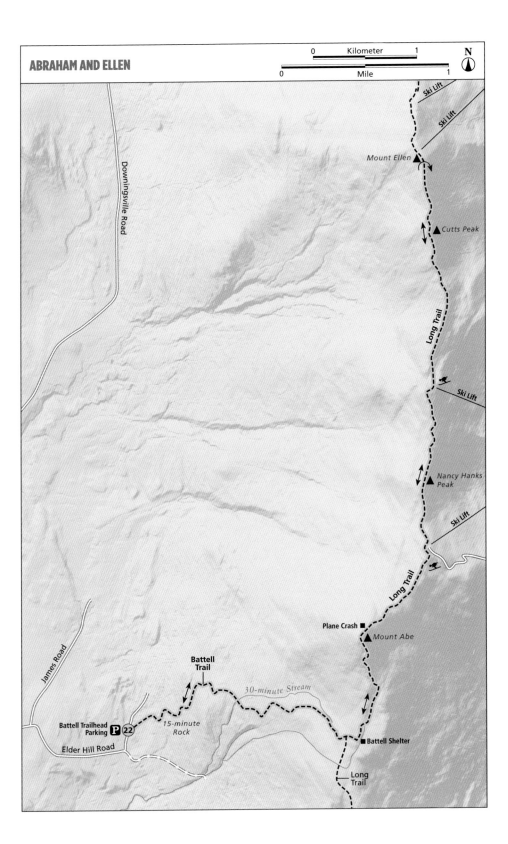

0 Kilometer 1

0 Mile 1

N

Ski Lift

Ski Lift

Mount Ellen ▲

▲ Cutts Peak

Long Trail

Ski Lift

▲ Nancy Hanks Peak

Ski Lift

Long Trail

Plane Crash ■

▲ Mount Abe

Downingsville Road

James Road

Battell Trail

30-minute Stream

Battell Trailhead Parking **P** 22

15-minute Rock

Elder Hill Road

■ Battell Shelter

Long Trail

1.9 Pass the Battell Shelter.

2.6 Arrive at Mount Abraham's summit; cross over and continue north.

2.7 A left-hand spur will bring you to the plane crash site in 50 yards.

3.3 Stay left at the ski area building and follow the white blazes.

3.8 Cross over nondescript Nancy Hanks Peak.

4.4 Pass another ski area lift operation.

5.3 Cross over Cutts Peak.

5.8 Arrive at Mount Ellen; continue 100 yards down to the open ski lift then turn around and retrace your steps.

8.3 Turn right into the woods at this last open ski area.

9.0 Cross over the Mount Abraham summit.

9.7 Pass the Battell Shelter.

9.8 The Long Trail bears left; continue straight downhill on the Battell Trail.

10.6 Cross "30-minute stream" on a small footbridge.

11.2 Pass "15-minute rock."

11.6 Arrive back at the parking lot.

New Hampshire:
White Mountains

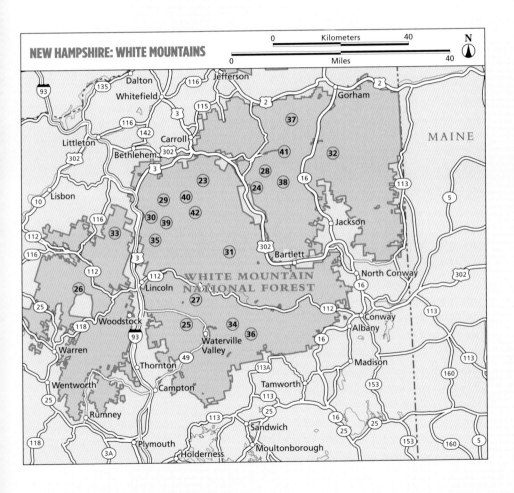

23 Mount Hale

Some days you need a shorter/easier hike below tree line; this one is perfect.

Start: Hale Brook Trailhead
Distance: 4.0 miles out and back
Summit elevation: 4,054 feet
4,000-footers rank of the 115: 92
Elevation gain: 2,246 feet
Difficulty: Easy
Hiking time: 3–4 hours

Trails used: Hale Brook Trail
Nearest town: Twin Mountain
Views: Not many
Water sources: Hale Brook at 0.8 mile
Canine compatibility: Very good
Special considerations: None

Finding the trailhead: To reach the town of Twin Mountain from the north, take exit 36 off I-93 to NH 141. Continue 0.7 mile then turn onto US 3 North for 9.7 miles. From the south, take exit 35 to US 3 North and travel 9.9 miles. From the intersection of US 302 and US 3 in the town of Twin Mountain, take US 302 East for 2 miles to Zealand Road, on your right (closed in winter). Take this road for 2.5 miles to a small parking lot. GPS (parking lot): N44°14'11.09" / W71°29'12.87"

The Hike

Granted, this is not the most exciting hike in the White Mountains, but at least it doesn't take that long. It's a great workout, as the relatively short ascent covers nearly 2,300 vertical feet on the Hale Brook Trail (parking on Zealand Road), following the yellow trail markers. Keep in mind that in winter, you have to add the road walk, since Zealand Road is gated. This trail follows the brook and is scenic and mellow at first. Once you cross the brook, however, the grade steepens as you ascend a series of switchbacks until you reach the summit clearing. The last time I hiked Mount Hale it was pouring rain, so even though it was not that cold, I found myself shivering as I approached the summit. After reaching the large clearing marked by a huge cairn (alas, there are no views) where three trails intersect, I ducked into the small area just before the summit to change into a dry shirt and new jacket. Feeling much revived, I descended via Hale Brook and made it back to my car in just over an hour from the summit. Take care at the summit to return the way you came. To the left of the summit cairn is the Lend a Hand Trail if you're in the mood to head toward Zealand Hut (2.7 miles according to the sign). If you take the trail behind the cairn, it follows an unofficial trail called the Fire Warden's Trail down to the Seven Dwarfs Motel parking.

DID YOU KNOW?

Mount Hale was named for Edward Everett Hale, an American author and Unitarian minister who happened to be the grand-nephew of Revolutionary War spy Nathan Hale.

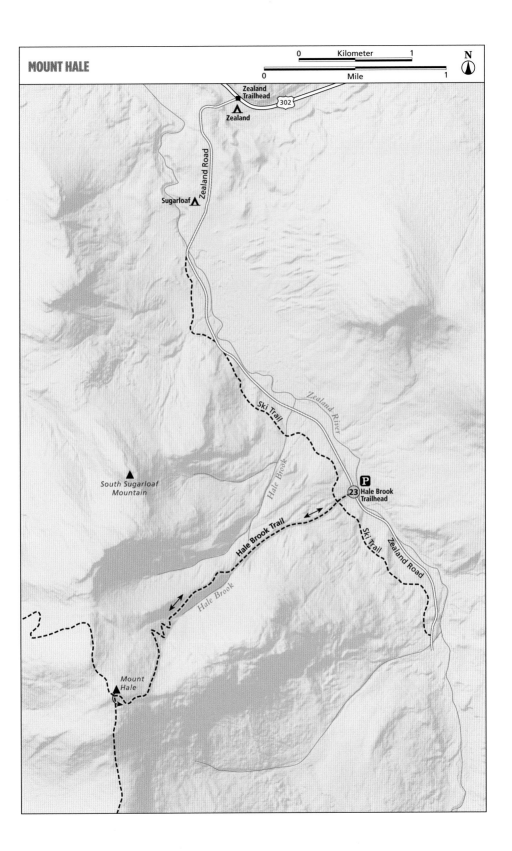

MOUNT HALE

0 — Kilometer — 1

0 — Mile — 1

N

Zealand
Trailhead
Zealand
302

Zealand Road

Sugarloaf

Ski Trail

Zealand River

South Sugarloaf
Mountain

Hale Brook

P
23 Hale Brook
Trailhead

Hale Brook Trail

Ski Trail

Zealand Road

Hale Brook

Mount
Hale

Michele atop the cairn at Mount Hale's summit DEAN J. OUELLETTE

Miles and Directions

0.0 Start from the trailhead and head west.

0.1 Cross the ski trail.

0.8 Cross Hale Brook.

2.0 Arrive at the summit of Mount Hale; return the way you came.

4.0 Arrive back at the trailhead.

24 Mount Jackson

This hike is one of the easiest on the Northeast 111 list, but you get a lot of "bang for your buck," with scrambles near the top and cool lookouts. This is a good one for kids who are just getting into hiking.

Start: Webster-Jackson Trailhead
Distance: 4.4 miles out and back
Summit elevation: 4,052 feet
4,000-footers rank of the 115: 93
Elevation gain: 2,184 feet
Difficulty: Easy
Hiking time: 3–5 hours

Trails used: Webster-Jackson Trail, Mount Jackson Branch
Nearest town: Twin Mountain
Views: Excellent
Water sources: A brook at the beginning of the hike; again shortly after the trail splits
Canine compatibility: Very good
Special considerations: None

Finding the trailhead: To reach the town of Twin Mountain from the north, take exit 36 off I-93 to NH 141. Continue 0.7 mile then turn onto US 3 North for 9.7 miles. From the south, take exit 35 to US 3 North and travel 9.9 miles. From the intersection of US 302 and US 3 in the town of Twin Mountain, take US 302 East for 8.4 miles; the AMC Highland Center will be on your right. Continue another 0.4 mile to a parking area on your right.

If traveling from the south or east, take US 302 West 16.7 miles from Attitash ski area in the town of Bartlett. The parking area will be on your left. GPS (parking lot): N44°12'51.73" / W71°24'27.50"

The Hike

Although some hikers tack this one on to the finale of a Presidential Traverse, we ran out of steam on our traverse and saved it as its own hike. It's nice to have an easy hike when you don't have all day to complete a peak. Incidentally, the mountain is not named for President Andrew Jackson but for Charles Jackson, a nineteenth-century geologist for the State of New Hampshire. You can do a loop that also tags Pierce or Webster, but if you want a quicker hike, we recommend the out-and-back up and down the Webster-Jackson (W-J) Trail, right across the street from the AMC Highland Center. Follow the Webster-Jackson Trail (just off US 302, with parking across

DID YOU KNOW?

The Appalachian Trail crosses Mount Jackson's summit. If you wanted to do a northbound Presidential Traverse, this would be your starting point—Jackson all the way to Mounts Adams and Madison.

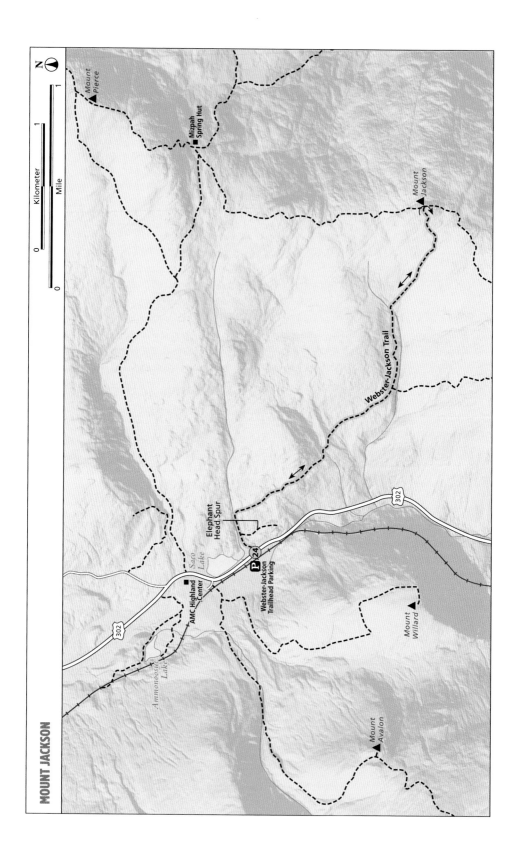

MOUNT JACKSON

N

Kilometer

0   1

0   1

Mile

Mount
Pierce

Mizpah
Spring Hut

Mount
Jackson

Webster-Jackson Trail

Elephant
Head Spur

302

24

Webster-Jackson
Trailhead Parking

AMC Highland
Center

Saco
Lake

Ammonoosuc
Lake

302

Mount
Willard

Mount
Avalon

Dean on Mount Jackson's summit MICHELE HERNANDEZ BAYLISS

the street). The trailhead is on the Saco Lake side; the trailhead sign is just south of there.

Heading up the first steep section, you will find the spur trail to the Elephant Head lookout. The next one (Bugle Cliff) is only 0.1 mile and a more spectacular lookout; that's the one we recommend if you have to choose one. As you follow the W-J trail, remember to bear left at the first junction to head up Jackson. Straight will lead you to Webster via the Webster Cliff Trail, which is even steeper. Don't underestimate this trail—it may be short, but there are several steep sections.

When you near the peak, you can enjoy the exciting rock scramble before the summit and 360-degree views from the bald summit toward the Mizpah Hut, the southern Presidentials, and Mounts Willey, Field, and Tom. To the north you can see Mount Washington, and western views stare right into the Pemigewasset Wilderness and the Bonds. On a clear day you can see east to Maine. For a White Mountain ascent, the gain is moderate, but in terms of feel, I would rate this trail much steeper/rougher than, say, Mount Waumbek, which is a gentler grade overall. The Appalachian Trail crosses the summit, which you could follow north to all the Presidentials should you desire. This hike is fairly quick; we'd allow 3–5 hours total. The loop to Mount Webster is a neat trail, but it is fairly challenging terrain-wise and adds almost an hour to the hike.

Miles and Directions

0.0 Start from the parking lot. Cross the road and head north 50 yards to the trailhead for the Webster-Jackson Trail

0.1 The Elephant Head spur heads off to the right; continue straight.

1.3 The Webster-Jackson Trail splits; bear left on the Jackson Branch.

2.2 Reach the summit of Mount Jackson. Return the way you came.

3.1 The Webster Branch comes in from the left; continue heading down.

4.4 Arrive back at the parking lot.

Option

Make a loop hike and go over Mount Webster via the Appalachian Trail and Mount Webster Branch. Distance: 5.6 miles; elevation gain: 2,407 feet.

25 Mount Tecumseh

When you don't have a lot of time and want a quicker 4,000-footer, this is your best bet. It's considered the "easiest" of the New Hampshire peaks.

Start: Waterville Valley ski area
Distance: 4.5 miles lollipop
Summit elevation: 4,004 feet
4,000-footers rank of the 115: 110
Elevation gain: 2,194 feet
Difficulty: Easy-moderate
Hiking time: 3–4 hours
Trails used: Mount Tecumseh Trail

Nearest town: Waterville Valley
Views: Okay
Water sources: A few stream crossings on the way up
Canine compatibility: Very good
Special considerations: Not much; when the hut is open, sometimes there are fun snacks for purchase.

Finding the trailhead: From I-93 take exit 28 and follow NH 49 East toward Waterville Valley. Just before the town of Waterville Valley, 10.2 miles from the interstate, turn left onto Tripoli Road. In 1.2 miles, bear left off Tripoli Road and onto the ski area road. Passing several parking lots on your left, bear right at 0.7 mile. In another 0.2 mile, the trailhead will be on your right; look for a place to park in the lots to your left. GPS (parking lot): N43°57'59.53" / W71°31'36.21"

The Hike

There are not many shorter hikes on the Northeast 111 than Tecumseh, the "shortest" of the New Hampshire 48 in height and also in terms of time it takes to hike. But a word of caution: Although short, it's not the easiest hike. Why? Because the top half is pretty much a giant staircase that makes you feel like you are on a stair climber the entire way (most of the 2,200 feet of gain seems to be on this section). The last time we hiked this was on an 80-degree, hot, and humid summer day, and it almost killed me. In fact, even though it's easy, it never feels easy to me. There are two main approaches—one from Waterville Valley, one from Tripoli Road (that way is longer, with more ups and downs)—but since you cannot access Tripoli Road in winter, we will cover the more common route. After parking in the Waterville Valley ski area, look for the trail on the right side, across from parking lots 1 and 2. This trail is very popular, so you should see other hikers almost any day of the year.

The first mile is fairly gradual until you reach the lookout to the ski slopes on your left. This is a good spot to gaze up and down the ski slope (although some hike

DID YOU KNOW?

Mount Tecumseh's name comes from a Shawnee Native American leader who fought the colonialists in the early 1800s and was killed in the Battle of the Thames in 1813.

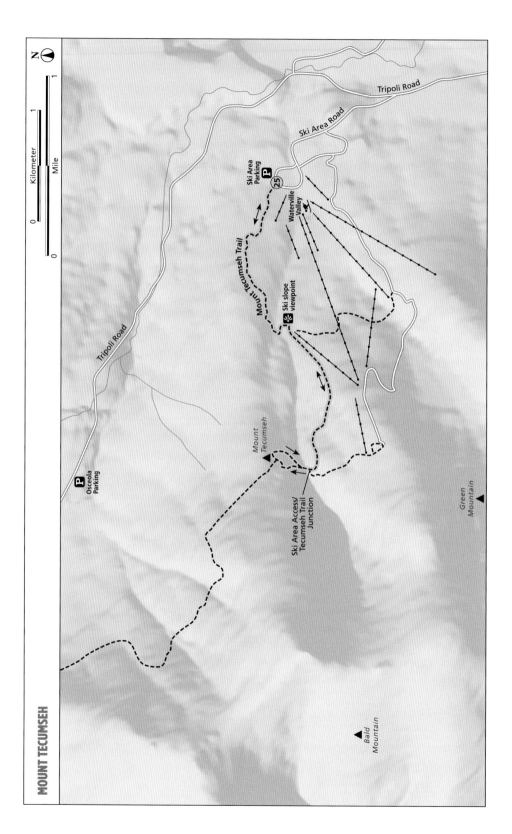

MOUNT TECUMSEH

N

0   Kilometer   1

0   Mile   1

Osceola Parking

Tripoli Road

Tripoli Road

Ski Area Parking

Ski Area Road

25

Waterville Valley

Mount Tecumseh Trail

Ski slope viewpoint

Mount Tecumseh

Ski Area Access/ Tecumseh Trail Junction

Bald Mountain

Green Mountain

Heart-shaped rock on the trail up to Mount Tecumseh DEAN J. OUELLETTE

down the ski slope, we prefer the trail). The trail now takes a major right-hand turn, and the staircase section starts in earnest with a very steep section. When it evens out, you come to a sign indicating two ways to the summit. Though we have done it both ways, we recommend taking the first left and winding up the loop clockwise—it's a bit more gradual and more scenic. It's only 10–15 minutes from this junction to the summit. Though small, the summit does provide some nice views, and it is worth taking a break from the climb to gaze upon the Tripyramids and Osceolas, with a glimpse of the Lafayette Ridge. Then you can either follow the gradual route you took up or, if this is your first time, continue over the summit to the right to take the very short but steep return loop, which takes you back to the junction in about 10 minutes. From there you can enjoy a relaxing descent. (**Note:** Remember to fork left at the junction with the ski trail.) The return is easily done in just over 1 hour, and even at a moderate pace, most hikers finish this 4.5-mile round-trip hike in 3–4 hours.

Miles and Directions

0.0   Start from the parking lot and head northwest.

1.1   Arrive at a short spur on your left to viewpoint from a ski slope.

2.0   At the intersection with the ski area access trail, to your left, bear right, heading northeast.

2.1   At the split in the trail, bear left and continue to the summit.

2.2   At the summit, continue northeast and follow the trail around.

2.4   Arrive back at the split that comes in from your right.

2.5   Bear left at the ski area access trail.

3.4   Spur to the ski slope view is on your right.

4.5   Arrive back at the parking lot.

Option

Change it up and start the hike from Tripoli Road. Distance: 5.4 miles; elevation gain: 2,442 feet. GPS (parking lot): N43°59'29.07" / W71°34'42.41"

26 Mount Moosilauke

This New Hampshire peak offers a huge payoff for a relatively easy hike, with a 360-degree view from the wide-open summit toward Vermont to the west and the Kinsmans and the Lafayette Ridge to the north/northeast.

Start: Moosilauke Ravine Lodge hiker parking
Distance: 7.5-mile loop
Summit elevation: 4,802 feet
4,000-footers rank of the 115: 20
Elevation gain: 2,522 feet
Difficulty: Easy
Hiking time: 5–7 hours
Trails used: Gorge Brook Trail, Appalachian Trail, Snapper Trail, Carriage Road
Nearest town: Lincoln

Views: Superb
Water sources: A few brook crossings at the start
Canine compatibility: Very good
Special considerations: The road to the trailhead is not plowed in winter. Parking is available by the generosity of the Moosilauke Ravine Lodge. Please be respectful and obey all signage.

Finding the trailhead: From I-93, take exit 32 and travel west on NH 112 (Kancamagus Highway) toward the town of Woodstock. In 0.5 mile, at the stoplight intersection with US 3, continue straight for 2.6 miles then bear left, heading south on NH 118. Travel another 7.2 miles to the hard-to-see right turn onto Ravine Road. Travel this dirt road for 1.5 miles; park in the designated hiker areas. GPS (parking lot): N43°59'34.67" / W71°48'55.95"

The Hike

As a Dartmouth alum, this mountain holds a special place in my heart; it brings back memories of freshman trips and our reunion at the Moosilauke Ravine Lodge. The Dartmouth Outing Club made these trips memorable by serving green eggs and ham for breakfast (Theodore Geisel, aka Dr. Seuss, is a Dartmouth alum too) and encouraging all "tripees," no matter what their trip was, to hike Moosilauke. Because the summit is entirely open, it is often windswept in any season, so be sure to bring extra warm gear. Snow lasts here well into spring, as you can see by the photo, taken in late March.

When the road to the Moosilauke Ravine Lodge is open (all but winter), the easiest and most pleasant route up is to go to the back of the lodge, head over the clearly marked hiker bridge, and bear right to follow a gentle path that follows Gorge Brook. Soon the trail parts ways from the brook and ascends gently through beautiful sections of woods as you progress up the flank. Take the time to appreciate some of the gorgeous viewpoints, one of which stares into the Sandwich Range, the other toward the Lafayette Ridge with Mounts Lincoln and Lafayette.

You know you are getting close when you hit a section of switchbacks and steeper sections (the last of which provides a great view behind you). The final section is

Michele's German shepherd, Argos, enjoying Mount Moosilauke's summit in early spring
MICHELE HERNANDEZ BAYLISS

one of my favorite sections in the White Mountains. You dip back below tree line through a beautiful tunnel of sorts as you head toward the alpine area below the summit. Breaking out of tree line here always takes my breath away—the summit cone beckons over a windswept alpine area and you head toward the summit sign, typically 2 to 2.5 hours later. No matter the season, the views are incredible in every direction. Staying off the alpine vegetation, take a seat and enjoy the views. Although the gain is 2,522 feet, it's quite gradual with the exception of a few steep but short switchbacks, making it less painful than many other hikes.

Though you can descend via the same route, we always follow the Appalachian Trail/Carriage Road over the summit, heading south toward South Peak, a subpeak of Mount Moosilauke. Taking care to follow the trail and avoid the fragile alpine vegetation, you follow the gentle downhill into another tunnel until you reach the junction for South Peak. Although this peak doesn't "count" for any list, the views back toward Moosilauke are worth the 10-minute scramble to the summit. The rest of the hike is scenic and easy as you head down the Carriage Road until you reach the left-hand junction for the Snapper Trail, which winds downhill until you return to the junction from earlier in the day and connect back up with the Gorge Brook Trail back to the lodge. This hike typically takes us 5–7 hours, but that accounts for generous summit breaks to enjoy the views.

DID YOU KNOW?

Constructed in the 1800s, the Carriage Road was built to get visitors to a hotel (the Tip Top House) that used to be on the summit.

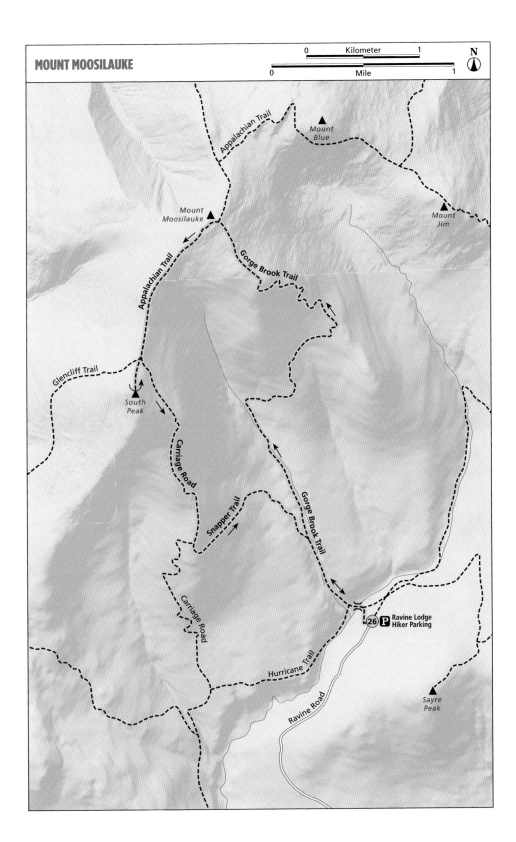

MOUNT MOOSILAUKE

0 Kilometer 1

0 Mile 1

N

Appalachian Trail

Mount
Blue

Mount
Moosilauke

Gorge Brook Trail

Mount
Jim

Appalachian Trail

Glencliff Trail

South
Peak

Carriage Road

Snapper Trail

Gorge Brook Trail

Carriage Road

26

Ravine Lodge
Hiker Parking

Hurricane Trail

Ravine Road

Sayre
Peak

Summit sign and elevation on the Moosilauke summit MICHELE HERNANDEZ BAYLISS

Miles and Directions

0.0 Start from the parking lot and head down toward the lodge.

0.2 After crossing the bridge, keep right on the Gorge Brook Trail as the Hurricane Trail bears left.

0.7 The Snapper Trail comes in on your left; stay right on Gorge Brook.

1.5 The Gorge Brook Trail bears right heading away from the brook.

3.4 The trail opens up above tree line.

3.5 Arrive at Mount Moosilauke's summit. Head south on the Appalachian Trail.

4.3 The Carriage Road bears left here; continue straight to grab a view from South Peak.

4.5 Arrive at South Peak. Turn around and head back the way you came.

4.7 Make a sharp right turn to head down the Carriage Road.

5.9 Turn left onto the Snapper Trail

6.8 Meet back up with the Gorge Brook Trail; continue down.

7.3 Turn left at the junction with Hurricane Trail and cross back over the bridge.

7.5 Make your way through the small roads around the lodge and arrive back at the parking lot.

Option

For a longer loop hike, try taking the Asquam Ridge Trail over Mount Jim, connecting with the Appalachian Trail, and summiting Mount Moosilauke from the north. Then continue down the Carriage Road Trail. Distance: 9.4 miles; elevation gain: 2,790 feet.

27 Osceola and East Osceola

Though East Osceola's peak is not that exciting, Mount Osceola is awesome, with a huge viewing platform where you can relax and enjoy the views. Plus you get to attempt the "chute" between the two peaks if you are up for the challenge.

Start: Greeley Ponds Trailhead
Distance: 6.8 miles out and back
Summit elevation: Osceola: 4,315 feet; East Osceola: 4,156 feet
4,000-footers rank of the 115: Osceola: 54; East Osceola: 73
Elevation gain: 3,026 feet
Difficulty: Moderate
Hiking time: 6–7 hours

Trails used: Greeley Ponds Trail, Mount Osceola Trail
Nearest town: Lincoln
Views: Very good
Water sources: A few streams at the start
Canine compatibility: Very good except for the "chute"
Special considerations: There is a modest fee to park in the parking lot.

Finding the trailhead: From I-93, take exit 32 to NH 112 (Kancamagus Highway). Travel east on NH 112 through the town of Lincoln and in 10 miles reach the Greeley Ponds Trailhead, on your left. GPS (parking lot): N44°3'48.71" / W71°35'17.11"

The Hike

We have done these peaks from both sides, although never as a traverse, which would require a long car shuttle. Because Tripoli Road is closed in winter, we typically start at the Greeley Pond side. Follow the Greeley Pond Trail, which is nearly flat until you reach a junction. If you continue straight on the Greeley Pond Trail, you reach a set of ponds that are perfect for letting your dog take a swim if you have time on a hot summer day. But if you are focused on peak-bagging, bear right on the Osceola Trail and start the ascent. Though gentle at first, it quickly becomes very steep. You ascend 2,000 feet in short order, so it's a real lung burner. Every time you round a turn, the trail keeps its relentless grade. Finally, after 45 minutes to 1 hour from the junction, you arrive at a small clearing in the trees with a sign and a cairn; this is the summit. Though the summit itself has no view, there are a few viewpoints nearby that we seek out before continuing the steep and rocky descent to the col between Osceola and East Osceola. Right before you head down, there are tremendous views over to Osceola. On a clear day you stare straight into Owl's Head, Mount Garfield, and the Twins.

Before long you come to the famous "chute" section (see photo). Although in summer and fall it's fairly easy to climb straight up the chimney (I don't love exposure, but in the chimney you are kind of wedged in and there are handholds, so it is hard to fall), we usually (and always in winter) veer toward the right. This is the only way my

Dean scampering up the steep chute between Mount Osceola and East Osceola
MICHELE HERNANDEZ BAYLISS

dog can make it up and down. Even the bypass is tough and can require crampons and ice axes in winter. You head up a very steep ledge and then fork left up more rocks, scrambling to the top where it joins back with the top of the chimney. This section is a no-go for many dogs.

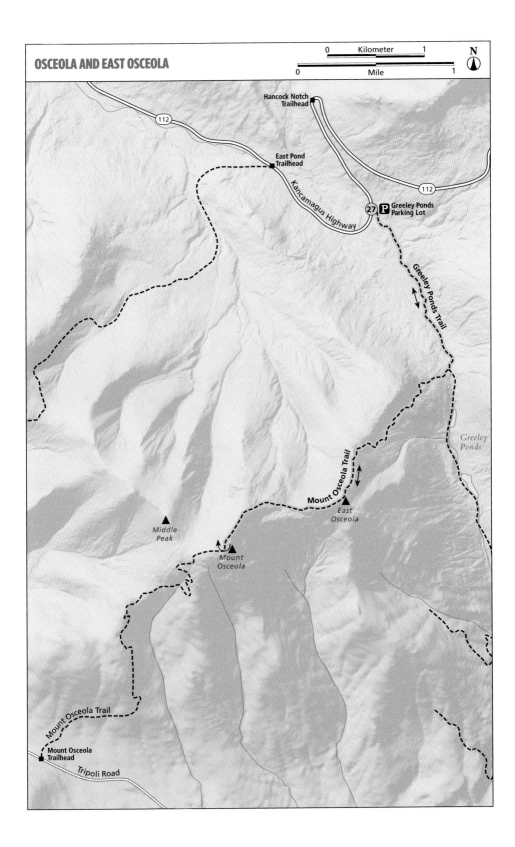

OSCEOLA AND EAST OSCEOLA

Hancock Notch
Trailhead

112

East Pond
Trailhead

Kancamagus Highway

112

27 P Greeley Ponds
Parking Lot

Greeley Ponds Trail

Greeley
Ponds

Mount Osceola Trail

East
Osceola

Middle
Peak

Mount
Osceola

Mount Osceola Trail

Mount Osceola
Trailhead

Tripoli Road

Once you have ascended the chimney, you still have the final rocky, staircase-like climb up to Osceola, but it's very rewarding to hit the last section and exit onto the very large platform. The real summit is not actually on this ledge but behind, where you follow the trail another minute or so to the actual summit—a rock marked with fire tower footings. Once you tag the summit, enjoy the views back at the viewing ledge. Due east there are views of Waterville Valley and the Tripyramids, with Mount Washington to the north over the Hancocks and Mount Carrigan. If you were to do a traverse, it's just over 3 miles down the Osceola Trail to Tripoli Road. This route tends to be very crowded; most hikers just want a great view on a short hike and will often come up this side.

The return up to East Osceola is tough on the legs, and then you tackle the steep descent. It's always a relief to hit the junction with the Greeley Pond Trail, where the rest is flat. The "easier" hike is to just hike Osceola by itself from Tripoli Road and back, but then you would orphan East Osceola.

Miles and Directions

0.0 Start from the parking lot and head south on the Greeley Ponds Trail.

1.2 Turn right onto the Mount Osceola Trail.

2.4 Cruise over the summit of East Osceola.

3.4 Arrive at the summit of Mount Osceola; turn around and retrace your steps.

4.4 Cross the summit of East Osceola again.

5.6 Turn left onto the Greeley Ponds Trail.

6.8 Arrive back at the parking lot.

Option

Change it up and hike up from Tripoli Road. Distance: 7.4 miles; elevation gain: 2,848 feet. GPS (parking lot): N43°59'29.07" / W71°34'42.41"

28 Pierce and Eisenhower

You get a true taste of New Hampshire's majestic Presidentials in a hike that is not super grueling yet features world-class vistas.

Start: AMC Highland Center parking lot
Distance: 8.4 miles out and back
Summit elevation: Pierce: 4,310 feet; Eisenhower: 4,761 feet
4,000-footers rank of the 115: Pierce: 55; Eisenhower: 21 (tied)
Elevation gain: 3,221 feet
Difficulty: Moderate
Hiking time: 7–8 hours

Trails used: Crawford Path, Appalachian Trail, Mount Eisenhower Loop Trail
Nearest town: Twin Mountain
Views: Superb
Water sources: Small streams at the beginning of the hike; nothing once up on the ridge
Canine compatibility: Good
Special considerations: There is a lot of above-tree line walking over to Eisenhower, with not much shade available.

Finding the trailhead: To reach the town of Twin Mountain from the north, take exit 36 off I-93 to NH 141. Continue for 0.7 mile then turn onto US 3 North for 9.7 miles. From the south, take exit 35 to US 3 North for 9.9 miles. From the intersection of US 302 and US 3 in the town of Twin Mountain, take US 302 East for 8.4 miles; the AMC Highland Center will be on your right. If traveling from the south or east, take US 302 West 17.1 miles from the Attitash ski area in the town of Bartlett. The parking area will be on your left. GPS (parking lot): N44°12'51.73" / W71°24'27.50"

The Hike

These are two of my favorite peaks in the White Mountains. Though you can do a loop going up Edmands Path and down Crawford Path, we typically do an out-and-back to avoid the need for a car shuttle. From the Highland Center parking lot, travel east, following the Crawford Path signs and cross US 302. You'll enter the woods and travel for 0.2 mile to the connector trail, which enters on your left. Follow the Crawford Path another 1.5 miles to the sign for the Mizpah Hut and Cutoff Trail; bear left to stay on the Crawford Path. I love this trail; it's very gentle (by mountain standards)—to the point where you can almost forget you are ascending a 4,000-foot peak.

Continue up a gently sloped but ever steeper trail for another hour or so until you arrive at the junction with the spur trail. In winter it can sometimes be hard to find the right-hand turn to the Webster Cliff Trail (also the Appalachian Trail), but just head 90 degrees from the trail and you should have no trouble finding the very short (5 minutes or so) winding trail to the actual summit of Mount Pierce. It's much windier on the summit, so we usually add a layer at the junction before the spur trail to the summit, marked by a cairn. Because this is one of the "easiest" peaks to climb, it's not unusual to see scores of people on the summit during popular hiking months.

Giant cairn on Mount Eisenhower's open summit, with Mount Washington and the northern Presidentials in full view to the north MICHELE HERNANDEZ BAYLISS

Even in winter, we typically see many hikers on Pierce though many fewer continue on to Mount Eisenhower (maybe because when you look up at Eisenhower from Pierce, it is imposing).

The next section of the Crawford Trail is spectacular—you are well into the alpine/over–tree line area, with occasional ducking into low trees. Sometimes with deep snow, it's hard to follow the path in and out of the trees, but once you arrive at the sign announcing that the summit is 0.3 mile, it's easier to follow the trail as it snakes straight up the side of Eisenhower. The switchbacks are super fun as you climb, although keep in mind that you are totally exposed to the elements in all seasons; be careful. Once you break out onto the summit, you follow the rock path right to the enormous cairn that marks the summit. Be aware of possible wasp nests in the warmer weather—we almost got stung as we took photos. Eisenhower has spectacular 360-degree views. Mount Washington looks so close, yet it's a fairly good hike to continue on to Monroe and Washington from here (it is the southern half of a "Presi traverse"). If you've arranged a car shuttle, you can loop down the other side of Eisenhower and take the Edmands Path (or do the 2.3-mile road walk), but we usually just reverse and head back down.

> ## DID YOU KNOW?
> The Crawford Path is considered the oldest maintained footpath in the United States.

PIERCE AND EISENHOWER

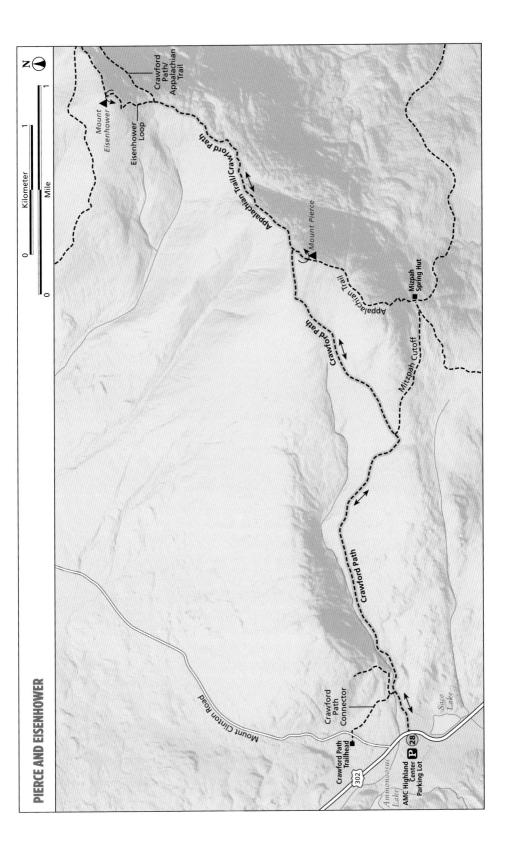

N

Kilometer
0   1

Mile
0   1

Mount Eisenhower

Eisenhower Loop

Crawford Path/ Appalachian Trail

Appalachian Trail/Crawford Path

Mount Pierce

Appalachian Trail

Mizpah Spring Hut

Crawford Path

Mitzpah Cutoff

Crawford Path

Mount Clinton Road

Crawford Path Connector

Crawford Path Trailhead

302

AMC Highland Center Parking Lot

P 28

Saco Lake

Ammonoosuc Lake

View from Mount Eisenhower looking toward the path to Mount Pierce's summit
MICHELE HERNANDEZ BAYLISS

Gazing back on Pierce, it looks like a small bump and nothing more. Once you have taken in the magnificent views, head back down the steep side of Eisenhower; follow the trail back to the Pierce turnoff and the relatively gentle downhill back to your car.

Miles and Directions

0.0 Start from the AMC parking lot and cross the road to start on the Crawford Path.

0.2 Junction with Crawford Connector on your left; continue straight.

0.4 Spur trail to Gibbs Falls.

1.6 Crawford Path–Mizpah Cutoff Trail junction; bear left and stay on the Crawford Path.

2.7 Junction with trail to Mount Pierce summit to your right; travel south.

2.8 Mount Pierce summit; head back toward the junction.

2.9 Bear right on the Appalachian Trail/Crawford Path.

4.0 At the Crawford Path–Mount Eisenhower Loop Trail junction, bear left toward the summit of Eisenhower.

4.3 Reach the summit of Mount Eisenhower; retrace your steps.

4.6 Crawford Path enters from your left; continue heading south.

5.7 At the junction for Mount Pierce, bear right and continue downhill.

6.8 The Mizpah Cutoff Trail comes in from your left; continue down.

8.2 The Crawford Connector is on your right; continue straight, toward the road.

8.4 Arrive back at the AMC parking lot

Option

For a loop hike, you'll need a shuttle car at the Edmands Path Trailhead (GPS: N44°14'56.53" / W71°23'28.28"). From Mount Eisenhower, take the Edmands Path down. Distance: 7.4 miles; elevation gain: 3,107 feet.

29 Mount Garfield

This is one of my favorite New Hampshire hikes. It's relatively easy, but you get an amazing summit, with views right into Franconia Ridge and the Twins.

Start: Garfield Trailhead on Gale River Loop Road

Distance: 9.4 miles out and back

Summit elevation: 4,488 feet

4,000-footers rank of the 115: 36

Elevation gain: 2,928 feet

Difficulty: Moderate

Hiking time: 6–7 hours

Trails used: Mount Garfield Trail, Appalachian Trail/Garfield Ridge Trail

Nearest town: Twin Mountain

Views: Excellent

Water sources: Several water sources on the hike up toward the ridge

Canine compatibility: Very good

Special considerations: The road is closed in winter, adding 2.4 miles to your trip.

Finding the trailhead: To reach Gale River Loop Road from the north, take exit 36 off I-93 to NH 141; continue for 0.7 mile then turn onto US 3 North for 4 miles. From the south, take exit 35 to US 3 North for 4.5 miles; Gale River Loop Road will be on your right. On Gale River Loop Road, travel south for 1.2 miles; you'll see the trailhead on your right after a bridge crossing. From the town of Twin Mountain and the intersection of US 3 and US 302, travel south on US 3 for 5.5 miles; Gale River Loop Road will be on your left. GPS (parking lot): N44°13'43.84" / W71°37'58.94"; (winter parking): N44°14'37.22" / W71°38'20.99"

The Hike

I'm writing this on the same day I just got back from my friend's New Hampshire "grid" finish on Mount Garfield. It was a good reminder that although this hike is easy, in winter you have to factor in the extra 1.2-mile walk each way from the gate to the "summer" parking, making this a 11.8-mile round trip rather than 9.4 miles.

One of the steepest sections is the 5 minutes of "up" from the parking area. The sign indicates that it's 4.8 miles to the junction with the Garfield Ridge Trail and 0.2 mile from there to the summit. The first section is lovely as you hike above one of the branches of the Gale River and wind through the woods. After a few downs and ups, you level out and then follow a relatively flat path for several miles. I'm always surprised by how fast the miles go for the first half of this hike. For the last few miles, you reach a series of gentle switchbacks that make the elevation gain relatively painless. No section by itself is very steep, but there are some uphill sections interspersed with flat sections. Overall, I would venture to say this hike has the mildest uphill sections of any New Hampshire peak.

You will know you are close when you hit the sign for the Garfield tentsite, which means you are only about 15 minutes away from the junction. One of the last curves to the left features a route out to Garfield Pond, to the right, which is a worthwhile

Concrete summit on Mount Garfield, looking toward Owl's Head, center, and Mounts Flume and Liberty in the distance MICHELE HERNANDEZ BAYLISS

detour if you have the time. After what seems like the tenth switchback, you level out and reach the junction with the Garfield Ridge Trail. Though it's tempting to layer up when it's windy or cold for the final stretch, we wait until the very top—you will sweat on this final steep section. On the bright side, although it's a tough uphill scramble, it does not take long. In 10 minutes or so, you break out above tree line to breathtaking views of Mounts Lafayette and Lincoln. It's only a short walk from here to scramble up to the concrete foundation that marks the summit.

This is a spectacular summit, so take the time to enjoy the views in every direction. I love staring into the Twins and Owl's Head, and this is one of the best vantage points of "Southwest" Twin—a subpeak I had to bushwhack to for my friend's Trailwrights 72 Summit Club.

DID YOU KNOW?

The section of trail down from Lafayette to Garfield on the Appalachian Trail is one of the most difficult sections of the entire AT. Mount Garfield is the "bridge" between the Franconia Ridge and the Twins.

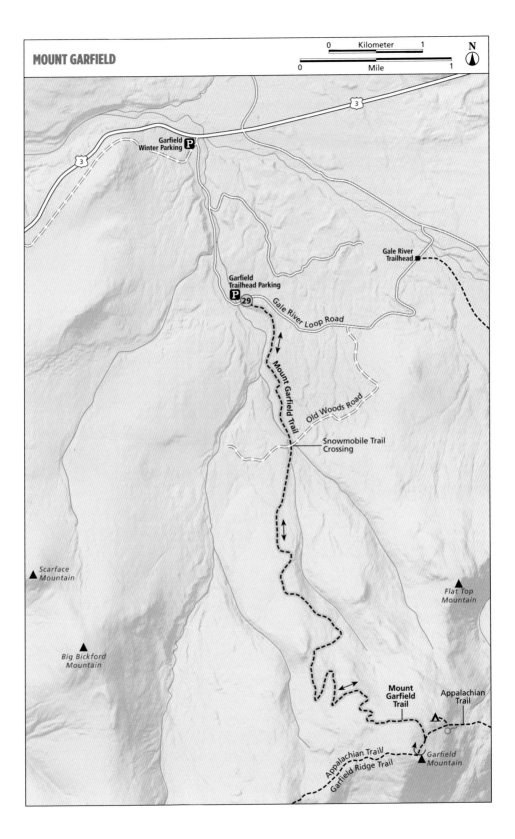

MOUNT GARFIELD

0 Kilometer 1

0 Mile 1

N

Garfield
Winter Parking P

3

3

Gale River
Trailhead

Garfield
Trailhead Parking
P 29

Gale River Loop Road

Old Woods Road

Snowmobile Trail
Crossing

Mount Garfield Trail

Scarface
Mountain

Flat Top
Mountain

Big Bickford
Mountain

Mount
Garfield
Trail

Appalachian
Trail

Appalachian Trail/
Garfield Ridge Trail

Garfield
Mountain

Miles and Directions

0.0 Start from the parking lot and head south on the trail.

0.5 Old trail to the right; bear to the left and stay on main trail.

1.1 Cross an old woods road/snowmobile trail.

4.6 Bear right at this junction with the Appalachian Trail.

4.7 Summit of Mount Garfield. Retrace your steps of the summit cone, turn right, and head downhill.

4.8 Junction with the Mount Garfield Trail; keep to the left. (If you need water, go right down the Appalachian Trail for 0.2 mile to the spring then return to this junction.)

8.3 Old road crossing

9.4 Arrive back at the parking lot.

Option

For a loop hike, continue down the Appalachian Trail and then take the Gale River Trail, which comes in from your left at mile 6.9. At the Gale River Trail parking, turn left onto Gale River Loop Road and walk 1.7 miles back to your car. Distance: 12.3 miles; elevation gain: 3,454 feet.

30 Lafayette and Lincoln

This loop hike deserves its title as the most iconic hike in the Northeast due to the spectacular ridge walk with views to almost every mountain in the state.

Start: Lafayette Place east parking lot
Distance: 8.0-mile loop
Summit elevation: Lafayette: 5,242 feet; Lincoln: 5,089 feet
4,000-footers rank of the 115: Lafayette: 8; Lincoln: 10
Elevation gain: 3,828 feet
Difficulty: Difficult
Hiking time: 5–7 hours
Trails used: Old Bridle Path, Greenleaf Trail, Franconia Ridge Trail/Appalachian Trail, Falling Waters Trail
Nearest town: Lincoln
Views: Excellent

Water sources: Not much until you get to the Greenleaf Hut, where during the summer months they have tap water for hiker use. Nothing on the ridge until you're coming down to the stream well below the summit of Little Haystack.
Canine compatibility: Not the best for dogs. Watch your dog's paws; this hike is mostly above tree line, and hot sharp rocks can burn and cut them.
Special considerations: Extremely busy during the summer months. A shuttle is sometimes offered if the lots become full.

Finding the trailhead: From I-93 and points north, travel 3.8 miles from exit 34A to a trailhead sign indicating "Bridle Path/Falling Water." If traveling south on I-93, continue 2.3 miles from exit 34B to a sign for Lafayette Place Campground. If parking here, you'll need to walk through a tunnel under the highway to reach the trailhead. GPS (parking lot): N44°8'31.14" / W71°40'52.98"

The Hike

This hike is a real leg burner, no matter which direction you tackle the loop. In any season, it pays to get an early start to avoid thunderstorms up on the Franconia Ridge in summer and dwindling daylight in winter. There have been many deaths and injuries on this hike (and dozens of rescues), so check the forecast and then check it again.

I'm writing this section the day after my seventh hike of this loop, and my legs are reminding me that there is a lot of elevation gain. We did it in January after a recent snowstorm, which drove home the point that, thanks to the smoother path in winter and the fact that our snowshoes have televators on them, the ascent can actually be easier in winter.

The trail starts up a short hill to the start of both hikes, 5 minutes up the path. At this point, you can go left to ascend the Old Bridle Path or right to ascend the Falling Waters Trail. We prefer the Old Bridle Path. Though it's mild for the first half hour or so, the path gets brutally steep as you approach the AMC's Greenleaf Hut (closed in winter). There are several fantastic viewpoints where you can catch your breath and look directly into the incredible Lafayette/Lincoln ridge rising to your right. There

Dean, Heather, and Michele atop Mount Lafayette's summit MICHELE HERNANDEZ BAYLISS

are also some great left-hand views toward Cannon Mountain and the skiway and back toward the Kinsmans.

After a very steep 2-plus-hour climb on this section, the path finally levels out to the hut, a welcome sight. This is a good spot to reassess the weather. If winds are high or a storm is coming, do not hesitate to turn around and descend the way you came rather than risk death. Though there is a trail that heads left, you want to head right from the hut (not behind it; there is no trail there) to continue on a bumpy section with a few ups and downs and short flats through the woods before you break out onto the flank of the mountain. You basically head toward a pile of rocks, only to discover you still have a bit more to go before finally leveling out atop Mount Lafayette. What a spectacular summit it is. You get to experience the very best New Hampshire has to offer for the next 1.7 miles (according to the sign) along the Franconia Ridge Trail, which is also the Appalachian Trail. Toward the southwest is the bald summit of Mount Moosilauke; due west is the Kinsman Ridge and the "Cannonballs," which you can see in profile between the Kinsmans and Cannon Mountain. After enjoying the summit, head south to pick up the Appalachian Trail and descend the summit cone of Lafayette.

DID YOU KNOW?

Ty Gagne's fantastic book *The Last Traverse* features this hike in reverse as it recounts the tale of two hikers who did not heed the weather, and the tragic result.

We can't emphasize enough how tremendous a ridge walk this is. You may hardly notice the fact that you still have to climb a subpeak right after you descend Lafayette, then descend that, then head up again to summit Lincoln Peak. The view here is every bit as fine as Lafayette, with more southerly views and usually less wind. Then there's one last section to reach Little Haystack, another fine lookout. This is where it is easy to lose the trail, so head right (west) from the summit to pick up the Falling Waters Trail, marked by a sign. If you continued south, you would have almost 2 more miles to traverse before reaching the Liberty Springs Trail.

Within 5 minutes you will descend below tree line. The Falling Waters Trail is gorgeous, but in winter it has some very icy pitches you must take care on. In summer the steep pitches also require care so that you don't face-plant on a protruding rock or root. The waterfalls and pools will dazzle as you head back to the bridge where the Old Bridle and Falling Waters Trails intersect and then turn left for the final short section back to your car. Your legs will recover quickly, though you will be left with a lifetime of memories of the views from the iconic and magnificent Franconia Ridge section of this hike.

View toward the summit of Mount Lafayette from Franconia Ridge MICHELE HERNANDEZ BAYLISS

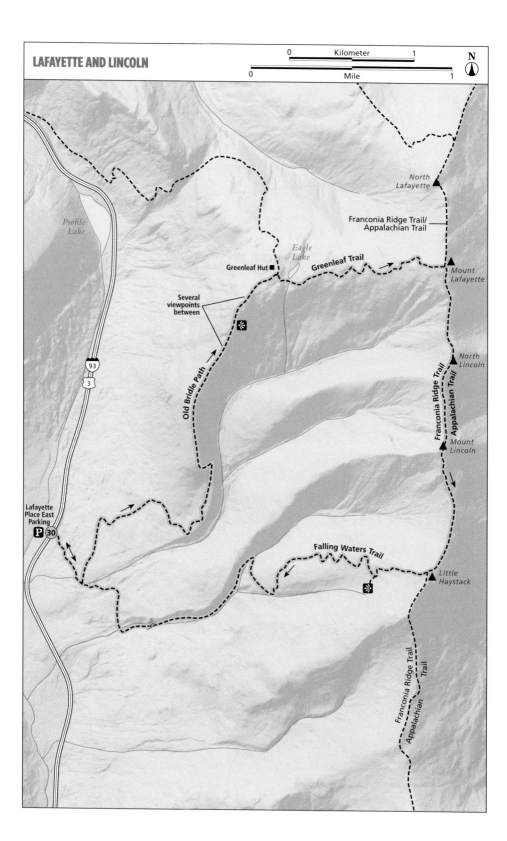

LAFAYETTE AND LINCOLN

0 — Kilometer — 1
0 — Mile — 1

N

Profile Lake

93
3

North Lafayette

Franconia Ridge Trail/
Appalachian Trail

Eagle Lake

Greenleaf Hut ■   Greenleaf Trail   Mount Lafayette

Several viewpoints between

Old Bridle Path

Franconia Ridge Trail   Appalachian Trail

North Lincoln

Mount Lincoln

Lafayette Place East Parking
P 30

Falling Waters Trail

Little Haystack

Franconia Ridge Trail   Appalachian Trail

Miles and Directions

0.0 Start heading east out of the parking lot on a paved path that turns to dirt.

0.2 Turn left at the junction with the Falling Waters Trail.

1.7 First good viewpoint to the left of the Franconia Ridge.

2.5 The last of several views of the ridge.

2.7 Arrive at the Greenleaf Hut. Take the Greenleaf Trail east, down the hill, and pass Eagle Lake.

3.2 The trail moves above tree line.

3.7 Arrive at the junction with the Franconia Ridge and Appalachian Trails; turn right and arrive at the Mount Lafayette summit. Continue south.

4.1 Pass over the hump of North Lincoln.

4.6 Arrive at the Mount Lincoln summit. Continue on the Appalachian Trail.

5.2 Arrive at the Little Haystack summit. Turn right and head west down the hill on the Falling Waters Trail.

5.5 Pass a short spur trail to shining rock lookout.

6.8 Pass several cascading waterfalls.

7.8 Arrive back at junction with the Bridle Path; bear left.

8.0 Arrive back at the parking lot.

31 Mount Carrigain

Despite its length (10 miles when the road is open; closer to 14 miles in winter), you are rewarded with a spectacular fire tower with among the best views anywhere in the White Mountains.

Start: Signal Ridge Trailhead on Sawyer Road
Distance: 10.0 miles out and back
Summit elevation: 4,680 feet
4,000-footers rank of the 115: 27
Elevation gain: 3,312 feet
Difficulty: Difficult
Hiking time: 5-7 hours
Trails used: Signal Ridge Trail
Nearest town: Bartlett
Views: Good once at the top of the tower

Water sources: There are several streams and crossings. Sometimes difficult to cross during periods of high water; extreme caution must be exercised.
Canine compatibility: Very good
Special considerations: Sawyer River Road is closed late fall until early spring. Plan accordingly; the road walk will add 4.0 miles round-trip to this hike.

Finding the trailhead: From the north, travel on US 302 East from the top of Crawford Notch, where the AMC Highland Center is located, for 10.7 miles; Sawyer River Road will be on your right. If traveling from the south or east near North Conway, take US 302 West for 6.4 miles from the Attitash ski area in the town of Bartlett. From US 302, travel down Sawyer River Road for 2 miles to reach the summer lot. Winter parking is just off of US 302. GPS (summer parking lot): N44°4'10.58" / W71°23'1.77"; (winter parking): N44°5'11.11" / N71°21'6.66"

The Hike

Though the mileage can seem off-putting, this hike is not as tough as you might think thanks to the almost entirely flat first section, which provides a great warm-up. *Note:* Sawyer River Road is not open in winter; you'll have to walk 2.0 miles one way to reach the trail.

I love the flat section of Signal Ridge Trail, which goes very quickly until you reach the junction with the Carrigain Notch Trail (which you do not want to take). Now the fun begins. Whatever elevation you have not gained starts here; the next section is quite steep, though not technically difficult in any way. Almost all the elevation gain takes place in this section, as you will soon see. One of the best parts of this hike is the incredible open and flat ridgelike section about 0.5 mile before the actual summit, where you have near 360-degree views of the Pemigewasset Wilderness. This section can be colder and windier than the actual summit, so add a layer if needed to cross the beautiful ridge, from which you can see the fire tower straight ahead. Though it looks intimidating, it's only 0.4 mile from here to the summit. This is a great spot to take a break to enjoy the views—and celebrate the fact that you do not have a ton of elevation left.

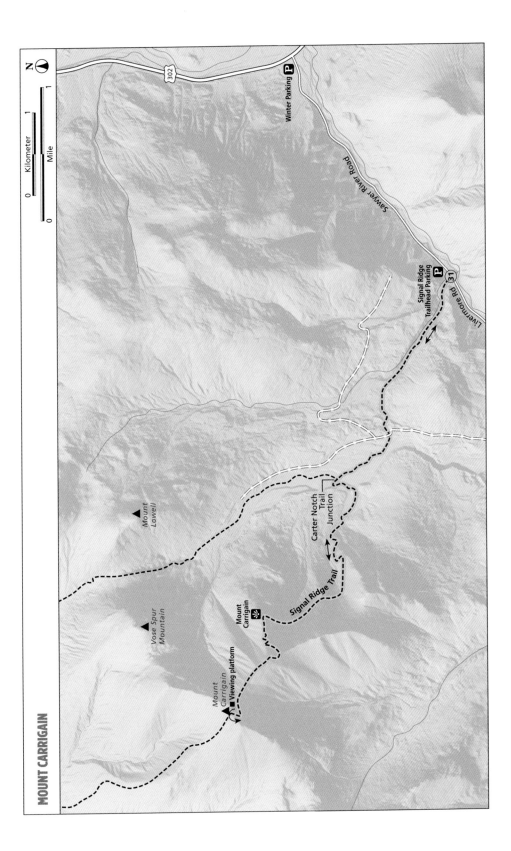

MOUNT CARRIGAN

302

Winter Parking

Sawyer River Road

Signal Ridge Trailhead Parking

Livermore Rd

31

Carter Notch Trail Junction

Signal Ridge Trail

Mount Carrigain

Mount Lowell

Vose Spur Mountain

Mount Carrigain
Viewing platform

N

Kilometer

Mile

0   1

0   1

Michele and Dean atop the cool tower on Mount Carrigain's summit, four days before New Hampshire spring MICHELE HERNANDEZ BAYLISS

After you reach some outbuildings, you continue up the last steep pitch to the small summit, dominated by a huge fire tower. This is one of the perks of Mount Carrigain. Climb the very high tower and take photos from the platform; you can see Vose Spur (a subpeak of Carrigain); Mounts Tom, Field, and Willey; the southern Presidentials; Chocorua to the southeast; and the Bonds and Franconia Ridge to the northwest. This hike is best done on a clear day to enjoy the views; otherwise you will be in a fire tower surrounded by mist and fog, as has happened to us more than once. (This mountain was our final New Hampshire peak in our first nonwinter round, and I remember it mostly for the intense rain.) The last time I did this hike, it was gorgeous—and reminded me to never do this hike again in terrible weather.

Once you get down the steep sections (careful on the rocks, which can be slippery), you get to enjoy the flat section and stretch your legs a bit. Despite the mileage, this hike is typically done in 5 hours or so; closer to 7 hours in winter with the extra road walk.

Miles and Directions

- **0.0**   Start from the parking lot and head west on the Signal Ridge Trail.
- **1.4**   Cross an old logging road; continue on the path.
- **1.9**   The Carter Notch Trail comes in from the right; continue straight.
- **4.4**   View of Mount Carrigain.
- **5.0**   Summit of Mount Carrigain. Turn around and retrace your steps back to the car.
- **8.1**   Pass the Carter Notch Trail.
- **10.0**   Arrive back at the parking lot.

DID YOU KNOW?

The mountain was named for Phillip Carrigain, New Hampshire's secretary of state in the early 1800s.

32 Carter Dome

This is another of my favorite New Hampshire hikes. It is relatively easy, has great views, and has a cool loop option that you can take to vary the trails a bit.

Start: Nineteen Mile Brook Trailhead
Distance: 9.7-mile loop
Summit elevation: 4,832 feet
4,000-footers rank of the 115: 18
Elevation gain: 3,479 feet
Difficulty: Difficult
Hiking time: 6–7 hours
Trails used: Nineteen Mile Brook, Carter Dome Trail, Appalachian Trail/Carter Moriah Trail
Nearest town: Gorham

Views: Excellent (clearing/ledge with a view a few feet from the summit cairn)
Water sources: Several water sources on the hike up toward the ridge; nothing on the ridge until arriving at Carter Notch
Canine compatibility: Very good
Special considerations: Not much, but when the hut is open, sometimes there are fun snacks for purchase.

Finding the trailhead: From the north in the town of Gorham, take NH 16 south for 6.9 miles. If traveling from the south, from the town of Jackson, travel north on NH 16 for 13 miles, passing the Pinkham Notch Visitor Center at mile 9.3 and Wildcat ski area at 10.1 miles. GPS (parking lot): N44°18'7.99" / W71°13'15.58"

The Hike

Like the start of the Wildcat Ridge hike (see appendix A, p. 215), you head up the gently sloping Nineteen Mile Brook Trail. But this time, instead of bearing right for Wildcat Ridge at the junction, you head left on the Carter Dome Trail and follow it for just under 1 hour until you reach the Zeta Pass intersection, where you follow Zeta Pass and then head left. Though optional, we always take the scenic short-but-steep section to Mount Hight (not an official peak)—it has a beautiful alpine summit, and the climb is not that bad. Then continue over the summit to head toward Carter Dome so you have the choice of two "loops" for your return. I love this section of trail from Hight to Dome; it follows a ridge, so there is not a ton of elevation gain to reach Carter Dome, and it's scenic. After some easy walking, you reach the approach to Carter Dome (only a short final uphill section) and then the huge summit cairn, which is in an enclosed area and thus shielded from high winds. Right before the summit, on the right is a gorgeous lookout toward the Presidentials—don't miss it. There are almost always some aggressive gray jays that will eat the food right out of your hands. Now you have two choices. If it's not super snowy or muddy or icy, it's fun to continue over the summit and descend to the Carter Moriah Trail, where you hit the junction for Wildcat A and descend the entirety of the Nineteen Mile Brook Trail back to your car.

Michele on a rainy day in the clearing that marks the summit of Carter Dome
DEAN J. OUELLETTE

We usually take the "easy" loop back toward Hight, turning left at the junction to the Carter Moriah Trail back to Nineteen Mile Brook and then back to the junction on the Carter Dome Trail, where you came up. The section of trail is beautiful, but winter can bring very tough sideways-slanted snow that makes it challenging, though not as challenging as the back side of Carter Dome toward the hut. The remaining section down Nineteen Mile Brook Trail goes quickly, and typically you can do the entire loop in 6–7 hours.

DID YOU KNOW?

Mount Hight features 360-degree views of the northern Presidentials, Carter Notch, and the Carter Moriah Range. On a clear day, you can see Maine to the east.

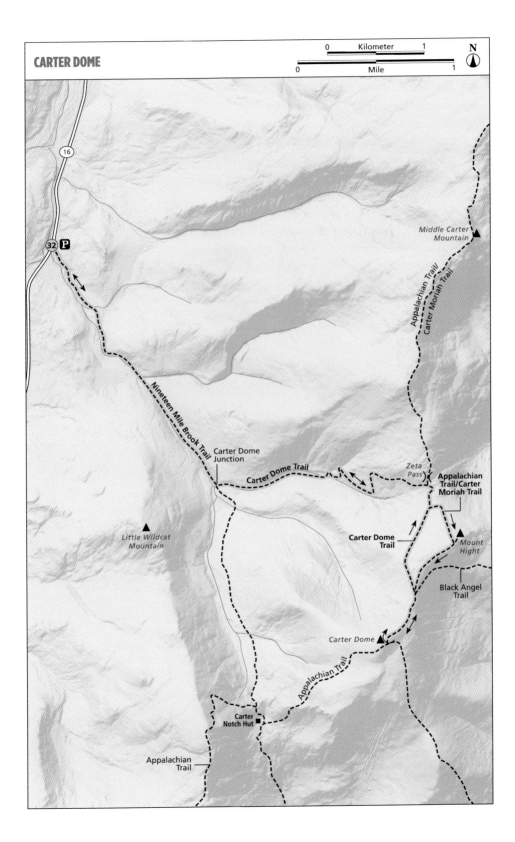

Kilometer

Mile

N

16

32 P

Middle Carter Mountain

Appalachian Trail/ Carter Moriah Trail

Nineteen Mile Brook Trail

Carter Dome Junction

Carter Dome Trail

Zeta Pass

Appalachian Trail/Carter Moriah Trail

Little Wildcat Mountain

Carter Dome Trail

Mount Hight

Black Angel Trail

Carter Dome

Appalachian Trail

Carter Notch Hut

Appalachian Trail

Miles and Directions

0.0 Start from the trailhead and head southeast on the Nineteen Mile Brook Trail.

1.9 At the split, go left up the Carter Dome Trail.

3.6 At Zeta Pass and the junction with the Appalachian Trail, turn right and head south.

3.8 Split from the Carter Dome Trail; turn left and go uphill to reach the Mount Hight summit.

4.2 Cross the open summit of Mount Hight.

4.6 Meet back up with Carter Dome Trail, on your right; the Black Angel Trail comes in on your left. Continue south on the Appalachian Trail.

5.0 Arrive at the Carter Dome summit. Return the way you came.

5.4 Arrive back at the junction and bear left on the Carter Dome Trail, bypassing Mount Hight.

5.9 The Appalachian Trail comes in from your right; continue straight.

6.1 At Zeta Pass, turn left and head downhill on the Carter Dome Trail.

7.8 Back at the junction with the Nineteen Mile Brook Trail, bear right.

9.7 Arrive back at the trailhead.

Option

Follow the Appalachian Trail down to Carter Notch Hut and follow the Nineteen Mile Brook Trail back to your car. Distance: 9.5 miles; elevation gain: 3,571 feet.

33 North Kinsman and South Kinsman

There are several fun hikes you can do to reach the Kinsmans from Cannon Mountain via the Kinsman Trail (also part of the Appalachian Trail), which goes up and down over the "cannonballs" to the out-and-back we describe.

Start: Mount Kinsman Trailhead off NH 116
Distance: 9.2 miles out and back
Summit elevation: North Kinsman: 4,293 feet; South Kinsman: 4,358 feet
4,000-footers rank of the 115: North Kinsman: 57; South Kinsman: 50
Elevation gain: 3,712 feet
Difficulty: Moderate

Hiking time: 6-7 hours
Trails used: Mount Kinsman Trail, Appalachian Trail/Kinsman Ridge Trail
Nearest town: Franconia
Views: Great
Water sources: Better fill up before you go.
Canine compatibility: Very good
Special considerations: None

Finding the trailhead: From the intersection of NH 18 and NH 116 in the town of Franconia, travel south on NH 116 for 4.6 miles; the parking area will be on your left. GPS (parking lot): N44°9'54.37" / W71°45'57.22"

The Hike

My favorite way to climb the Kinsmans is from NH 116, which has a spacious parking area right next to the Tamarack Tennis Camp. Although there is over 500 feet more elevation gain from this side, I find the grade is easier overall than from the east and the terrain more forgiving. The eastern side has some very rugged sections that lose and gain altitude that I don't enjoy quite as much, especially when it's muddy.

From the parking lot, the trail starts out flat with only a few gradual ramp-like ups and downs through fern and hemlocks until after 1 hour or so, when you hit the junction for Bald Peak at 2.1 miles. The trail winds through beautiful woods; about 0.5 mile in, you can see the old trail (blocked off by logs) that comes in on the left. Shortly after, you pass an old sugarhouse and, following the blue blazes, reach the junction for Bald Peak (to the right) and Kinsman, straight up.

Along the way you enter the White Mountain National Forest, and cross three streams, the last of which is Flume Brook (you can take a short detour here and walk to the top of Kinsman Flume). Many hikers who are not obsessed with high peaks make a day out of hiking to Bald Peak. From the junction sign, it's only a 5-minute walk to the lookout on Bald Peak and well worth it as a destination hike.

The sign announces that it's only 1.6 miles to the Kinsman Ridge, which sounds promising, except this section always seems to take longer than it should. On the bright side, it's beautiful in any season, with gorgeous woods. There are some flat sections between the steeps, which always makes it seem a bit easier, although the steep sections are fairly steep. Finally, about 2.5 hours from the parking lot, you hit the ridge junction where this trail meets up with the Appalachian Trail. Instead of taking a left toward Cannon Mountain, you turn right to rise up another 450 feet/20–25 minutes to North Kinsman. The summit is the obvious high point; one of our favorite lookouts, to the left down a steep nob, features amazing views of Lafayette, Lincoln, and Cannon on a clear day.

Once you get to North Kinsman, you have done the majority of the elevation gain (3,300 feet). The ridge to South Kinsman is fairly easy by White Mountain standards as it bounces up and down the ridge to South Kinsman. Beware the "false" summit on the left just before the real summit with a large cairn. Many hikers stop here; however, the actual summit is another 5 minutes up a gradual hill. In winter this ridge typically is either very icy or filled with deep snow, so be careful with your footing. On a clear day, the open summit of South Kinsman offers 360-degree views of Mount Moosilauke to the south, Vermont to the west, and the Lafayette Ridge to the east.

The return trip isn't that bad, with a bit more gain to reclimb north and then the 450 feet down to the junction, where you head left back down to NH 116. In good conditions, this hike takes 6–7 hours, with an elevation gain of almost 4,000 feet.

Heather and Michele by Lonesome Lake JOYCE MAILMAN

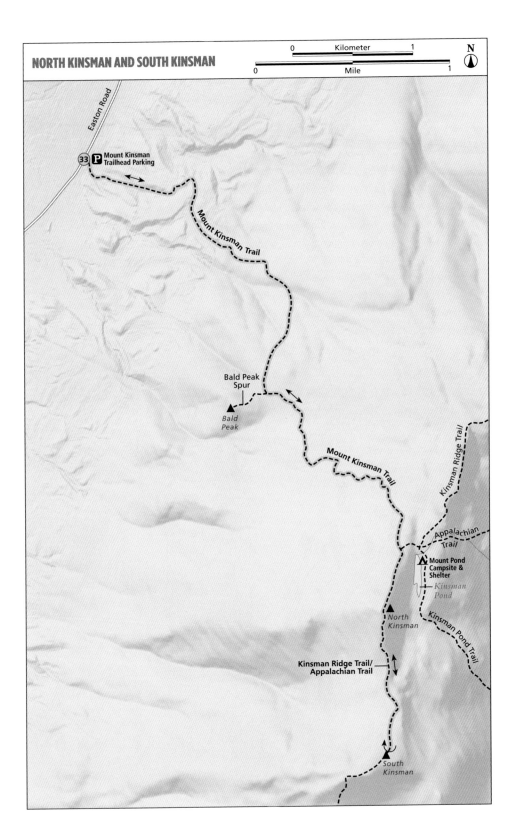

Kilometer

0   1

0   Mile   1

N

Easton Road

33 P Mount Kinsman
Trailhead Parking

Mount Kinsman Trail

Bald Peak
Spur

Bald
Peak

Mount Kinsman Trail

Kinsman Ridge Trail

Appalachian
Trail

Mount Pond
Campsite &
Shelter

Kinsman
Pond

North
Kinsman

Kinsman Pond Trail

Kinsman Ridge Trail/
Appalachian Trail

South
Kinsman

Miles and Directions

0.0 Start from the parking lot and head east.

2.1 Turn left at the junction with a short spur (0.2 mile one way) to Bald Peak.

3.5 Arrive at the junction with the Appalachian Trail/Kinsman Ridge Trail; turn right.

3.8 Arrive at the North Kinsman summit; continue heading south.

4.6 Arrive at the summit of South Kinsman; a short walk farther affords views from all directions. Turn around and retrace your steps.

5.4 Back at the North Kinsman summit.

5.8 Turn left at the junction with the Kinsman Ridge Trail

7.2 At the junction with the Bald Peak spur, bear right.

9.2 Arrive back at the parking lot.

Option

Hike over Cannon Mountain, then the Kinsmans, and out at Lafayette Place Campground with a car shuttle. Distance: 10.1 miles; elevation gain: 4,345 feet.

34 North Tripyramid and Middle Tripyramid

This is one of the prettiest fall hikes of all time—and with so many loop options, there are several exciting routes you can take to hit both of these 4,000-footers in a day.

Start: Livermore Trailhead
Distance: 11.5-mile lollipop
Summit elevation: North Tripyramid: 4,140 feet; Middle Tripyramid: 4,110 feet
4,000-footers rank of the 115: North Tripyramid: 76 (tied); Middle Tripyramid: 80
Elevation gain: 3,030 feet
Difficulty: Moderate
Hiking time: 5–6 hours
Trails used: Mount Tripyramid Trail, Scaur Ridge Trail, Livermore Road 53

Nearest town: Waterville Valley
Views: Good
Water sources: A few streams on the way toward the mountains
Canine compatibility: Very good
Special considerations: In the winter, Livermore Road is a cross country ski trail so be respectful of other users. There is a nominal fee to park in this lot.

Finding the trailhead: From I-93, take exit 28 and follow NH 49 East toward Waterville Valley. Just before the town of Waterville Valley, at 10.2 miles from the interstate, turn onto Tripoli Road, on your left. In 1.2 miles, bear right and stay on Tripoli Road. In 0.6 mile turn right onto West Branch Road; in 200 feet, Livermore Trailhead parking will be on your left. GPS (parking lot): N43°57'56.87" / W71°30'49.15"

The Hike

We have done this pair in every season and on every trail, including the infamous North Slide. My favorite route is the loop that bypasses the slide for the Scaur Ridge Trail, hits North and Middle, and continues on to loop over to South Peak (not an official peak) and down the South Slide. Though the mileage sounds long, almost half of the mileage is on an old logging road and is fairly flat, so the hike typically takes 5–6 hours.

From the parking lot off Tripoli Road, follow the Livermore Road until you see the junction to the right for the Pyramid Trail to the South Slide. You can hike the loop counterclockwise, but we recommend continuing left to follow the Scaur Ridge Trail. You will notice the North Slide turnoff on your right. In summer and in dry weather, you can take this route if you want a serious rock-climbing route, but it is *not* easy. We made a mistake the first time we did this, in early winter with loose snow, and it took 3 hours to cover this near-vertical section. This is the only hike on this list where I thought I might actually have to get rescued. When we did it in summer on dry rock, it was a lot of fun, but it still has some scary, exposed, super steep sections.

Donna and Alexia (Michele's daughter) picking their route carefully up the North Slide amid the fall foliage MICHELE HERNANDEZ BAYLISS

Scaur Ridge is a very nice and well-graded trail, so we recommend this route, which winds around toward the right (on the ascent you'll see some impressive views of the North Slide, which looks vertical from this angle) as you climb up to where you will see the Pine Bend Brook Trail coming in from the left. Though you are less than 1 mile from the summit of North Tripyramid, this section is steep and challenging, with some exciting rock scrambles as you head up. In winter, this entire stretch is challenging for route finding on the saddle before you hit the top; you have a few areas of open woods, and it can be hard to stay on the trail. The summit itself is anticlimactic—it is treed and marked with a large cairn. If you head out a few feet to the right, there are some views and you can see where the North Slide trail comes up. When we finally staggered up this trail in winter, a small group of hikers by the cairn looked at us like we were crazy.

Continuing down a gentle slope, you reach a saddle section and, soon after, the left-hand junction with the Sabbaday Trail. Heading up a short but steep section brings you to the summit of Middle Tripyramid, which has a large viewing rock you can climb up to. Now the trail heads very steeply down toward the subpeak of South Tripyramid, where you bear right and head down the South Slide, which is scree and boulder filled, so take your time. We usually take a lunch break on top of the slide

DID YOU KNOW?

The route up the North Slide is considered the most technical/difficult route in the White Mountains alongside the Huntington Ravine Trail up Mount Washington and the Great Gulf Trail.

NORTH TRIPYRAMID AND MIDDLE TRIPYRAMID

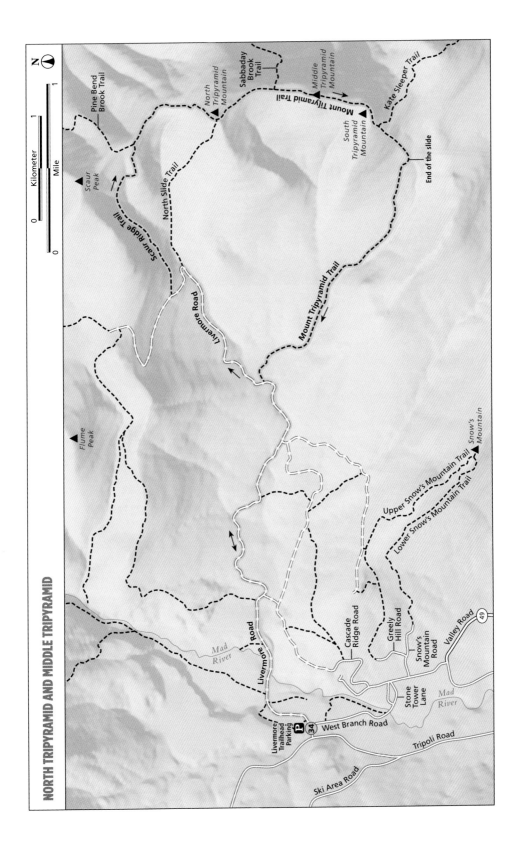

Another reason to hike in the fall—gorgeous foliage on a mid-October Tripyramid hike
Michele Hernandez Bayliss

to enjoy the expansive views. The slide is not long, but it takes a good half hour to descend before you level out to easy walking on the beautiful Tripyramid Trail back to the logging road, so mostly flat/downhill easy walking. In fall, this section was truly spectacular, with some of the best foliage ever.

Miles and Directions

0.0 Start from the parking lot and head east on the open road that doubles as a cross-country ski trail in winter.

2.7 Stay on the road as the Mount Tripyramid Trail to South Tripyramid bears right.

3.6 The road turns sharply left and the North Slide Trail continues east; stay on the road.

3.9 Leave the road by bearing right onto the Scaur Ridge Trail.

5.0 The Pine Bend Brook Trail comes in from your left; continue on the Scaur Ridge Trail.

5.7 Arrive at the summit of North Tripyramid; continue on toward Middle Tripyramid.

6.1 The Sabbaday Brook Trail is on your left; continue straight.

6.4 Arrive at the summit of Middle Tripyramid and continue your journey.

6.7 Cross over South Tripyramid and start heading down.

6.9 The Kate Sleeper Trail is on your left; continue down the slide.

7.1 End of traveling on the slide.

8.9 Arrive back at the forest road; turn left to head back to the parking lot.

11.5 Arrive back at the parking lot

Option

If you're feeling brave, try the North Slide route. Distance: 10.6 miles; elevation gain: 3,017 feet.

35 Liberty and Flume

This loop is much less traveled than its northern brothers Lafayette and Lincoln, but the views are fantastic and the hike features some of the nicest trails in the White Mountains.

Start: Lincoln Woods parking lot
Distance: 9.7 miles point to point
Summit elevation: Liberty: 4,459 feet; Flume: 4,328 feet
4,000-footers rank of the 115: Liberty: 37; Flume: 52
Elevation gain: 3,801 feet
Difficulty: Moderate
Hiking time: 7–8 hours
Trails used: Lincoln Woods Trail, Osseo Trail, Franconia Ridge Trail, Liberty Springs Trail/

Appalachian Trail, Franconia Notch Bike Path, White House Trail
Nearest town: Lincoln
Views: Excellent
Water sources: Several water sources on the hike up toward the ridge; again at Liberty Springs tentsite
Canine compatibility: Good
Special considerations: This hike requires having a vehicle at the Liberty Springs parking lot. There's a modest fee to park at Lincoln Woods.

Finding the trailhead: From I-93, take exit 32 to NH 112 (Kancamagus Highway). Travel east on NH 112 for 5.3 miles through the town of Lincoln to reach Lincoln Woods parking, on your left. GPS (Lincoln Woods parking lot): N44°3'48.71" / W71°35'17.11"

To leave a vehicle at the Liberty Springs parking lot: From I-93 and points north, take exit 34A to US 3 and travel south 0.3 mile; turn left into the lot. Traveling from the south on I-93, take exit 34A and travel 0.4 mile; the parking area will be on your left. GPS (Liberty Springs parking lot): N44°6'2.84" / W71°40'54.34"

The Hike

Though we love the Flume Slide Trail route, depending on conditions it can be very icy, slippery, and challenging, so we will focus on one of our very favorite trails: the Osseo Trail.

Unlike most trails in the White Mountains, this route features a large parking area complete with restrooms, ranger cabins, and an official visitor center. Leaving Lincoln Woods, you cross the bridge and head down the super flat Lincoln Woods Trail. This section is also the final section of a Bonds Traverse; later in the day, you might see bedraggled hikers staggering out.

The Osseo Trail junction is a flat walk from the parking area on the Lincoln Woods Trail and only takes 40 minutes. In fact, it's easy to miss, so keep your eyes peeled for that left-hand exit by some running water.

The trail starts gradually and winds up and around a brook. The grade is gentle for at least the first hour and gives your legs a chance to warm up. When the grade finally gets steep, there are switchbacks that ease the pain and some super fun

Michele on the final approach to Mount Flume's rocky summit DEAN J. OUELLETTE

ladders that make this trail part of the "Terrifying 25" list. Please note that dogs may have problems with the ladders (though most have steps, not rungs), so take that into consideration. After ascending a series of ladders, a perfect viewpoint looks to the east and provides an unusual angle to Owl's Head and the Pemigewasset Wilderness. Ascend a few more ladders until the grade flattens, and before you know it (typically 2.5–3 hours), you find yourself at the junction. This is also where the Flume Slide Trail comes in from the left. The hard part is done! Your reward is the final 10 minutes or so as you exit onto a super rocky and exposed section—this is

DID YOU KNOW?

Until you hit the Liberty Springs Trail, this hike is part of the 30-plus-mile "Pemi-Loop" trail that hard-core hikers often attempt as a day hike.

Awesome ladders on the Osseo Trail heading up Mount Flume (also part of the "Terrifying 25" list) Dean J. Ouellette

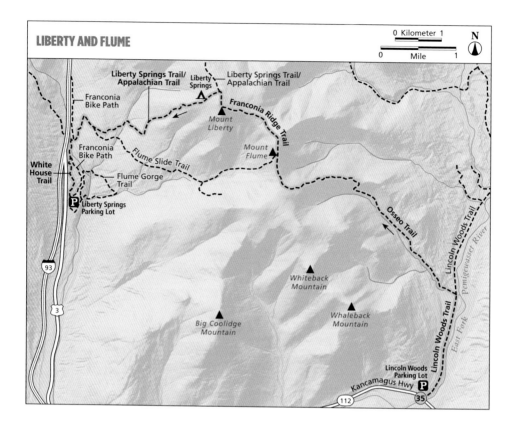

not quite the summit, but you can see it up ahead. Though it does look scary from this vantage point, the actual exposure is really not bad (leash your dog!) as long as you stay in the trail. Climb the rocklike staircase up the breathtaking final stretch to the summit.

Once you have enjoyed the spectacular views of the Lafayette Ridge and Pemigewasset Wilderness (the Bonds and Owl's Head), head down a gentle descent to the saddle between Flume and Liberty. Except for a 5- to 10-minute climb at the end, the total gain is manageable and typically takes 30–45 minutes to arrive at the summit of Liberty. Again, the views are incredible, and you basically stare right up the Lafayette Ridge.

Continue in the same direction another 10 minutes until you hit the junction with the Liberty Springs Trail (straight would continue to Lincoln/Lafayette along the Franconia Ridge Trail) and take a left. You are now on the Appalachian Trail (AT), so this section is usually quite crowded, especially in spring/summer. After a few minutes you will come to the Liberty Springs tentsite, where you can fill up with water (pump or purify it). From here it's a rocky descent on the Liberty Springs Trail/AT. Because the views are so good on both peaks, you want to allow 8 hours for this hike, although your actual hiking time will be more like 7 hours. If you only want to hike Mount Flume, it's actually longer to do an out-and-back on the Osseo Trail (closer to 11 miles round-trip, 7–8 hours). Hiking just Mount Liberty as an out-and-back is under 11 miles, about 7 hours.

Miles and Directions

0.0 Start from the Lincoln Woods lot and make your way past the ranger station and down toward the river.

0.1 Cross a bridge over the East Branch Pemigewasset River; turn right onto the Lincoln Woods Trail.

1.4 Turn left onto the Osseo Trail.

5.0 The Flume Slide Trail is on your left; stay on the Osseo Trail.

5.1 Reach the summit of Mount Flume.

6.1 Reach the summit of Mount Liberty.

6.3 Turn left onto the Liberty Springs Trail/Appalachian Trail.

6.6 Arrive at the Liberty Springs tentsite and spring.

8.4 The Flume Slide Trail comes in on your left; continue downhill.

8.9 Take a left onto the Franconia Notch Bike Path.

9.2 Turn right onto the White House Trail.

9.7 Arrive at the Liberty Springs parking lot.

Option

Instead of a car shuttle, try an out-and-back hike from the Liberty Springs parking lot. Distance: 9.0 miles; elevation gain: 4,102 feet.

36 Whiteface and Passaconaway

If you love ledges and rock scrambling, this hike provides some real thrills; plus you get to grab two peaks on this nice loop hike.

Start: Ferncroft Road parking lot
Distance: 11.0-mile loop
Summit elevation: Whiteface: 4,015 feet; Passaconaway: 4,060 feet
4,000-footers rank of the 115: Whiteface: 103; Passaconaway: 88 (tied)
Elevation gain: 3,972 feet
Difficulty: Difficult
Hiking time: 8–10 hours

Trails used: Ferncroft Road, Squirrel Bridge Road, Blueberry Ledge Trail, Rollins Trail, Dicey's Mill Trail
Nearest town: Chocorua
Views: Good
Water sources: At the beginning; again where the Rollins and Dicey's Mill Trails meet
Canine compatibility: Good
Special considerations: None

Finding the trailhead: From the west and I-93, take exit 24 and head south on US 3 for 4.5 miles. Turn left onto NH 113 toward Sandwich and continue 11.7 miles. In the town of Center Sandwich, turn left, staying on NH 113. In 3.7 miles bear left onto NH 113A. In 6.7 miles turn left onto the unpaved Ferncroft Road. From the east and the town of Chocorua at the intersection of NH 16 and NH 113, head west on NH 113 for 2.9 miles. Turn right and head west for 6.5 miles on NH 113A toward Wonalancet to get to Ferncroft Road. Continue on Ferncroft for 0.6 mile; turn right onto Soring Brook Road 337 and you will see the parking lot. GPS (parking lot): N43°54'49.51" / W71°21'27.89"

The Hike

There is a roomy parking lot here, but get here early in peak season (summer/fall)—it fills up, and they ticket cars parked on the street. We have done this hike five different ways, but my favorite way is still going up the Blueberry Ledge Trail and looping down Dicey's Mill Trail. Note that the upper sections of the Blueberry Ledge Trail are very challenging and can be dangerous when wet or icy. You want to ascend the dangerous part rather than descend, which is why we climb the Blueberry Ledge Trail first. The first part is fairly easy (though it can be hard to follow in fall when the leaves are down) until the steep climbing starts. The trail alternates between rocky ledges and flatter switchbacks until you reach the first obstacle, Blueberry Ledge. After a short and fun scramble, you continue on until the super steep section around a huge boulder that looks impossible. Luckily, you can use a downed tree to pull yourself up. Shorter people (like me) often need a little push/brace to get up to the first rock, so this may be an area that requires a bit of teamwork. In fact, the "easiest" hike I've had of this steep section was in winter, when we could just televate our snowshoes and step up carefully. You would not want to slide down, and descending this section in snow/ice is not recommended. After a few short but very steep sections (enjoy the

At the end of the hike, looking back at Mount Whiteface in the clouds DEAN J. OUELLETTE

view from each ledge), you come out to a rock ledge summit where you can take a break and enjoy the views. The true summit is along the Rollins Trail (which you will cross on your way to Passaconaway), so take note to tag the real summit if you are doing an out-and-back.

I love the ridge from here along the Rollins Trail, though it is not totally flat, to be sure. When you reach the junction for Dicey's Mill (you will come back to this point in order to descend), bear *left* to do the short climb to Passaconaway, about 30 minutes. The other loop trail is much harder, so unless you want more of a challenge, we wouldn't bother. Though the summit itself has no view, there is an incredible view if you continue another 5–10 minutes. We noticed it when we came up the other way from the Kancamagus Highway one year, and it's worth the extra walk. Heading back to Dicey's Mill, you follow this path; it's rocky at first and then gorgeous woods and a nice end to this heart-pumping hike. It's roughly 2–2.5 hours from the junction. No

DID YOU KNOW?

Five mountains in this part of the Sandwich Range are *not* 4,000-footers: Mount Chocorua, Mount Kancamagus, Mount Paugus, The Sleepers, and Sandwich Mountain.

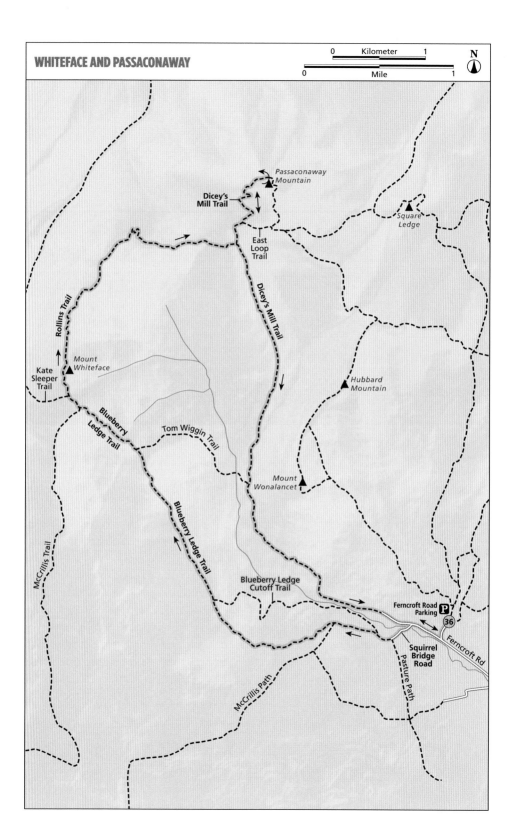

0   Kilometer   1

0   Mile   1

N

Passaconaway Mountain

Dicey's Mill Trail

Square Ledge

East Loop Trail

Dicey's Mill Trail

Rollins Trail

Kate Sleeper Trail

Mount Whiteface

Hubbard Mountain

Blueberry Ledge Trail

Tom Wiggin Trail

Mount Wonalancet

McCrillis Trail

Blueberry Ledge Trail

Blueberry Ledge Cutoff Trail

Ferncroft Road Parking

36

Squirrel Bridge Road

Ferncroft Rd

Pasture Path

McCrillis Path

drama on this trail—just the few remaining miles through some private land (hikers are allowed, so be respectful) and the final walk out to the parking lot. In fall, the hike is even more spectacular. It's not unusual for this hike to take 8–10 hours, so budget extra time to navigate the ledges and rocks and to take in the views from all the ledges and the special lookout on Mount Passaconaway.

Miles and Directions

0.0 Start from the parking lot and head north onto Ferncroft Road.

0.3 Turn left onto Squirrel Bridge Road.

0.5 Access the Blueberry Ridge Trail (the Pasture Path turns to the left).

0.6 The Blueberry Cutoff Trail heads off to the right; continue on the Blueberry Ridge Trail.

0.9 The McCrillis Path comes in on your left (not to be confused with McCrillis Trail).

1.9 The Blueberry Cutoff Trail comes in from your right.

3.1 The Tom Wiggin Trail comes in from your right; continue straight.

3.6 Junction with the McCrillis Trail; turn right onto the Rollins Trail.

3.7 The Kate Sleeper Trail enters from your left; continue straight.

3.9 Cross over the summit of Mount Whiteface and continue on the Rollins Trail.

5.9 T junction with the Dicey's Mill Trail; turn left.

6.1 At a junction with the East Loop, turn left and stay on the Dicey's Mill Trail.

6.7 Reach the summit of Mount Passaconaway; retrace your steps.

7.3 Bear right and continue down the Dicey's Mill Trail.

7.5 The Rollins Trail comes in on your right; continue down Dicey's.

9.1 The Tom Wiggin Trail takes off to your right.

10.5 Back to Ferncroft Road.

11.0 Arrive back at the parking lot.

Option

Want more of a challenge? Find yourself near the Kancamagus side of this mountain range? Try an out-and-back from the Oliverian Brook Trail. Distance: 14.1 miles; elevation gain: 4,354 feet. GPS (Oliverian Brook Trailhead parking A): N43°59'35.98" / W71°21'1.80"

37 Madison and Adams

Any time of year, this iconic New Hampshire hike in the northern Presidential Range features world-class views, high alpine environment, and challenging elevation gain.

Start: Appalachia parking lot
Distance: 9.1-mile loop
Summit elevation: Madison: 5,363 feet; Adams: 5,798 feet
4,000-footers rank of the 115: Madison: 5; Adams: 2
Elevation gain: 4,953 feet
Difficulty: Difficult
Hiking time: 6–8 hours
Trails used: Valley Way Trail, Osgood Trail, Gulfside Trail/Appalachian Trail, Lowe's Path, Airline Trail
Nearest town: Gorham

Views: Superior
Water sources: A few water sources on the hike up toward the ridge. In summer months, fill up at the Madison Hut.
Canine compatibility: Not the best due to many sharp (hot in summer) rocks that can cut dogs' paws
Special considerations: Many trails converge on this route; be sure you are going the correct way. Lots of above-tree line exposure; watch out for bad weather—this route can be dangerous during storms. When the hut is open, sometimes there are fun snacks for purchase.

Finding the trailhead: From the intersection of US 3 and US 302 in the town of Twin Mountain, go north on US 3 for 2 miles. Turn right onto NH 115 North; continue for 9.8 miles and come to the intersection with US 2. Bear right onto US 2 East and travel 7.1 miles; the Appalachia Trailhead parking will be on your right. From the town of Gorham, travel west on US 2 from the intersection of NH 16 and US 2 for 5.3 miles; the parking lot will be on your left. GPS (parking lot): N44°22'17.05" / W71°17'20.32"

The Hike

This is one of our favorite hikes, especially in winter, and we have hiked these peaks in a half dozen ways. My all-time favorite route is via the very long and challenging Madison Gulf Trail, but that is an expedition of its own. Between the two standard approaches, I prefer ascending via Valley Way for two major reasons: It's more sheltered from high winds, and the grade is so perfect that even though you ascend more than 4,000 vertical feet, it always feels a lot easier than the tougher ascent on the Airline Trail (which I prefer on the descent).

From Appalachia, both trails start off together for the first few minutes until you cross the old railroad bed/Presidential Range Rail Trail. Valley Way bears left. Enjoy the gentle grades as you follow the blue blazes to stay on the main trail. Once you near Durand Ridge, the trail gets steeper and you can catch glimpses of Mount Madison. If you are seeking excitement, you can bear left on the Watson Path, which heads directly to the summit of Madison without passing the hut, but the route is much harder.

You'll know you are fairly close when you see the sign for the Valley Way tent-site and the trail steepens a bit. Just when you start to think the trail couldn't go up anymore, you break out of the woods within sight of the Madison Hut around the 2.5-hour mark. This is a good time to take stock of the weather; the rest of the hike is above tree line—very exposed—and can be dangerous in bad weather. There have been many deaths and many rescues in the northern Presidentials. The Gulfside Trail will be on your right (also the Appalachian Trail), but you want to bear left right before the hut to catch the Osgood Trail for the final 20–25 minutes or so up the rocky ascent of Madison.

Once you reach the sign, you are at the summit and can take in the views toward Mount Washington, the auto road, Mount Adams (your next objective), and great views of the very steep Star Lake Trail and Star Lake. Be sure to head back toward Adams, as the Osgood Trail does continue over the summit! The rocky descent can be hard on your knees, but before you know it, you will be back at the hut.

Though we have climbed the Star Lake Trail to Adams several times, it is much harder than the Gulfside Trail. For a first hike, we recommend following the Gulfside Trail toward Adams to the intersection with the Airline Trail. Though you can follow

View toward Mount Madison, Madison Hut, and Star Lake from Mount Adams's summit
MICHELE HERNANDEZ BAYLISS

Michele trying not to fall to her death while climbing up a steep section of the exciting Madison Gulf Trail DONNA DEARBORN

the steep ascent to Adams from here, we prefer to follow Gulfside a little farther toward Thunderstorm Junction (marked by a gigantic cairn); from there it's an easier 10-minute scramble to the top. Enjoy the views from the second-highest mountain in the Whites. You can always descend straight to Airline if you prefer to make a mini-loop or retrace your steps back to Thunderstorm Junction. I much prefer descending Airline to ascending, as you have such incredible views along the exposed ridge.

Take care to stay on Airline and not branch off on any of the smaller trails. You will also see the intersection on the left to the very fun "Chemin des Dames" scramble, which is part of the Terrifying 25 along with the King Ravine Trail. After 2–2.5 hours or so, you will arrive back at the rail trail and then Appalachia, where your car awaits after completing this classic White Mountain hike of two of the most well-known peaks.

Miles and Directions

0.0 Start from the parking lot and head south.

0.2 Pass the Sylvan Way junction.

0.6 The Fallsway Trail bears off to your left to view Tama Falls.

0.7 The Fallsway Trail comes back in from your left.

0.9 Junction with the Randolph Path.

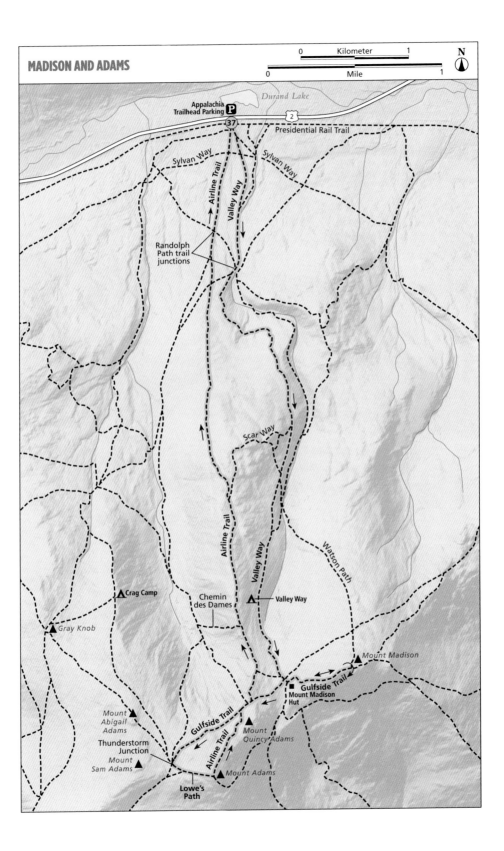

MADISON AND ADAMS

0 Kilometer 1

0 Mile 1

N

Durand Lake

Appalachia Trailhead Parking

2 Presidential Rail Trail

Sylvan Way

Sylvan Way

Airline Trail

Valley Way

Randolph Path trail junctions

Scar Way

Airline Trail

Valley Way

Watson Path

Crag Camp

Chemin des Dames

Valley Way

Gray Knob

Mount Madison

Gulfside Trail

Mount Madison Hut

Mount Abigail Adams

Gulfside Trail

Mount Quincy Adams

Thunderstorm Junction

Airline Trail

Mount Sam Adams

Lowe's Path

Mount Adams

2.0 The Scar Trail enters from the right; bear left and continue on Valley Way.

2.3 The Watson Path heads to the right; continue straight on up Valley Way.

2.6 The Lower Bruin Trail enters in on your left; continue straight.

3.0 The Valley Way tentsite spur heads back and to your right.

3.1 The Upper Bruin Trail enters on your right; continue straight.

3.5 Intersection with several trails and the Madison Hut; follow the Osgood Trail/Appalachian Trail toward Mount Madison.

3.9 Arrive at Madison's summit; retrace your steps back to the hut.

4.3 At the Madison Hut, follow the Gulfside Trail/Appalachian Trail south.

4.5 The Airline Trail branches off to your right; continue on Gulfside.

4.6 The Airline Trail bears left to go up Mount Adams; continue on Gulfside.

5.1 Arrive at the large cairn at Thunderstorm Junction; turn left on the Lowe's Path toward Mount Adams.

5.2 The Israel Path comes in on your right; continue upward.

5.3 Arrive at Mount Adams's summit; turn toward the north and follow cairns on the Airline Trail down.

5.7 At the Gulfside Trail, turn right, heading back toward the Madison Hut.

5.8 Airline continues down on your left; don't go down the King's Ravine Trail.

6.0 The Airline cutoff comes in from the right; continue down Airline.

6.3 The Chemin des Dames Trail enters steeply from the left.

6.4 The Upper Bruin Trail is on your right.

7.0 The Scar Trail bears right; bear left and stay on the Airline Trail.

8.2 Intersection with the Randolph Path; continue down Airline.

8.5 Intersection with Beechwood Way; continue down Airline.

8.9 Intersection with Sylvan Way; continue toward parking lot.

9.1 Arrive back at the parking lot.

Option

Head up the Watson Path straight to Mount Madison's summit then down to the Madison Hut. Distance: 8.8 miles; elevation gain: 4,943 feet.

DID YOU KNOW?

You can visit some very cool huts/shelters on the north side of Mount Adams maintained by the Randolph Mountain Club: The Perch, Crag Camp, The Log Cabin, and Gray Knob.

38 Mount Isolation

If you enjoy above-ridgeline hikes, you can take the more challenging route up Boott Spur and the Glen Boulder Trail (around 5,000 feet of vertical gain); but if you need a more protected hike, you can take the Rocky Branch route, which has minimal exposure.

Start: Rocky Branch Trailhead off NH 16
Distance: 13.5 miles out and back
Summit elevation: 4,005 feet
4,000-footers rank of the 115: 108 (tied)
Elevation gain: 3,533 feet
Difficulty: Difficult
Hiking time: 9–10 hours
Trails used: Rocky Branch Trail, Isolation Trail, Davis Path

Nearest town: Jackson
Views: Excellent
Water sources: Several water sources on the hike up toward the ridge; nothing on the ridge
Canine compatibility: Good
Special considerations: Several water crossings that are difficult to impossible during spring or high-water times

Finding the trailhead: From the north in the town of Gorham, take NH 16 south, passing Pinkham Notch on your right at 10.6 miles. At 14.7 miles, trailhead parking will be on your right. If traveling from the south, travel north from the town of Jackson on NH 16 for 5.2 miles. Parking will be on your left. GPS (parking lot): N44°12'16.40" / W71°14'25.57"

The Hike

No one jumps for joy about hiking Mount Isolation, although it can be quite pleasant in the right conditions. This hike is not at all fun if it's very wet. The Rocky Branch Trail becomes a running stream, and if you hike up the Glen Boulder route, the rocks will be super slippery coming down. (**Note:** If you don't mind a car shuttle, you can climb up via the Glen Boulder Trail and then descend Rocky Branch. This route features just over 3,800 feet of vertical versus almost 5,000 feet if you do Glen Boulder out and back, because you face a return gain of 1,500 vertical feet to climb Boott Spur.)

Though it's almost 3 miles longer, I prefer the out-and-back from Rocky Branch Trail—the gain is "only" 3,400 feet, but it's spread out so it doesn't feel that bad. Plus, in winter, when it's broken out, you can save about 45 minutes by taking the Engine Hill Bushwhack, which cuts out some of the nasty sections of the Rocky Branch Trail. You should allow 9–10 hours for this nearly 15-mile hike.

Quite a lot of the elevation gain takes place up front as you ascend the Rocky Branch Trail for about 2 hours. Maps show a feature called Engine Hill, where a bushwhack (more obvious in winter) can save you some stream crossings and tough terrain to join up with the Isolation Trail. In winter we missed it on the way up but found it on the way back, saving a good 45 minutes.

The summit marker lets you know you have arrived. MICHELE HERNANDEZ BAYLISS

I was pleasantly surprised at how mild the Isolation Trail is; it's nice this far into a long hike to have relatively flat sections that are also protected from the wind (good thing for us, as we last did this in minus-zero temps on a windy day). When you reach the Davis Path, fork left for just under 1 mile to reach the short, unnamed spur trail that pops you out atop Isolation's rocky summit. This is a beautiful summit because it is so remote and has unusual views of Mount Washington. Typically the return trip shaves off a little time (though you still have an annoying almost 300-foot climb toward the end of the hike). Even so, this hike normally takes 9–10 hours, a little less if you do the traverse rather than the out-and-back.

Miles and Directions

0.0 Start from the parking lot and head north on the Rocky Branch Trail.

0.5 The Avalanche Ski Trail enters from the left.

0.7 The Avalanche Ski Trail bears right; go left to stay on the Rocky Branch Trail.

2.7 Reach the height of land at Engine Hill.

3.5 Turn sharply right at the intersection with the Isolation Trail.

5.6 At the Davis Path junction, turn left and follow the Davis Path.

6.75 Short spur to the Mount Isolation summit; retrace your steps.

7.6 Turn right at the Isolation Trail junction.

10.0 Turn left at the Rocky Branch Trail junction.

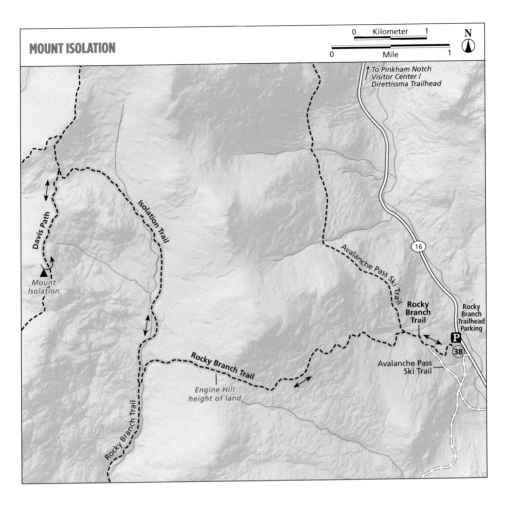

10.8   Arrive back at the Engine Hill height of land.

12.8   The ski trail enters from your left.

13.0   Bear right as the ski trail goes straight.

13.5   Arrive back at the parking lot.

Option

Park at the Direttissma Trailhead and take the Direttissma Trail to the Glen Boulder Trail to Davis Path. Distance: 10.2 miles; elevation gain: 4,798 feet. GPS (parking lot): N44°15'17.20" / W71°15'13.79"

DID YOU KNOW?

Though Isolation is the second-shortest mountain in the Whites, it is the highest peak in the Montalban Ridge. It is also one of the most remote peaks in the White Mountains.

39 Owl's Head

This is the longest hike in the White Mountains, so you get the satisfaction of completing a less-hiked peak with fewer people.

Start: Lincoln Woods parking lot
Distance: 15.4 miles out and back
Summit elevation: 4,025 feet
4,000-footers rank of the 115: 99
Elevation gain: 3,260 feet
Difficulty: Difficult
Hiking time: Hours
Trails used: Lincoln Woods Trail, Black Pond Trail, Black Pond Bushwhack, Lincoln Brook Trail, Brutus Bushwhack, Owl's Head Path

Nearest town: Lincoln
Views: Okay
Water sources: Several water sources up to the point of the steep climb to the summit
Canine compatibility: Good
Special considerations: This is an unmarked, unmaintained trail, so take care. There's a modest fee to park at Lincoln Woods.

Finding the trailhead: From I-93, take exit 32 to NH 112 (Kancamagus Highway). Travel east on NH 112 for 5.3 miles through the town of Lincoln to reach Lincoln Woods, on your left. GPS (parking lot): N44°3'48.71" / W71°35'17.11"

The Hike

This hike gets a bad name. It's the longest out-and-back of the NH 4,000 footer list, but I don't mind it because the majority of the mileage is flat until you reach the slide. I would point out that it's still shorter than Allen Mountain in the Adirondacks, and the terrain is much flatter. You may have caught a glimpse of Owl's Head and the Pemigewasset Wilderness if you climbed Mounts Liberty or Lafayette or Mount Lincoln, which stares right down at Owl's Head, which looks like a bump rather than a mountain from up high.

There are two accepted bushwhacks that shorten the 18-plus miles to around 15-plus miles, but keep in mind that in fall, when there are leaves on the ground, or if they are not broken out in winter, they can be hard to follow. The benefit of the Black Pond Bushwhack is that you bypass some of the tricky water crossings that can be deal breakers on this hike.

From the Lincoln Woods parking lot, you cross the bridge and head out on the Lincoln Woods Trail for a nice flat start until you take a left on the Black Pond Trail. Then you follow the herd path/bushwhack an additional 1 mile or so until you connect with the Lincoln Brook Trail (bring a map and compass and a GPS log if you can). The trail is fairly unremarkable, so much so that you may not notice that you just kept going straight to stay on it until you hit Lincoln Brook. The next section is pretty straightforward until you reach the Owl's Head Path (the avalanche slide),

Dean and his children heading up the steep slide toward the summit
MICHELE HERNANDEZ BAYLISS

which is 1 mile of *very* steep rubble (see photo). We usually opt for the Brutus Bush-whack, which is also very steep but a bit shorter with a few switchbacks. Then we bear left to head for the summit, bearing north on the ridge for 5–10 minutes. Since the summit is treed, it's not very exciting, but there are great views toward Lafayette and Lincoln from the slide on the way down. On the way up, at about 3,400 feet, the Brutus Bushwhack meets the Owl's Head slide at a large boulder. It's actually easier to find the Brutus Bushwhack on the way down from that boulder than on the way up. If you really want to find the start of the Brutus route, look sharply right after Lincoln Brook (there used to be a jumble of smallish boulders, but those were gone last time we hiked it). There may be a small cairn, but don't count on it. I find it a tad easier, as did Brutus, the dog for whom that route is named. Fun fact: On a winter hike several years ago, we met a gentleman named Kevin whose dog was the Brutus of the Brutus Bushwhack, a Newfoundland! That made it easy to find the path that day.

DID YOU KNOW?

Until 2005 the "official" summit of Owl's Head was actually not the highest point, which was discovered to be 0.2 mile north. But not to worry, anyone who hiked it before 2005 can still count the old peak as the summit.

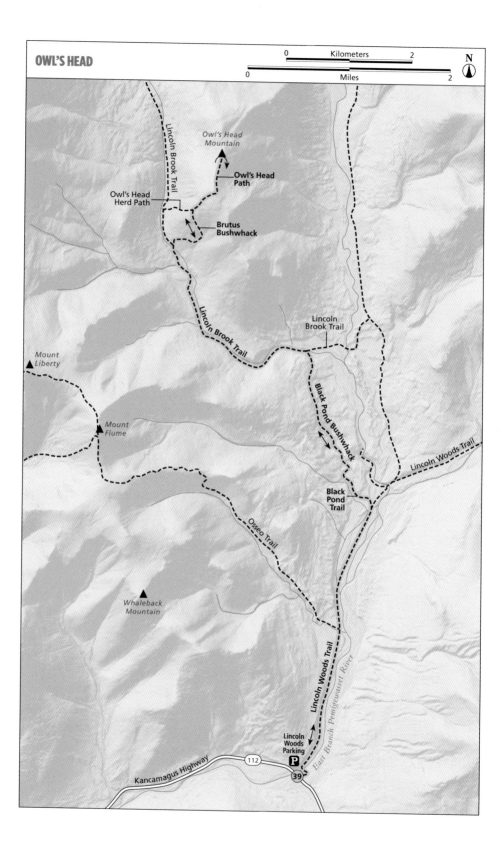

OWL'S HEAD

Kilometers

0   2

0   Miles   2

N

Owl's Head
Mountain

Owl's Head
Path

Lincoln Brook Trail

Owl's Head
Herd Path

Brutus
Bushwhack

Lincoln Brook Trail

Lincoln
Brook Trail

Mount
Liberty

Black Pond Bushwhack

Lincoln Woods Trail

Mount
Flume

Black
Pond
Trail

Osseo Trail

Whaleback
Mountain

Lincoln Woods Trail

East Branch Pemigewasset River

Lincoln
Woods Parking

P

Kancamagus Highway

112

39

View from the slide toward the Lafayette Ridge, towering above
MICHELE HERNANDEZ BAYLISS

Miles and Directions

0.0 Start from the edge of the parking lot and head toward the ranger station.

0.1 Make your way across the bridge over the East Branch Pemigewasset River and turn right onto the Lincoln Woods Trail.

1.4 On your left is the Osseo Trail; continue straight.

2.6 Bear left here to go to Black Pond.

3.3 Arrive at Black Pond; make your way on the south side and follow the herd path.

4.4 Arrive at the junction with the Lincoln Brook Trail; turn left and follow.

6.4 Take the Brutus Bushwhack; follow this trail uphill.

7.3 Arrive at the ridge; turn left—you're almost there.

7.7 Arrive at the summit of Owl's Head; turn around and retrace your steps.

8.9 Turn left at the junction with the Lincoln Brook Trail.

11.0 Locate the small rock cairn to follow the bushwhack herd path.

12.0 Arrive back at Black Pond; follow the marked path from here.

12.8 Arrive at the Lincoln Woods Trail; turn right and follow this flat path.

14.0 Pass the Osseo Trail, on your right.

15.3 Turn left to recross the bridge over the river.

15.4 Arrive back at the parking lot.

Option

Unsure about the Black Pond Bushwhack? Take the Lincoln Brook Trail from the Lincoln Woods Trail and go up the Owl's Head Herd Path instead. Distance: 17.4 miles; elevation gain: 3,202 feet.

40 South Twin and North Twin

South Twin has one of the best views in all of the White Mountains and lies at the confluence of many routes that crisscross this area.

Start: Gale River Trailhead on Gale River Loop Road

Distance: 12.4 miles out and back

Summit elevation: South Twin: 4,902 feet; North Twin: 4,761 feet

4,000-footers rank of the 115: South Twin: 13; North Twin: 21 (tied)

Elevation gain: 4,111 feet

Difficulty: Difficult

Hiking time: 8–9 hours

Trails used: Gale River Trail, Appalachian Trail, Twinway Trail, North Twin Spur

Nearest town: Twin Mountain

Views: Excellent

Water sources: Several water sources on the hike up toward the ridge; again at the Galehead Hut during summer months

Canine compatibility: Very good

Special considerations: The road is closed in winter, adding 5.8 miles to your trek. Or you could walk alongside US 3 for 0.3 mile, adding only 3.8 miles round-trip.

Finding the trailhead: To get to Gale River Loop Road from I-93, from the north take exit 36 to NH 141 for 0.7 mile then US 3 North for 4 miles. From the south, take exit 35 to US 3 North for 4.5 miles; the road will be on your right. From the town of Twin Mountain and the intersection of US 3 and US 302, travel south on US 3 for 5.5 miles; the road will be on your left. At Gale River Loop Road, travel south for 2.9 miles; you'll see the trailhead on your right. GPS (parking lot) N44°13'43.84" / W71°37'58.94"; (winter parking): N44°14'37.22" / W71°38'20.99"

The Hike

We have done these mountains lots of different ways (including a brutal winter hike from Zealand Hut to the Bonds, out and back to the Twins—more than 22 miles), but the easiest way is from the Gale River Trail, which is mild by White Mountain standards. It's close to 5 miles on the rock-filled trail up to the Galehead Hut, but the first few miles are fairly flat, so you get a nice warm-up. When you reach the junction for the Garfield Ridge Trail, bear left toward the hut; it takes 3–3.5 hours, and the last part of the ascent to the hut is quite steep. When you arrive, you can decide if you want to take the mile-long round-trip leg up Galehead, a wooded peak, or prioritize

DID YOU KNOW?

North Twin Mountain is one of the "optional" mountains of a Pemi-Loop hike. Some hikers opt to skip the out-and-back to North Twin, as even the "short" Pemi-Loop hike is an enormous undertaking.

Gorgeous early spring on the open summit of South Twin, with snowcapped Mount Washington behind MICHELE HERNANDEZ BAYLISS

reaching North Twin. We typically enjoy a scenic break at the hut and then head up one of the steepest pitches in the Whites—the Twinway ramp to South Twin. In winter this hike is almost easier, as you can use televators to lessen the incline, but in warmer weather it's just a brutal uphill. On the positive side, when you near the top, the final walk to the summit is one of the finest sections in the White Mountains. It's one of the most spectacular summits in the range, with views everywhere you look. It's worth hanging out on the spectacular summit of South Twin to enjoy the views of the Bonds and Presidentials—and catch your breath. The ridge walk to North Twin is not exactly a ridge, but it's easy and does not take that long to do the out-and-back. (**Option:** You can make a loop with a car shuttle down the North Twin Trail, but there is a very tough river crossing we typically try to avoid.) North Twin has a short spur, so make sure you actually tag the summit before climbing about 350 feet of elevation to return to South Twin.

The ramp descent is tough on the knees, but the going is much easier after that, heading back down the Gale River Trail. This hike usually takes 8–9 hours due to some steep sections, not to mention that you will want to spend some time both at the hut and on top of South Twin to enjoy the views.

Miles and Directions

0.0   Start from the parking lot and head east on the trail.

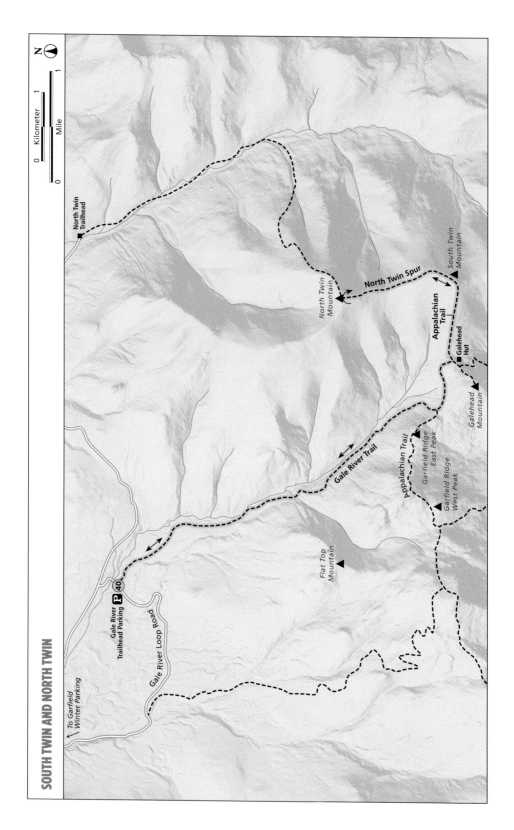

SOUTH TWIN AND NORTH TWIN

North Twin Trailhead

North Twin Spur

North Twin Mountain

South Twin Mountain

Appalachian Trail

Galehead Hut

Galehead Mountain

Gale River Trail

Appalachian Trail

Garfield Ridge East Peak

Garfield Ridge West Peak

Flat Top Mountain

Gale River Trailhead Parking

P 40

To Garfield Winter Parking

Gale River Loop Road

N

0 Kilometer 1

0 Mile 1

3.8 At the junction with the Appalachian Trail (AT), bear left and continue on the AT.

4.3 Arrive at a junction with the Twinway and spur to the Galehead Hut. Bear right if you want to stop at the hut; otherwise bear left and head west toward South Twin.

5.0 Arrive at the summit of South Twin. Bear left and follow markings toward the north on the North Twin Spur.

6.2 Arrive at a junction with the North Twin Trail. Turn left here—the summit is a few steps away. Retrace your steps.

7.4 Back at South Twin, bear right and head down toward the Galehead Hut.

8.1 At the spur to the hut, bear right and continue on the AT.

8.7 At the junction with the Gale River Trail, bear right and follow the Gale River Trail back to the parking lot.

12.4 Arrive back at the parking lot.

Options

1. To add Galehead Mountain to this hike, follow signs and the trail west from the Galehead Hut to the mountain's summit. Distance: 0.8 mile; elevation gain: 286 feet.

2. If the water crossings aren't too bad, try this hike from the North Twin Trail. Distance: 10.7 miles; elevation gain: 3,778 feet. GPS (parking lot): N44°14'16.12" / W71°32'50.39"

Donna, her dog, Eva, and my dog, Argos, dealing with the notorious water crossing on the descent from North Twin in April MICHELE HERNANDEZ BAYLISS

41 Monroe, Washington, and Jefferson

You get to climb the highest mountain in the Northeast, known for having some of the worst weather in the world, and combine it with two other impressive peaks—all in a doable day hike.

Start: Ammonoosuc Trailhead on Base Station Road
Distance: 12.6-mile loop
Summit elevation: Monroe: 5,385 feet; Washington: 6,288 feet; Jefferson: 5,715 feet
4,000-footers rank: Monroe: 4; Washington: 1; Jefferson: 3
Elevation gain: 5,300 feet
Difficulty: Difficult
Hiking time: 8–10 hours
Trails used: Ammonoosuc Ravine Trail, Mount Monroe Loop, Appalachian Trail, Crawford Path, Gulfside Trail, Mount Jefferson Loop, Jewell Trail
Nearest town: Twin Mountain
Views: Superior

Water sources: During the summer months, available at the Lakes of the Clouds Hut and at the top of Mount Washington inside the information center
Canine compatibility: Not recommended for dogs in summer months unless booties are worn. The hours on sharp rocks above tree line can damage their paws.
Special considerations: Mount Washington is notorious for some of the nastiest weather on the planet. Great care and planning should be done prior to ensure that the weather will be nice enough for your hike. You are above tree line, with no shade for most of this hike. There is a modest fee to park in this lot.

Finding the trailhead (located near the Mount Washington Cog Railway Station):

Turn onto Base Station Road, 4.5 miles east on US 302 from the intersection of US 3 and US 302 in the town of Twin Mountain and 4 miles west on US 302 from the Crawford Notch Information Center. The parking lot is located on the right, 5.5 miles from the intersection with US 302 and just before the Cog Railway Base Station. A modest fee for the White Mountain National Forest is required to park in this lot. GPS (parking lot): N44°16'0.37" / W71°21'40.60"

The Hike

Crawford Notch has several campgrounds as well as the official AMC Highland Center, so you can stay overnight and get an early start for any hike up Mounts Monroe, Washington, and Jefferson. You can pay to park right at the Washington Base Station (recommended for restrooms and being right by the trail). It's easy to pick up the Ammonoosuc Ravine Trail right from the parking lot near the Washington Cog Railway Station. In about 1 hour you arrive at the spectacular Gem Pool and waterfall. From here the trail gets incredibly steep for the final section to the Lakes of the Clouds Hut. In winter this section often requires microspikes or actual crampons. In bad visibility, take extreme care when you break out of the cover of the Ammonoosuc Trail above tree line; it is very challenging in whiteout conditions or fog to find the exact point where you reenter the woods below the hut. Many hikers have

Summit area near Mount Jefferson where tons of trails intersect and Mount Washington peeks out MICHELE HERNANDEZ BAYLISS

gotten lost and needed rescue because they could not relocate the trail, even though they had just ascended. Our recommendation is to put a sign here marking the entry below tree line.

In colder weather, hikers layer up at the hut before heading up toward the right via the Crawford Path and then the Monroe Loop Trail. Although it looks intimidating, the hike up to Mount Monroe from the hut is gradual and typically takes only 15–25 minutes. In winter you can often just take a shortcut/direct route right up the flank rather than winding up the Crawford Path. From Monroe the views back toward Lakes of the Clouds and Mounts Washington/Jefferson/Clay are spectacular on a clear day. Keep in mind that Monroe is very close to Washington, which features some of the most extreme weather in the world, so the winds can be fierce in fall/winter/spring. Looking toward Eisenhower, you can also see the two subpeaks, "Little Monroe" (not an official peak) and Franklin southwest of the summit.

Once you descend Monroe, you can either retrace your steps back on the Ammonoosuc Trail or continue on to Mount Washington. Take the Crossover Trail to the actual Appalachian Trail and then fork right to the Gulfside Trail. That last section takes longer than you think, as the elevation gain is quite a lot from the col up to

Donna, Michele, and Eva on the summit of Mount Jefferson, with Mount Washington directly behind DONNA DEARBORN

Washington. In summer you are likely to have a huge crowd up here, since many drive up the auto road or ride the cog railway. You can take pride in knowing that you made it up the old-fashioned way—on foot. After taking the mandatory summit picture atop Mount Washington, follow the gentle descent toward Jefferson. You can either tag Clay (not an official peak) or save your legs a little elevation by skirting it. Either way, you have to descend into Sphinx Col before you head up the last short but steep climb on Jefferson.

From here, if you were smart enough to spot a car (in winter you can't access the road) at the end of the Caps Ridge Trail, you can take a very scrambly descent down the Caps Ridge Trail to your car. We usually return down Jefferson, head toward the Jewell Trail, and descend back to the Washington base station. Typically it takes us 8–10 hours to complete this loop. The hike is difficult, with more than 5,000 feet of vertical gain, but you do get bragging rights to summitting the tallest peak in the White Mountains plus two other presidents.

DID YOU KNOW?

The flat area called Monroe Lawn, south of Monroe's summit, features a few rare plants, including a species of cinquefoil that somehow survives the freezing cold winters high in the mountains.

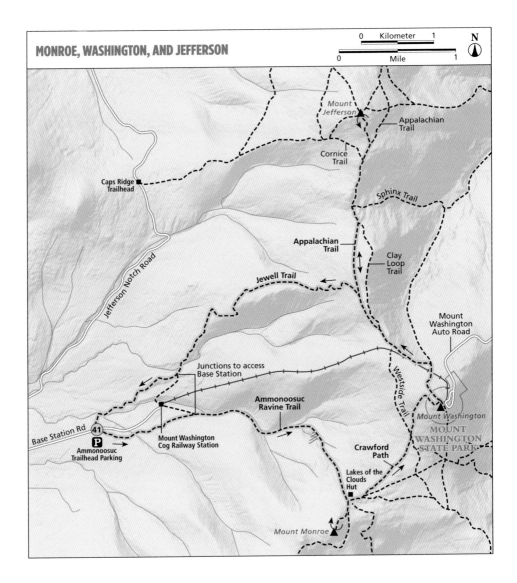

Miles and Directions

0.0 Start from the parking lot and head northeast on the Ammonoosuc Ravine Trail.

0.9 The Ammonoosuc Link comes in from your left; bear right and continue following the stream.

1.9 Cross the stream and pass the Gem Pool.

2.0 A short spur trail on your right leads to a beautiful cascading waterfall.

2.8 Break out above tree line to the Lakes of the Clouds Hut; bear right on the Monroe Loop Trail.

3.1 Mount Monroe summit; turn around and head down off the summit.

3.4 Back at the hut, walk west on the Crawford Path, passing Lakes of the Clouds on your right and, in a short distance, the lower lake on your left.

3.5 Junction with the Tuckerman Crossover Trail and Camel Trail. Bear left and stay on the Crawford Path.

4.2 The Davis Path comes in from your right and, in a few paces, Westside Path from your left. Bear right and continue on the Crawford Path/Appalachian Trail (AT).

4.7 The AT veers to the left; continue heading uphill on the Crawford Path.

4.9 Work your way around the buildings and roads to find the summit of Mount Washington.

5.1 Connect back up with AT as it enters from your left.

5.2 Cross over the railroad tracks for the cog railway.

5.3 Intersection with the Great Gulf Trail; bear left and parallel the train tracks.

5.7 The Westside Trail enters from your left.

5.8 The Mount Clay Loop heads off to the right; stay left on the Gulfside Trail.

6.1 At the junction, the Jewell Trail heads off to your left. Remember this junction—you'll be going down this trail later.

6.7 The other end of the Mount Clay Loop enters from your right.

6.9 Pass the Sphinx Trail junction, on your right.

7.3 The Cornice Trail comes in from the left; continue straight.

7.4 Take the Jefferson Loop, on the left, and head to the summit.

7.7 Arrive at the summit of Mount Jefferson; retrace your steps back to the Jewell Trail.

8.0 At the Gulfside junction, bear right.

8.7 At the Clay Loop, bear right.

9.4 At the Jewell Trail junction, turn 120 degrees right and follow this path downhill.

9.7 You're back below tree line.

11.7 The Jewell Link (quick exit to the base station) is on your left; continue straight.

12.6 Cross the Base Station Road and arrive back at the parking lot.

Options

1. Spot a car at the Caps Ridge Trailhead and exit from Jefferson via the Caps Ridge Trail. Distance: 10.0 miles; elevation gain: 4,860 feet. GPS (trailhead parking): N44°17'48.12" / W71°21'12.93"

2. Add Mount Clay to this adventure. It's not a Northeast 4,000-footer because of elevation rules, but this 5,525-footer is a fun peak to bag. Total mileage with Clay: 12.9 miles; elevation gain: 4,495 feet.

42 Bond Traverse (Bond, West Bond, Bondcliff, Zealand)

The Bonds are the hardest/most-remote mountains to tackle in the Whites, with the biggest payoffs in terms of views, remote wilderness, and physical challenge.

Start: Zealand Trailhead
Distance: 18.5 miles point to point with a car shuttle
Summit elevation: Bond: 4,698 feet; West Bond: 4,526 feet; Bondcliff: 4,265 feet; Zealand: 4,260 feet
4,000-footers rank of the 115: Bond: 26; West Bond: 34; Bondcliff: 59; Zealand: 60
Elevation gain: 3,927 feet
Difficulty: Strenuous
Hiking time: 10–13 hours
Trails used: Zealand Trail, Twinway Trail, Bondcliff Trail, Lincoln Woods Trail

Nearest town: Twin Mountain at start; Lincoln at finish
Views: Excellent
Water sources: A few spots along the way. Zealand Hut is a good spot to fill up, as well as a spur trip to Guyot Shelter to fill up at the spring. Once down from Bondcliff, there are several stream crossings to take advantage of.
Canine compatibility: Yes, though it's a very long hike and the rocks make it hard on paws, so this is not our top canine choice.
Special considerations: This hike requires a car shuttle. There's a small fee to park at Lincoln Woods.

Finding the trailhead: *Zealand Road parking:* To get to the town of Twin Mountain from the north, take exit 36 off I-93 to NH 141 for 0.7 mile then onto US 3 North for 9.7 miles. From the south, take exit 35 to US 3 North for 9.9 miles.

From the intersection of US 302 and US 3 in the town of Twin Mountain, take US 302 East for 2 miles to Zealand Road, on your right (closed in winter). Take this road for 3.5 miles to the end, where there's a small parking lot. GPS (parking lot): N44°13'29.40" / W71°28'43.12"

Lincoln Woods parking: From I-93 take exit 32 to NH 112 (Kancamagus Highway). Travel east on NH 112 for 5.3 miles through the town of Lincoln to reach Lincoln Woods, on your left. GPS (parking lot): N44°3'48.71" / W71°35'17.11"

The Hike

The Bond Traverse is no light undertaking. I prefer doing it as a long day hike, because when we camped at Guyot, it seemed harder with heavier packs. Keep in mind that in winter, route finding can be tough (one year it took us 7 hours *just* to get to Guyot); you also have an extra road walk in winter. You will want to spot a car at Lincoln Woods, where you will emerge 10–13 hours later. I 100 percent recommend starting at Zealand Road rather than Lincoln Woods; the elevation gain is almost 1,000 feet less from this side, and you get most of your elevation gain done in the first half of the day.

The hike starts nice and easy on Zealand Road, and much of the Zealand Trail is mostly flat. In just over 1 hour or so, you hit the junction with the A–Z Trail, where

Michele perching on the famous rock cliff on the way up Bondcliff Donna Dearborn

you bear right onto the Twinway (keep your eyes peeled for moose!) and then a steep but short ascent to the hut. It typically takes us under 1.5 hours to arrive at the hut. Now the climbing starts as you head up a steep incline to the Zeacliff Viewpoint, which is worth a short detour to check out Zealand Notch and Mount Carrigain. The climb moderates a bit (though there are some fun ladders) until you reach the small spur trail to Zealand Mountain, which is a very short, flat walk of 5–10 minutes. Zealand Mountain is just a treed summit (though it does have a cool hand-carved sign), so head back to the Twinway and continue a bit more climbing to the base of Guyot and head up. The section from Zealand to Guyot has quite a lot of ups and downs. It's not super steep, but your legs may be feeling the elevation by now.

It's exciting to finally reach the Bondcliff Trail over the bald summit, where you head left (lots of exposure here) toward the sign for the Guyot campsite. It's a long way down, so if you don't need to stop, keep going toward the West Bond Spur. It's a short but steep climb and, annoyingly, you have to head *down* before the short "up" to West Bond, whose small summit has great views of Bondcliff, Bond, the Twins, Franconia Ridge, and Guyot. Once you rejoin the Bondcliff Trail, you head up a beautiful section of trail to summit Bond. Now you can take a breath, as most of the climbing is done, and enjoy the 360-degree views toward the Presidentials, Franconia Ridge, and all the surrounding mountains, some of which you have just climbed.

Staring out toward Bondcliff is inspiring. This is my favorite view of the day and my favorite part of the Bond Traverse. In truth, it's one of the best spots in the entire

White Mountains. Even though the steep descent is tough, you will hardly notice it as you get more and more spectacular views. Due to the boulders and rocks, it's not a quick descent; it can be brutally hot in summer, so bring plenty of water. The climb toward Bondcliff goes a lot faster, and of course you have to take the time to step out onto the famous rock ledge before the summit for a photo. The first part of the descent from Bondcliff is tough and features a few small cliffs (one jokingly called the

Michele, Donna, and intrepid hiker Eva on Bond's summit on a Bond Traverse hike
Donna Dearborn

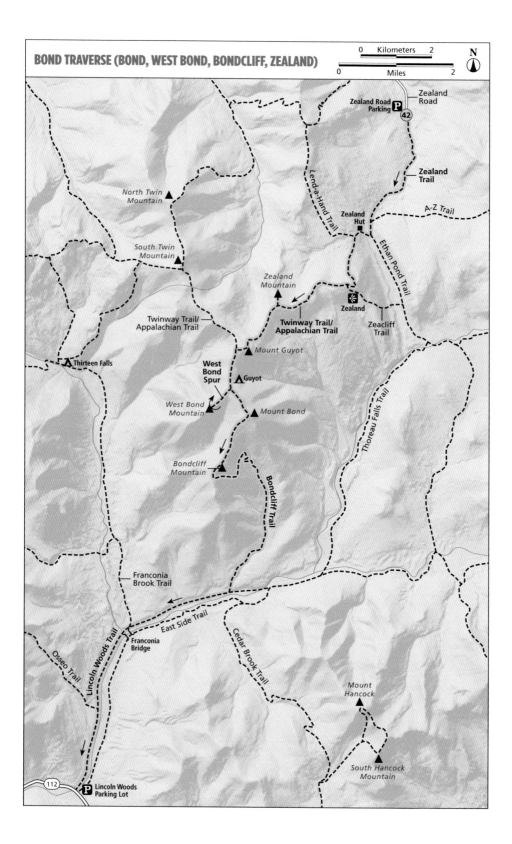

BOND TRAVERSE (BOND, WEST BOND, BONDCLIFF, ZEALAND)

Kilometers 0 — 2

Miles 0 — 2

N

Zealand Road Parking **P** 42

Zealand Road

Zealand Trail

Lend-a-Hand Trail

A-Z Trail

Zealand Hut

Ethan Pond Trail

North Twin Mountain

South Twin Mountain

Zealand Mountain

Twinway Trail/ Appalachian Trail

Twinway Trail/ Appalachian Trail

Zealand

Zeacliff Trail

▲ *Mount Guyot*

Thirteen Falls

West Bond Spur

Guyot

West Bond Mountain

▲ *Mount Bond*

Thoreau Falls Trail

Bondcliff Mountain ▲

Bondcliff Trail

Franconia Brook Trail

East Side Trail

Franconia Bridge

Cedar Brook Trail

Osseo Trail

Lincoln Woods Trail

Mount Hancock

112 **P** Lincoln Woods Parking Lot

South Hancock Mountain

Hillary Step) you have to downclimb. Once you get beyond the obstacles, it's easy hiking down on a wooded trail in the Pemigewasset Wilderness. Once you hit the major stream crossing, you are close to the final stretch, which is still several miles but totally flat. At least you can find water here to pump if you have run out. When you reach the Franconia River footbridge, you have just under 3 miles of flat left to power through. You *will* make it!

Miles and Directions

0.0   Start from the Zealand Road parking lot and head south on the Zealand Trail.

1.6   Cross a pleasant boardwalk over a swampy area.

2.3   Come to the Zealand–A-Z Trail junction; continue straight.

2.5   At the Zealand–Ethan Pond Trail junction, bear right, heading northwest toward the Zealand Falls Hut.

2.7   Arrive at the Zealand Falls Hut.

2.8   Come to the Lend-a-Hand Trail, on you right; continue straight.

3.7   Arrive at the Zeacliff Viewpoint and admire the view. Turn sharply right, heading west.

3.9   The Zeacliff Trail comes in on your left; continue straight.

5.3   Take a right onto the Zealand Spur Trail.

5.4   Reach the Zealand summit.

5.5   Back at the junction, turn right and continue to the Guyot summit.

6.5   Walk over the bare summit of Mount Guyot.

6.6   At the T intersection with the Bondcliff Trail, turn left, heading south.

7.2   The Guyot Campsite Spur is on your left (0.3 mile down to campsites and a spring).

7.3   Take a right onto the West Bond Spur Trail.

7.8   Reach the West Bond summit.

8.2   At the junction, turn right and continue the easy uphill to the Bond summit.

8.8   Arrive at the Bond summit. On this mostly bald summit, head southwest, down toward now-visible Bondcliff.

9.8   Arrive at the remarkable open summit of Bondcliff. Follow rock cairns toward the south and off the open summit into the trees.

13.8   Cross a small bridge and then make a right-hand turn to start the flat walk out on an old railroad bed.

15.6   Come to and cross the Franconia River footbridge.

18.4   Near the end of this trail, turn right onto the large bridge spanning the East Branch Pemigewasset River.

18.5   Arrive at the Lincoln Woods parking lot.

Maine

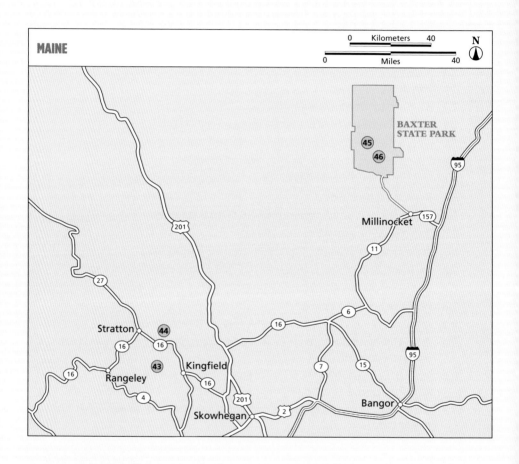

43 Mount Abraham

The Fire Warden's Trail provides an epic alpine ascent that will accelerate your heartbeat, especially if the weather is bad.

Start: Fire Warden's Trailhead
Distance: 7.8 miles out and back
Summit elevation: 4,049 feet
4,000-footers rank of the 115: 94 (tied)
Elevation gain: 2,864 feet
Difficulty: Moderate, though final ascent is difficult.
Hiking time: About 7 hours
Trails used: Fire Warden's Trail

Nearest town: Kingfield
Views: Excellent
Water sources: Several small stream crossings; the last is right before the campsite.
Canine compatibility: Very good
Special considerations: The road is rough and a snowmobile trail in winter. Take great care if you have a low-clearance vehicle.

Finding the trailhead: From the intersection of ME 27 and ME 16 in the town of Kingfield, travel on ME 27 North (ME 16 West) for 0.5 mile; turn left onto West Kingfield Road. Travel west on this road for 3.5 miles its end. Continue straight onto Rapid Stream Road. At 2.5 miles turn left; cross two bridges over Rapid Stream and immediately turn right. Travel up this road for 0.6 mile to reach the summer parking lot. GPS (parking lot): N44°58'5.18" / W70°15'38.45"

The Hike

In summer we did a traverse and hiked Abraham from the other side, but for winter we wanted to attempt the Fire Warden's Trail. Keep in mind that in winter, the road can be inaccessible. We four-wheeled it in the most hair-raising part of this hike in a Range Rover with studded snow tires, and, even so, we almost didn't make it. If you want to spot a car, you can do a loop hike over Abraham to Spaulding, Sugarloaf, and down to knock off three Maine high peaks (there are fourteen total in Maine).

The trail is moderate until you reach the campsite/privy area (at the 2.5-mile mark), where you start to go up. We had a hard time in winter; the snow was soft and we kept falling into the nonfrozen water, so it took us way longer. At about 0.75 mile past the campsite, you break tree line for the exciting final ascent right up the cone of the mountain. It is *steep*—and was scary in winter with the extreme wind and ice. There are a few false summits, so keep climbing until you reach the obvious summit with a sign. Don't hesitate to turn back if the weather is not favorable here. It's easy to

DID YOU KNOW?

Mount Abraham features Maine's largest alpine environment, not counting Katahdin. There are three distinct alpine communities with six rare plant species.

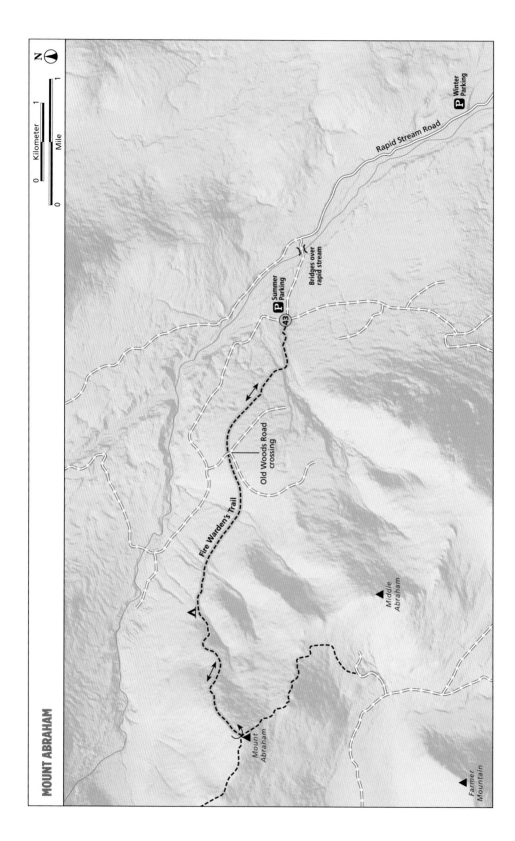

MOUNT ABRAHAM

N

Kilometer
0   1

Mile
0   1

Rapid Stream Road

P Winter Parking

P Summer Parking

43

Bridges over rapid stream

Old Woods Road crossing

Fire Warden's Trail

Mount Abraham

Middle Abraham

Farmer Mountain

View from the top of Mount Abraham (the tower has since collapsed) DEAN J. OUELLETTE

get lost, as several sets of cairns lead to the summit, with some marking the connector to the Appalachian Trail (AT), toward the north. From Abraham's summit you can see just about all the Maine high peaks.

My memories of this hike are foggy, as both Dean and I got sick on this hike from a nasty cold. We struggled up the cone in high winds and then struggled the whole way out. We both were sick for several days afterward, so this was not a pleasant hike for me the first time. (Dean just re-hiked it with Heather and loved it.) This route is a great hike with lots of alpine excitement to experience in one of Maine's largest wilderness areas.

Miles and Directions

- **0.0** Start from the parking lot and head out on the blue-blazed trail.
- **1.3** Cross the old woods road.
- **2.7** Pass a campsite to your right.
- **3.4** Move above tree line.
- **3.9** Reach the summit of Mount Abraham; retrace your steps.
- **5.1** Pass the campsite.
- **6.4** Cross the woods road again.
- **7.8** Arrive back at the parking lot.

Option

Trying the hike in the winter? Start at the winter lot on this road if it's plowed. Distance: 12.7 miles; elevation gain: 3,296 feet. GPS (winter parking lot): N44°56'47.77" / W70°13'36.93"

44 Avery Peak and West Peak

Maine's Bigelow Preserve is gorgeous—and a perfect fall hike if you are up for the challenge.

Start: Fire Warden's Trailhead
Distance: 9.7 miles out and back
Summit elevation: Avery Peak: 4,088 feet; West Peak: 4,150 feet
4,000-footers rank of the 115: Avery Peak: 84; West Peak: 74
Elevation gain: 3,249 feet
Difficulty: Difficult
Hiking time: 7–10 hours (more like 7–8 in summer without the 3-mile road walk)
Trails used: Fire Warden's Trail

Nearest town: Stratton
Views: Very good
Water sources: A few along the way; a small spring a short walk away in the col at the campsite
Canine compatibility: This one is fairly easy for dogs if they are in shape, as it's a steep climb.
Special considerations: The road leading to the trailhead is rough; a low-clearance car may have trouble during mud season.

Finding the trailhead: If traveling from the north, from the intersection of ME 16 and ME 27 in the village of Eustis, take ME 27 South (ME 16 East) for 4.6 miles to Stratton Brook Pond Road. If coming from the south, Stratton Brook Pond Road is 18.4 miles from the town of Kingfield on ME 27 North (ME 16 West). Continue on this road for 1.6 miles until you reach the parking area with trailhead signage. GPS (summer trailhead): N45°6'34.57" / W70°20'12.89"; (winter lot): N45°6'33.29" / W70°21'53.89"

The Hike

This was our first attempt at a Maine peak. Since we had finished our ADK Winter 46, we decided we might as well do some of the Maine peaks in winter, since it was early March—almost spring. The issue was that it had snowed 6–12 inches, so we ended up having to break trail on the steepest part of the climb. In winter you have to do an extra 3 miles, as the parking is at the beginning of the snowmobile path. After some easy walking, we found ourselves on the trail to get to the Fire Warden's Trail to the col. At the 2-mile mark, you reach the Horns Pond Trail junction but continue straight ahead. It was fast walking for the most part (even though we had to break trail in a few inches of snow), with a few uphills until the final mile mark. (This last section to the col is one of the steepest sections we had encountered, which says a lot, considering the Adirondacks are known for super steep trails.) We had heard there were many steep steps, but with the deep snow, we could not see them. Maybe the fact that we also had to kick steps in the snow as we made our way up had drained our energy. I think we may have stopped just short of the junction of the Bigelow Range Trail and the Appalachian Trail (AT), where it's a steep and rocky 0.4 mile (according to the sign) to Avery Peak.

Heather and Dean at the summit with a bird landing in the background Dean J. Ouellette

DID YOU KNOW?

Atop Avery Peak is a plaque honoring Myron Avery, who extended the northern terminus of the AT from Mount Washington to Mount Katahdin and founded the Maine Appalachian Trail Club.

AVERY PEAK AND WEST PEAK

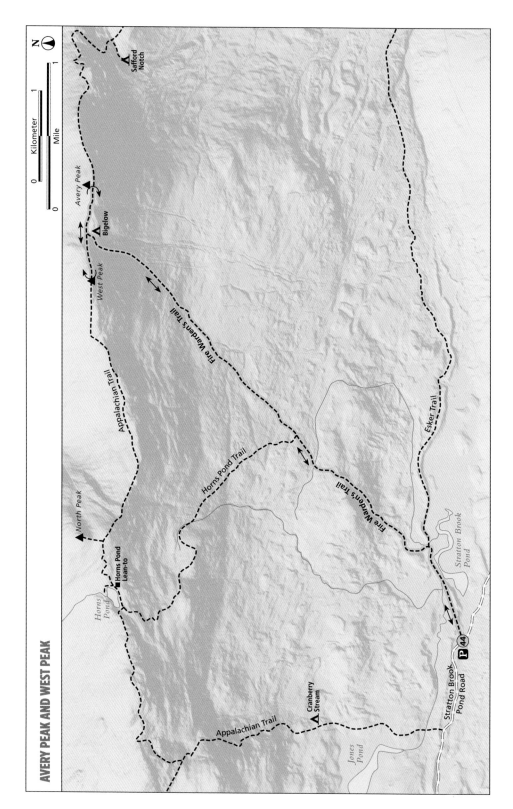

There was, in fact, so much snow that we could not see the well-marked junction for the AT, which turned out to be a bummer; we simply bushwhacked up toward what looked like a peak in the whiteout conditions. By the time we hit the ridge, we realized that the actual peak was not there, so we had to bushwhack through a thick copse of trees. Between bushwhacking, route finding, and trail breaking, it took us almost an hour to find the peak—and it was windy and cold, with no views. We snapped a picture and followed our trail (we still couldn't really see the actual trail) back to the col, where we took a short break. Luckily, the short trip to West Peak was much easier; we snaked our way up and finally got some blue skies and sun for a few minutes. It's a gorgeous peak, so take the time to enjoy the summit and views of Avery Peak. Fall/summer hikers do a longer loop to the Horns, but we descended the way we came. It took us 6 hours to hit Avery (without trail breaking and the winter road walk, it would be more like 4 hours) but only about 3.5 hours to get back to the car, as the descent was much faster with no trail breaking. One of our winter refrains was "Where are all the Maine hikers?" Though we hiked all the fourteen peaks in Maine, we often faced deep, unbroken snow and rarely if ever bumped into another hiker. This hike is very rugged and tough, with a lot of elevation gain—don't underestimate the Bigelows!

Miles and Directions

- **0.0** Start from the parking lot and head east on the Fire Warden's Trail.
- **0.7** Esker Trail junction; turn left and head north on the Fire Warden's Trail.
- **2.0** Horns Pond Trail is on your left; continue straight on the Fire Warden's Trail.
- **4.1** Arrive at the Bigelow campsite and col; go right toward Avery Peak.
- **4.5** Reach Avery Peak's summit; turn around and head back to the col.
- **4.9** At the junction, continue straight to get to West Peak.
- **5.1** Arrive at West Peak's summit; head back toward the col.
- **5.6** At the col, turn right and head back down the hill.
- **7.6** Continue straight past the junction.
- **8.9** At the junction, turn right and head west toward the parking lot.
- **9.7** Arrive back at the parking lot.

Option

Add an additional 3.0 miles if attempting this hike in winter, as you'll need to park close to ME 27.

45 North Brother

Baxter State Park is one of the most spectacular parks in the United States. North Brother is a less populated peak than Mount Katahdin, so you can appreciate the rugged beauty and true wilderness with unbelievable views of the Knife Edge.

Start: Marston Trailhead parking lot
Distance: 10.0-mile lollipop
Summit elevation: 4,143 feet
4,000-footers rank of the 115: 75
Elevation gain: 3,288 feet
Difficulty: Difficult
Hiking time: 7–9 hours
Trails used: Marston Trail, North Brother Trail, Mt. Coe Trail
Nearest town: Millinocket
Views: Excellent

Water sources: A few streams along the way down low
Canine compatibility: Dogs are not allowed in Baxter State Park.
Special considerations: Day-hike parking requires a permit. Go to the Baxter State Park website for reservations and up-to-date information. Spots fill up quickly, so arrive at the gate 1.5 hours before they open and wait in line. Take the time to learn what you can about the park by visiting baxterstatepark.org.

Finding the trailhead: In the town of Millinocket, where ME 157 crosses Millinocket Stream, head west on ME 157 for 0.4 mile then merge right onto Katahdin Avenue. Continue for another 0.6 mile then bear left onto Bates Street. Travel 0.9 mile on Bates Road; at the intersection with Stacyville Road, on your right, the road becomes Millinocket Road. In another 7.6 miles, stay right to access Baxter State Park Road. In another 8.3 miles, arrive at the Togue Pond Gatehouse to check in. From the gatehouse bear left on the Tote Road and travel 13.3 miles; parking for the Marston Trailhead will be on your right. GPS (parking lot): N45°56'21.24" / W69°2'29.18"

The Hike

After driving 8 hours from Vermont, we arrived at Baxter State Park to camp at Kidney Pond. What a beautiful site, often used for stargazing—we had ink-black skies and amazing views of the Milky Way. Though the rangers advise doing this loop counterclockwise so that you go *up* the Coe Slide, we wanted to make sure we hit North Brother, since that was our only "required" mountain. So we did the loop clockwise. If it's wet or icy, you will *not* want to descend the Coe Trail; in which case, you would simply reverse the direction.

From the parking area near Slide Dam (off the Tote Road), you follow the Marston Trail until the first junction. We chose to continue on the Marston Trail so we could reach North Brother first. This trail has it all—flats, steep sections, more flat, more steep; rinse; repeat. Beautiful woods and great scenery make this trail a joy, and you are far from civilization. When you hit the Coe Trail, you bear left to tackle the tough and rocky climb straight up to North Brother. When we did this in winter, the trail was not broken out; it took us more than 2 hours to do this section in subzero

View from the summit of North Brother, looking toward Katahdin's Knife Edge
MICHELE HERNANDEZ BAYLISS

temps as we fought our way inch by inch, with some heroic trail breaking by Dean. In summer we made good time and found ourselves on the rocky, windy, and rugged summit in about 40 minutes after the junction. The views toward the interior of the park are truly incredible as you gaze toward the Knife Edge and Katahdin from an unusual angle (see photo). It is a spectacular peak.

Heading back to the junction, continue straight to follow the Coe Trail toward South Brother. It's only 1 mile or so and pretty easy walking—first to the spur trail and then a short but steep climb to the South Brother summit. Back at the intersection of the Coe Trail, it's about a 1-hour walk (almost 2 miles) to reach the summit of Coe, which also has amazing views. When you reach the Oji Link Trail, you face a very challenging descent down the Coe Slide. It's pretty much straight down a slide. When we did it, it was very wet and slippery, so I ended up crab-walking/butt-sliding down parts of it. Doing this section was tiresome; suddenly it made sense why the

DID YOU KNOW?

North Brother is the northernmost mountain of the Northeast 111. Together with Fort Mountain and South Brother, they are called "the Brothers," although only North Brother is part of the official NE 111.

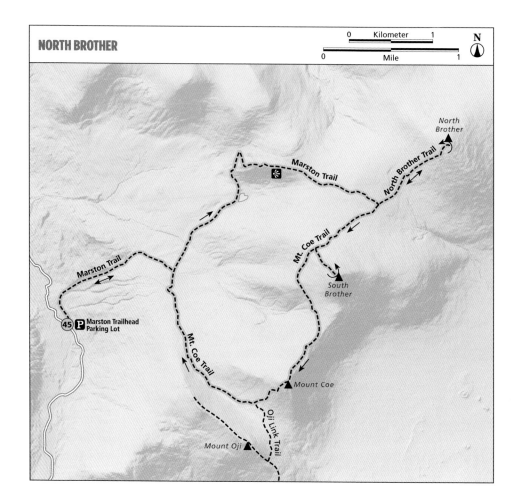

rangers recommend ascending this trail, but it was too late for us. On the bright side, when you finally reach the Marston junction, it's an easy walk back to the trailhead. We took our time on this loop, and it took us just under 9 hours in summer. In winter we could not do the loop due to unbroken snow, and we barely made it to North Brother and back to our campsite (which involved skiing in from a campsite for a 14-hour day). If it's rainy or icy, consider doing this hike in reverse so you don't injure yourself coming down the Coe Slide.

Miles and Directions

- **0.0** Start from the parking lot and head east after signing the register.
- **1.2** The Marston Trail splits; bear left.
- **2.5** Enjoy nice open views to the south.
- **3.4** Junction with the North Brother Trail; turn left.
- **4.1** North Brother's summit. Turn around and head back down.

4.8 At the junction with the Marston Trail, continue straight.

5.4 Arrive at a junction with a spur trail to South Brother; turn left and head uphill.

5.7 Arrive at South Brother's summit; turn around and head down.

6.0 At the junction, turn left.

7.1 Travel over the Mount Coe summit and continue on.

7.4 The Oji Link Trail comes in on your left; continue down the slide.

8.8 Back at the Marston Trail split, bear left.

10.0 Arrive back at the parking lot.

Option

Not up for a complete loop over the other mountains? Do an out-and-back of just North Brother. Distance: 8.3 miles; elevation gain: 3,058 feet.

46 Katahdin (Baxter and Hamlin)

This is probably the best hike in all of New England and certainly a highlight of the Northeast 111. Pick a good weather window and tackle the Knife Edge Trail while grabbing two of Maine's fourteen high peaks.

Start: Roaring Brook Campground parking lot
Distance: 10.0-mile loop
Summit elevation: Baxter: 5,267 feet; Hamlin: 4,751 feet
4,000-footers rank of the 115: Baxter: 7; Hamlin Peak: 23
Elevation gain: 4,412 feet
Difficulty: Difficult
Hiking time: 7–10 hours
Trails used: Chimney Pond, North Basin Cutoff, North Basin, Hamlin Ridge, Saddle, Knife Edge, and Helon Taylor Trails
Nearest town: Millinocket

Views: Superior
Water sources: A few streams along the way; may be something at Caribou Spring, but not guaranteed
Canine compatibility: Dogs are not allowed in Baxter State Park.
Special considerations: Day-hike parking requires a permit. Go to the Baxter State Park website for reservations and up-to-date information. Spots fill up quickly, so arrive at the gate 1.5 hours before they open and wait in line. Take the time to learn what you can about the park by visiting baxterstatepark.org.

Finding the trailhead: In the town of Millinocket, where ME 157 crosses Millinocket Stream, head west on ME 157 for 0.4 mile then merge right onto Katahdin Avenue. Continue for another 0.6 mile then bear left onto Bates Street. Travel for 0.9 mile on Bates Road; at the intersection with Stacyville Road, on your right, the road becomes Millinocket Road. In another 7.6 miles, stay right to access Baxter State Park Road. In another 8.3 miles, arrive at the Togue Pond Gatehouse to check in. From the gatehouse, bear right on the Tote Road and travel 7.9 miles to the end for Roaring Brook Campground parking. GPS (parking lot): N45°55'9.08" / W68°51'25.60"

The Hike

We recommend a loop hike that ascends Hamlin, continues on to Baxter, traverses the famous Knife Edge along with Pamola Peak and Chimney, and then returns via the Dudley Trail. Keep in mind that you have to apply for a permit, so plan ahead. In winter you need even more planning. Because the road is closed in winter, you have to hike into Chimney Pond. It is a 5- to 6-day undertaking and a rite of passage for Northeast 111 winter hikers.

In summer you park at Roaring Brook Campground and start on the Chimney Pond Trail. You then bear right onto the North Basin Cutoff Trail and left to the North Basin Trail to the Hamlin Ridge Trail shortly thereafter. The hike up Hamlin Peak is very rocky and scrambly, but nothing too steep. Walking past Hamlin Peak for 10 minutes, turn left onto the Northwest Basin Trail for almost 1 mile. You are now on the "table lands," a windswept section that can be fearsome in winter or in

Looking out toward the infamous Knife Edge from near Katahdin's summit
MICHELE HERNANDEZ BAYLISS

high winds. On the bright side, the terrain is fairly flat as you reach the sign for the Saddle Trail. From the Cathedral Trail Cutoff, it's only a short climb to the mother of all mountains, Baxter summit. Though I have done it in good weather, our winter hike featured wind gusts of over 60 miles per hour that blew us over more than once.

Normally the summit is quite crowded; several trails converge here and everyone wants a summit photo, as this is the end of the Appalachian Trail. Now you have to make a serious decision. Is the weather good? Trust me when I say you do not want to tackle the Knife Edge in super windy weather, or thunderstorms, or in the dark. More than a dozen people have died on the Knife Edge, and there have been many rescues. If you are afraid of heights, simply return the way you came—the Knife Edge is not for the faint of heart.

For me the Knife Edge was much easier than I thought. (There is one scary part with a steep drop-off, but the rock leans inward, so it would be very hard to fall off.) Though book time is 90 minutes, we crossed in 45 minutes flat. In fact, the hardest part was not the Knife Edge but the descent of Chimney Peak. There is one spot where, if Dean hadn't spotted me, I might not have made it with one big step down. If that wasn't bad enough, I didn't realize that I had to climb a vertical cliff up Pamola Peak right after the descent. Although the handholds were fine, it was very intimidating. I distinctly remember a woman looking down from above who was crying. Though I was scared, I made it up in about 5 minutes.

Once we got to the top of Pamola, I knew we were golden. You have two choices: Head down the Helon Taylor Trail back to the Roaring Brook Campground to your parked car, or do what we did, which was to head down the Dudley Trail, which was *not* easy at all but, compared to what we had already done, seemed less death-defying. It is a very rugged trail—even tougher when wet, requiring a few butt slides and crab walks to get down. We celebrated our regular season NE 111 finish as we played cards in the lean-to. For our winter hike we went up the Saddle Trail to Baxter and then returned down the Hamlin Ridge Trail. Hiking both in and out in a blizzard with below-zero temps and crazy (over 50 mile-per-hour) winds made for a brutal and most memorable winter experience.

Sign at Katahdin's summit, the northern terminus of the Appalachian Trail
MICHELE HERNANDEZ BAYLISS

KATAHDIN (BAXTER AND HAMLIN)

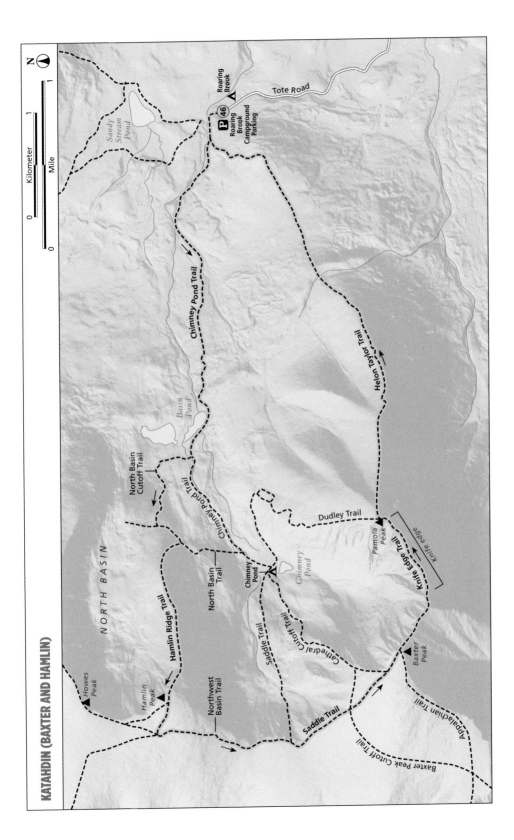

Miles and Directions

0.0 Start from the parking lot; head north toward the ranger station and sign in.

0.2 The Helon Taylor Trail comes in on your left; continue on the Chimney Pond Trail.

1.9 Short spur to a lookout at Basin Pond.

2.2 Turn right onto the North Basin Cutoff Trail.

2.8 Turn left onto the North Basin Trail.

3.0 Turn right at the junction with the Hamlin Ridge Trail.

4.1 Arrive at Hamlin Peak; continue straight.

4.3 Pass the North Peaks Trail that comes in from your right (Caribou Spring is on your left); walk another 40 feet and turn left onto the Northwest Basin Trail.

5.2 The Saddle Trail comes up from your left; continue up the mountain on the Saddle Trail.

5.6 Four-way intersection with the Baxter Peak Cutoff and Cathedral Trails; continue straight up the mountain.

5.9 The Cathedral Trail comes up on your left.

6.1 The Hunt Trail/Appalachian Trail comes in on your right as you arrive at the Baxter Peak summit.

6.4 Cross over the South Peak summit as you make your way toward the Knife Edge.

6.9 Arrive at the crux of the hike at Chimney Peak.

7.0 You made it to Pamola Peak; turn right and head down the Helon Taylor Trail.

9.8 Meet back up with the Chimney Pond Trail; bear right to get to the ranger station.

10.0 Arrive back at the parking lot.

Option

Didn't get up early enough to get to Roaring Brook or just looking for more of a challenge? Try going up the Hunt Trail/Appalachian Trail with all the finishing thru-hikers. Distance: 12.9 miles; elevation gain: 5,356 feet. GPS (parking lot): N45°53'7.87" / W69°0'0.60"

Appendix A: Bonus Hikes at a Glance to Complete the Northeast 111

The seventeen remaining hikes (twenty-nine mountains) that will get you to the NE 111

We saved this last batch for quick hiking notes, since they are either less spectacular or just more straightforward as hikes and don't need as much elaboration.

New York, Adirondacks

Street and Nye Mountains

Though not the most exciting pair of Adirondack hikes, at least you can knock both of them off in 5–7 hours, depending on conditions, as they clock in relatively short by Adirondack standards. From the trail register at Heart Lake near the Adirondack Loj, the main thing you want to remember is to bear *right* at the sign for Old Nye Ski Trail (we totally missed this and added 2 hours to our hike). Then you go straight toward Street and Nye rather than right to the Rock Garden Trail up Mount Jo. Though these are both considered herd paths, they are fairly well defined. This is one of those hikes where it's flat and then *up* until the fork. Take into consideration the one very tough water crossing of Indian Pass Brook—avoid after heavy rains/snow. When you reach the intersection, head left up the 0.5 mile or so moderate section to arrive at Street. You often have to crawl over and under fallen logs. Don't miss the viewpoint just over the summit. It should take 2–2.5 hours to reach Street from the Loj. Heading back down to the junction, it's even shorter to reach the summit of Nye. The only view is just below the summit, so of the two, we'd say Street is more exciting, with a cool perspective looking back toward Algonquin and Iroquois. Now it's a quick downhill walk to the start as you return via the section you climbed up earlier.

Seymour Mountain

I have actually grown to love this hike. Keep in mind that in winter, if Corey's Road is closed, you have to add an extra 6-mile road walk to a roughly 14-mile hike. Despite its length, it's fairly easy by Adirondack standards. You hike the majority of it on a more or less flat road (Blueberry Foot Trail) then bear right on the Ward Brook Truck Trail and continue to the Ward Brook Lean-to (avail yourself of the outhouse if needed). This is as close to a flat road as you will find in the Adirondacks. We like to call it "luxurious." We have reached the lean-to in 2 hours flat, but allow 2–3 hours. Just past the lean-to (less than 5 minutes up the road, just over a brook), you will see the small cairn on your right that marks the herd path up Seymour. You get a 20-minute warm-up before the slide starts in earnest. All the elevation gain (more than 2,000 feet) is over this section. Yes, it's steep, and often you have to duck under logs (in winter, we've had some epic butt slides down this steep section). Take it slow and enjoy the ascent, which bears right as it winds up the mountain. When you come to a Y junction, in nice weather you can head right to a fantastic lookout rock where you are treated to views of the other Sewards (Donaldson, Emmons, and Seward) and the remote Ouluska Pass. The summit is not far from here as you begin a fairly mild uphill section to reach the true summit, marked with a sign. There are views to be had from here as well if it's not too cold, so enjoy the view before the steep descent and return the way you came. Allow 7–9 hours for this hike, depending on your speed and conditions. On the bright side, the steep section is less than 1.5 miles, and most of the rest is flat.

Seward and Donaldson Mountains, Mount Emmons

Though these mountains are not the highest in the Adirondacks, this is always a tough hike. In winter, matters can be complicated if Corey's Road is closed at the gate; in which case you add almost 6 miles to an already super long hike (and it's *not* flat). When we did it in winter, the gate was open, and it still took us 13 hours. This hike is most pleasant in the fall, when the mosquitoes and mud are under control. For many, this can be a suffer-fest hike from the combo of blackflies, mosquitoes, mud, and mileage.

From the parking lot, you follow the red DEC-marked hiking trail on a flat road for just over 1 mile, where you take a right toward the Shattuck Clearing and the Calkins Brook Herd Path. You may not notice it now, but this trail does slope down—an elevation gain you will not appreciate later in the day—and then up and down and flat for 1.5–2 hours. Keep your eyes peeled when you get to the rocky decline section; you are looking for a "bucket" cairn that marks the Calkins Brook Herd Path—don't miss it! Make a left and head up the herd path. About 0.2 mile into the herd path is the water crossing; continue your climb through open, then thick woods to reach the Donaldson summit, although when we reach the cairn at the top of the ridge (about 10 minutes below Donaldson), we typically head left toward Seward first, as that is a tougher ascent—typically about a 2-hour climb from the bucket cairn, 3.5–4 hours from the start.

After a steep downhill to the col, you head up the bumps on Seward (the "Brothers"). This is a very tricky/cliffy climb with some technical scrambles. It takes 45 minutes to 1 hour from the cairn to the top, and equal care is required to descend the rocks and climb back up to the cairn. Ten minutes more brings you to the Donaldson summit, which is an open rock you climb onto for incredible views. After a short refueling, head down the ridge toward Emmons. In summer this can be a muddy mess, and though it's a ridge, there is a lot of up and down and some tough rock scrambles, so it's not particularly fast. You lose 200-plus feet of elevation, gain 150, and then have to reverse it. The out-and-back to Emmons typically takes 1.5–2 hours. Emmons itself is not very exciting, so only add it if you are peak-bagging. Don't be tempted to take a shortcut down from Emmons—several hikers have gotten lost in this area. The only way back is the way you came.

After you drag yourself back to Donaldson, you hang a left on Calkins, descend until the bucket cairn, then bear right, where you will notice the uphill parts as you return to the final junction. Head left on the final flat section to the parking area.

Mount Marshall

In the past, the most common route was the one between Iroquois and Marshall from Cold Brook Pass, but now most hikers choose the much easier route from Upper Works, across the Flowed Lands, to the cairn that marks the start of the path that follows Herbert Brook. We prefer this route, although you can also leave from the High Peaks Information Center, but it's longer (mostly for those camping) and a little more elevation gain. The Upper Works approach is fairly flat for the first few miles along the Calamity Brook Trail toward the Flowed Lands. In winter you can take a nice shortcut over the Flowed Lands to the lean-to to avoid a few ups and downs on the actual path. Keep an eye out for the cairn on the left just north of the bridge over Herbert Brook that marks the start of the herd path, which mostly follows the brook but can be hard to follow in winter before it is tracked out. The trail crosses the brook a few times, so try to follow the small cairns. One winter we ended up missing the top section of trail and taking a straight line up before we found the actual path on the way down. The top section is quite steep, though the hike only gains about 2,500 feet total over many miles. Although this hike is well over 10 miles, much of it is fairly flat, and the climb, though steep near the top, is not bad by Adirondack standards. Typical time for this hike is 7–9 hours. There is a good viewpoint just off the summit where you can gaze over toward Iroquois Peak, the Shepherd's Tooth, and western peaks like the Santanonis and Sewards.

Maine

Old Speck Mountain

This trailhead is about 4 hours north of us from Vermont. We hiked it on the way to the more northerly peaks in Maine. Because it's easy and fairly short, it's often crowded, as it's the only 4,000-footer in this area. It's the highest and most northeastern peak in the Mahoosuc Range of the White Mountains. This hike may be short, but it's not super easy; the elevation gain is close to 3,000 feet, so the trail is steadily up. The Appalachian Trail (AT) comes within 0.3 mile of a mile of Old Speck's summit. We took the Old Speck Trail to the AT and then the summit. There was a very cool fire tower on top, which we felt compelled to climb to get some views. If you want more of an adventure, you can do the Eyebrow Loop Trail up, which has some ladders and cliffs. Allow 5–6.5 hours round-trip.

Crocker and South Crocker Mountains, Mount Redington

In summer we did a five-day traverse to do the Crockers and Redington, so I can say firsthand that doing South Crocker this way is very hard. For winter we found what I think is the best route, starting from ME 27. What a great trail; after the first few steep sections, it's actually quite gradual, with some nice flats in the middle that make the mileage go fairly quickly. According to the sign, 5.2 miles later we found ourselves on top of North Crocker in some heavy snow and wind. What a beautiful ridge. We covered the distance to South Crocker in only 30 minutes, as it's fairly flat. Since it had only taken us 3.5 hours thus far, we decided to attempt Redington. To find the start of the herd path, start from the viewpoint to the left; the herd path is directly across on the right-hand side.

This is a brutal bushwhack, especially in winter when no one has been there before you. The trees are *thick*, and it's near impossible to stay on-trail. I'm not sure how we did it, but eventually we made it to the snowmobile trail. Compared to the whack down from South Crocker, the bushwhack *up* from the logging road wasn't as bad. Yes, there were some thick sections, but not super steep, and after about 40 minutes we found ourselves on the summit looking back at the Crockers. It was exhilarating the winter we did it, as not many hikers had made it up. Though the summit itself is unremarkable, you can find the old-fashioned summit canister and sign in. On the way down, we decided to take a "shortcut" down the woods road, which was probably the actual herd path. It wasn't as easy as you'd think—*very* deep snow, some spruce traps, and some tight squeezes—but we made it down to a lower point on the snowmobile trail. When we saw that the snowmobile trail branched right, we thought we might save some mileage by bushwhacking to the snowmobile trail rather than taking the right turn and going the whole way on the road (8-plus miles). Long story short: I would not recommend the shortcut; follow the CVR road!

We finally staggered back to the car 12 hours later. I suspect the "normal" time for this hike is way less when you don't have to deal with figuring out how to reach Redington. The Crockers by themselves are fairly easy, but adding Redington adds a fun challenge, as it's one of the hardest unmaintained trails to follow.

Sugarloaf and Spaulding Mountains

There are two ways to get up Spaulding: straight up on a very steep ski path from Sugarloaf Resort or the Appalachian Trail route from the Caribou Valley Appalachian Trailhead. We chose the ski path since it was slightly shorter and was accessible in winter, but it's definitely not easier, as it's basically straight up a steep slope. It is direct, though, and in winter you can count on the trail being broken since you are hiking on a ski slope. The road leading to the AT trailhead is very rough and you can't always depend on reaching it; the ski route is more reliable.

You start by taking the Tote Road Trail 2.5 miles up from the resort, about 90 minutes. We arrived at the ski hut on top and headed from there to the summit, only 150 yards. We tagged Sugarloaf and then (because there was a ton of new snow) floundered around looking for the trail to Spaulding. The best way to find the trail is to descend from the summit tower straight down the side that points toward Spaulding. There is very small flagging, and once you catch the trail, you'll see the blue blazes and then the white blazes of the AT. The first 0.5 mile is a steep descent to an intersection that indicates that you have 2.1 miles more to Spaulding, which is 2.7 miles from the summit of Sugarloaf. It took us 2 hours one way, but we had to make our way in deep snow (normally it would be more like an hour to the spur trail, which is quite short). For those who want a ton of additional mileage, you can continue just under 4 more miles (2 miles to the junction of the Abraham Side Trail and roughly 1.7 miles from there to the summit). The problem is that you'd then have to retrace your steps, making it a very long hike. Alternatively, you can do a traverse if you do a shuttle and descend the Fire Warden's Trail, which would save a lot of extra mileage. Retrace your steps along the AT until you reach the final junction, which is that 0.6-mile ascent back to the Sugarloaf junction.

The downhill section from the ski hut down can be very hard on your knees when there is no snow. In summer and fall, it might be easier to simply follow the AT from Caribou Valley—the grade is more moderate, and the total time will be quite similar.

Saddleback Mountain and Saddleback Horn

In winter (though you can ascend this way in summer too), we opted to buy uphill ski passes and ascend the Green Weaver Trail. In summer we took the Appalachian Trail (AT) route, since we did a multiday camping trip traverse to grab a bunch of Maine peaks. The base lodge is located at around 2,500 feet, so it's not as bad as the climb up Sugarloaf Mountain. After stopping in the warming hut, we headed up the tricolor steep section that takes you to the highest ski lift, where you pick up the trail. It's a fairly long ridge walk just to get to Saddleback Peak from the ski lift, so you are up there for a bit. It's a beautiful summit, but due to the high winds and low temps, we just blew by to look for the trail to the Horn, which follows the Appalachian Trail.

This is far from an easy ridge walk, and some very thick forest will prevent you from beelining the 1.7 miles (according to the summit sign) or so to the Horn. For the most part we stayed on the trail, but there was one section (we could tell from the armpit-deep snow) where we definitely lost the trail not far after leaving Saddleback. Because of a recent blizzard when we did this hike, there were two tricky spots that took about 15 minutes to get up maybe a 10- to 12-foot wall of snow. Once you get closer to the Horn, the route up is pretty obvious and you can actually see a few cairns. Like Saddleback, the Horn has lovely views and an open summit. Even with the trail finding and trail breaking, we made it back to the hut in 5 hours flat and then 45 minutes from there to the car, making this a doable hike in under 6 hours. In warmer weather, allow more time to take in the views.

In summer we experienced one of the worst thunderstorms of the summer just as we broke out onto Saddleback. We ended up sprinting down toward the Horn and then hurling ourselves off-trail to weather 45 minutes of terrifying thunder and lightning. We held a tarp over our heads as we hunkered down 20 feet off the trail in the woods. After our trip, we learned that the storm had knocked out electricity in half the state of Maine. **Bottom line:** Always watch the weather. These are very exposed peaks, and that was the closest we've come to being electrocuted!

New Hampshire

Mount Moriah

There are two main routes up to the summit using either the Stony Brook or Carter-Moriah Trail. Since Carter-Moriah is a bit shorter than Stonybrook, we tend to take this route. There are two parking areas at the Carter-Moriah Trailhead down Bangor Road.

I won't lie—this is not an easy hike. The trail is beautiful and traverses some incredible open woods and ledges with eye-popping views of Mounts Washington, Adams, and Madison. But it has a ton of up and down, or what hikers call "PUDS" (pointless ups and downs). Not to mention you get a bonus mountain that doesn't count—Surprise—even though you have to climb up and over it around 2 miles into the hike. We did love the ledges, which have amazing views, though they can be tough to scramble up (especially with ice). The final miles of this hike alternate very steep "up" sections with some rolling hills, more up; rinse, repeat. Just when I thought we had to be there, we caught a glimpse of the summit with one last short climb, which was a final down and longish up one last hill to the junction, where you see the continuation of the Carter-Moriah Trail straight ahead and the summit spur to the right. Luckily that last climb only takes a minute until you emerge onto a large rock with awe-inspiring views of the Pinkham Notch side of the Presidentials. The last time we did this hike, there was quite a lot of fresh snow; the climb took about 4 hours, but the descent took under 3. This hike has more than 3,000 feet of elevation gain (and some is on the way back), so allow 7–8 hours for the out-and-back.

Mount Waumbek

This is one of the "easiest" hikes in the White Mountains. Mount Waumbek is the second most northerly peak in the range and the shortest, at just over 4,000 feet. Though there are several long loop hikes you can do, the normal route (which starts right across from the Waumbek Golf Course) is a 2- to 2.5-hour hike up the Starr King Trail in Jefferson. About 1 mile from the Waumbek summit, you reach what looks like a stone pizza oven (actually the old shelter/hut) that marks the summit of non-4,000-footer Mount Starr King. This summit has more of a view, so gaze toward the Presidentials before heading down along a ridge to reach the rather unexciting summit of Waumbek, marked by a cairn. It's worth continuing 2 minutes past the summit to the awesome lookout that makes this hike totally worthwhile. Most hikers can do this in 4–5.5 hours, as the elevation gain is fairly gradual (2,600 feet).

Mount Cabot

Cabot is officially the northernmost peak in the White Mountains and the tallest in the Pilot Range. Though mileage-wise you might not guess, it's one of the easiest hikes in terms of gentle terrain. We actually did both Cabot and Waumbek in the same day (I don't necessary recommend this, but we were on a peak-bagging mission). From the parking area near York Pond, take the Bunnell Notch Trail. After no more than 10–15 minutes, you'll see the junction for York Pond, but you stay right to follow Bunnell until you reach the Kilkenny Ridge Trail. From here it's a relatively easy grade to the summit of Cabot. When you reach the Cabot Cabin, you are less than 0.5 mile from the summit and it makes for a nice break stop. There is a lookout just off the summit, so don't forget to check out the limited views before heading back. It usually only take 4–5 hours, as the grade is gentle. If you want a loop hike, you can continue over the ridge to climb both the Bulge and the Horn then bear right on the Unknown Pond Trail back to York Pond. You add more miles and a few hundred feet more of elevation gain, but it does make for a more interesting hike with additional views.

Galehead Mountain

Only those seeking to complete the forty-eight White Mountain peaks would bother with this mountain. There is not much of a view, and you basically have to climb all the way to the Galehead Hut to reach the base of the trail. From the hut, it's only a 25-minute or so climb on the Frost Trail to reach Galehead up a short but steep and switchbacked trail. Though the summit is completely treed in, there is a fantastic lookout toward the Twins, about 5 minutes from the summit. Most people simply tag Galehead when they are doing North and South Twin (or just South Twin), or they will do Garfield first then head over on the Garfield Ridge Trail to the hut to climb Galehead. The easiest route would be the Gale River Trail to the hut, then the Frost Trail to the summit of Galehead, and then up the steep section to South Twin Mountain from the hut.

South and Middle Carter Mountains

We often do Carter Dome with this hike as well, but to keep things a bit easier, we suggest the following loop hike. Start from the Imp Trail to the North Carter Trail (about 1.5 hours). Continue straight until you hit the Carter-Moriah Trail, which is also the Appalachian Trail (AT). Bear right and continue to the summit of Middle Carter. Though there are not many views, you will get some great viewpoints a bit past the summit. I love this section of trail, as the ridge is fairly moderate and the views are pretty nice when there is good visibility.

Continue to follow the AT on some easier terrain to reach South Carter Mountain. At this point you can either backtrack or continue forward to the junction with Carter Dome Trail/Zeta Pass where you will bear right on the Carter Dome Trail and continue until you reach 19-Mile Brook Trail, a relatively easy descent. Once you reach the bottom, you have a half-hour road walk unless you spotted a car, which would save you that last section.

North and South Hancock Mountains

The hardest part of this hike is crossing the traffic-filled "Kanc" (Kancamagus Highway) to get to the trail, which is directly across from the parking lot on the other side of the Kanc. This hike is spectacular in late summer/early fall as long as there has not been a ton of rain; there are several brook crossings, which can cause issues after winter with high snowmelt or after heavy rains.

This trail is easy by White Mountain standards because it's relatively flat at the beginning. When you reach the Cedar Brook crossing, take a left to head toward the Hancock Loop Trail. In short order, you follow this very nice trail until you reach the Hancock Loop Trail and continue until you reach a junction, where you have to decide in which direction you want to tackle both mountains. Though we have done the loop clockwise and counterclockwise (South Hancock first), we highly recommend bearing left and doing North Hancock first—it's very difficult to descend North Hancock thanks to its steepness and loose rocks and roots.

Almost immediately, the trail dips down a steep pitch before you start the climb in earnest. It is *steep*, with most of the gain on this section until you finally level out and reach the sign that indicates the outlook to the left and South Hancock to the right. Although this is the summit, we recommend saving your photos for the outlook, which is a 1-minute detour to the left. It is spectacular as you stare right at Mount Osceola and the Sandwich Range Wilderness.

From North Hancock, you bear right to follow the ridge. I love this section of trail, as you are high up on a ridge; though it is by no means totally flat. There are several up-and-down bumps with a final easy descent to South Peak. Just left of the summit is a great lunch stop/lookout.

At that point you have a very short and steep 0.5-mile section (great winter butt slide) until you return to the loop junction. Then head back to the junction with Hancock Notch (which you will not take) and another easy walk on the Hancock Ridge Trail back to the parking lot. The slight downhill pitch makes this section quite fast. We typically do it in 6–6.5 hours, 7 hours tops (including time for lunch breaks). Be careful recrossing the highway back to your car.

Mounts Tom, Field, and Willey

Though you can do these one at a time or in pairs, true peak-baggers combine all three peaks into a loop hike from the AMC Highland Center at Crawford Notch. Though the total elevation gain is close to 3,500 feet, it is fairly spread out so you don't do it all at once. Almost every time we have done this hike, it has either rained or been super cold, but there are some nice views along the way and pleasant trails.

You start out on the A-Z Trail and hike until you reach the junction for the spur trail to Mount Tom. The out-and-back is not super hard in terms of elevation gain.

If you continue on the A-Z Trail, you'd arrive at the Zealand Hut, a fun place to stay if you want to spend time in this area and bag the maximum number of peaks. It's a fairly easy trek from the junction to the summit of Field along the Willey Range Trail. If the weather is clear, you can usually see views to the Mount Washington Hotel from the summit. The toughest part is the up-and-down ridge walk out and back to Willey. There are also quite a lot of rocks and roots on this section. Though you can do a traverse with a car spot, we typically head back up to Mount Field and then loop around the Avalon Trail so we can do the short spur trail up Avalon if the weather is nice. The loop drops you back (with a steep final descent) to the junction you passed early in the morning, leaving only the easy 40-minute walk back to the AMC Highland Center.

This hike is pretty satisfying. In 6.5–8 hours or so, you can bag three high peaks with the elevation typically required for one peak.

Wildcat A and D

Though there are actually five Wildcats, only two of them (A and D) count for the 4,000-footer club. (Although the official form still has Wildcat E as the preferred mountain, on the AMC website's FAQ, they mention that it was replaced with Wildcat D.) My favorite is to do a car spot on NH 116 and start at the Nineteen Mile Brook Trail. You'll thank us later. This trail is very gentle by White Mountain standards and follows the brook until you reach a junction to the Carter Dome Trail. Stay right to continue on the Nineteen Mile Brook Trail until you reach the next junction for the Carter Hut (a *very* steep down, which you should avoid unless you want to visit the hut). So far the trail has been gentle, covering about 1,800 feet of ascent, but the best is yet to come—1,000 feet of ascent crammed into this steep ascent to the top of Wildcat A. Even with the ascent, we typically make it up in about 2 hours.

There is a small spur path to enjoy the view toward the Presidentials before getting back to business. The Wildcat Ridge is a bit of a wild ride. You will go up and down over Wildcat B and C before going down, down, down. And then down some more. About three times I thought we had finished all the down, but I was wrong. The col between C and D is by far the deepest. Then of course you have to ascend to reach Wildcat D, but at least this is the last climbing you will have to do on this hike.

Once you crest Wildcat D, make your way over to the viewing platform just above the ski area. Just at the bottom of the platform is a wooded area that is the trail to cut over to the ski trails. We do not recommend either ascending or descending the Wildcat Ridge Trail back to NH 116, as it can be nasty in any season (and *very* icy in winter, typically requiring crampons). Once you cut through this wooded path, you have to slide down a ledge (we did this on our butts in winter) to reach the ski trails and then basically stay right to follow Upper/Middle/Lower Polecat about 2,100 vertical feet down the mountain just short of 3 miles. Don't fret if you cross over to another trail (they all lead down), but try to stay by Polecat. This part went fast for us, though the last time we hiked, we got blasted by snow guns on the bottom half of the trail due to the light snow that winter. Despite the 3,000-plus feet of elevation gain, we typically do this hike in about 7 hours, though it can take longer depending on conditions. The skiway saves you some mileage and a perilous descent on the Wildcat Ridge Trail. Now when you hear the word "wildcat," you'll do what we do and emit a mewing cat sound like an actual wildcat to remind you how challenging this hike is.

Cannon Mountain

Attending Dartmouth College, I have distinct memories of viewing the New Hampshire state emblem: the "Old Man of the Mountain" profile from I-93 gazing up toward Cannon Mountain as you drove north through Franconia Notch. The granite formation was almost 46 feet tall by 29.5 feet wide and weighed in at over 7,165 tons. In May 2003 it fell, though I can still see it in my mind when I travel up the notch.

For some reason, I had never hiked it. When we did our winter blitz, we decided on the short, steep way up that starts at the Cannon Mountain Tramway. Following the Kinsman Ridge Trail, you basically go up a steep and rocky ramp. In winter this section is almost always extremely icy. The first time we did it, we used microspikes up and full crampons for the descent. Though it is steep, you are rewarded with unforgettable views right into the flank of Lafayette/Lincoln/Liberty/Flume and Franconia Notch from the top of the skiway.

If you want a longer loop, you can go over the "cannon balls" toward the Kinsmans following the Kinsman Ridge Trail, or you can bear left and follow the Hi-Cannon Trail to Lafayette Campground. The up and down via Kinsman Ridge typically takes under 3 hours, but the descent can grind your knees a bit. This is a perfect mountain for when you want a short hike with an amazing view.

Appendix B: Winter Gear

In summer there is more flexibility in gear, but in winter it helps to have some specialized clothing for both comfort and safety. We have spent years honing our winter kit, and we wanted to give some advice as to our favorite layering system and pieces of clothing.

The only way to dial in your kit is to hike often and test gear yourself. Dean, for example, typically wears a bit less than I do, as he likes to hike "cold" whereas I prefer to hike "hot." My theory is that women cool down faster than men, so I'd rather sweat a bit more than feel freezing cold. I actually generate a ton of heat when I hike in winter, which is something I did *not* expect! In fact, that's another reason I love hiking in winter—I feel that I'm beating winter by staying warm no matter how miserable it is outside. We have hiked in temps well below zero (minus 50°F with the windchill factor) on many occasions (almost every hike the winter of 2014–15 in New Hampshire and Maine) while keeping ourselves warm and fairly dry over 8- to 12-hour hikes.

Overall, winter hiking entails being prepared for *anything*—frigid temps, high winds, extreme wet (even on dry days, snow falls down from trees and many trails are closed in by snow-laden bushes and trees, so snow is perpetually being dumped on top of you), sleet, hail, deep snow, and long days. Having the right gear and learning how to layer has kept me alive on many an unpleasant winter day.

Base Layers

Wool is the key for base layers in winter unless you do not sweat at all. Some hikers swear by polypropylene or Capilene; I like those in any season BUT winter. I would also add they STINK (well, at least they smell like "hard work."). Wool does not. The real advantage of wool as a base layer is that it still insulates when wet. That means even after you sweat climbing up 3,000 feet with your winter backpack, your outer layer will keep you warm even if you are not dry. You just add an additional layer on top and, magically, you are warm. Wool does not wick as well as a synthetic, but on most hikes, by the end of the day, my wool layer dries out as the wind blows through my jacket. Even if it does not dry out, it preserves my body heat, and that's why it can save your life in winter. Keep in mind that a synthetic might wick out moisture, but in winter you have another layer over it, so it will simply wick right into that layer. In effect, the moisture has nowhere to go. Now you are wet and cold rather than wet and warm.

All wool is not created equal. I swear by the New Zealand company Icebreaker; their merino wool is softer and holds up better in my experience. It's not cheap, but my comfort level (and life) is worth a lot to me. Icebreaker's soft merino wool feels more like cotton. And they make it in different weights. If it's 20°F or above, I opt for their lighter top base layer and leggings (they use a number system, so 200); if it's below 20°F, I will wear the heavier top and bottom layer (260). We also wear Ice-breaker long underwear bottoms under our snow pants.

Snow Pants

You don't necessarily need Gore-Tex Pro (though I do love it) for winter as long as it has a good DWR (durable water repellent) finish. Our favorites are Norrøna (Norwegian), Helly Hansen (Norwegian), and STIO (American). My favorite pants from STIO are the Credential pants, which also feature a bombproof cuff and inner gaiter that helps you not slice your pants with crampons.

Wicking Soft-shell/Hard-shell Jacket

We both hike using a DWR or Gore-Tex outer jacket. For three winters I hiked in my RAB (fantastic British company) Baltoro soft shell, which featured polar-dry power-stretch fabric on the inside. That jacket might have been a tad too insulated, and after a few seasons it seemed to get more waterlogged, but it worked very well. Dean's go-to is the RAB Neo Guide jacket, which is very water resistant on the outside and sweat wicking on the inside (with pit zips too, of course), which keeps us drier on the trail. My two current favorites are the Helly Hensen Odin Mountain Infinity 3L Shell Jacket, which features their new Lifa Infinity Pro material—like Gore-Tex but has no chemicals and never needs reproofing—(the 9 World's Infinity Shell Jacket is also excellent), and the STIO Credential Jacket, which is extra-long in the back, perfect for deep snow and a backpack.

Vest

I swear by my Norrøna's Polartec hooded vest. It wicks like crazy and has a fantastic hood. When I'm done with a climb, I relish putting it on under my jacket for just enough extra warmth and great wicking.

Other Layers

We also swear by the Patagonia R1 Hoody, which had a gridded fabric to wick away sweat. It's perfect to add over your wool layer and under your jacket when it's super cold. My only critique is that it will smell bad after a certain number of hikes.

For the Summit

When it's super windy and we break tree line, we usually add a Gore-Tex windbreaker like the Arc'teryx (a Canadian company) Severe Weather (SV) or All-Around Jacket (AR) over our other jacket for a full windbreak. The power of two wind layers is amazing. Even in minus 40°F temps, that is usually my system. If I get cold on the way down or the summit is extra cold, sometimes I add the Arc'teryx Light Atom

Hoody, one of the best jackets of all time. Instead of down, it uses Coreloft (which can get wet without losing its insulation) and is so comfortable, I have slept in it.

Backup Layers

If it's over zero degrees, I carry a North Face Summit Series down jacket for emergencies. If it is below zero, I carry my super amazing Feathered Friends Volant Down Jacket (the Khumbu is one level warmer if you run cold), which I would use in case of injury to stay warm. It is a full expedition-level down jacket that could save your life. It may not be flattering, but it is the warmest piece of clothing I own. And for winter camping, I always bring it.

Socks

Icebreaker or Smartwool wool socks, always. Darn Tough (Vermont company) too. No blisters, bombproof.

Winter Hiking Boots

I swear by the Salomon Toundra Pro boot. Very waterproof and comfortable and easy to use with crampons/snowshoes and microspikes. You want to look for a boot that is waterproof and has 400 or 600 grams of insulation built for hiking. We both always use winter Gore-Tex Outdoor Research (another great company for gear for real hikers) gaiters, which cover the tops of our boots up to our knees. They are indispensable to keeping your feet warmer and dryer (your legs too).

Goggles and Balaclavas

On some of the very exposed peaks, goggles are lifesavers. The cheap pair I bought at first fogged up the moment I breathed hard (which is pretty much every step in winter hiking). For hiking, you want a tinted goggle that has ventilation so it won't block your vision when you exhale going uphill. The Oakley skiing goggles I bought were more expensive, but they work a lot better. Seirus makes the best face masks and balaclavas. If it's below 10°F, I typically wear a face mask and switch out for the balaclava on the summit.

Mittens

I say "mittens" intentionally, not "gloves," as the biggest problem I have had in winter is losing feeling in my fingers, which is never a good thing. I use very light wool Icebreaker mitten liners under my water-resistant Outdoor Research Overmitts. (I have two pairs—insulated Meteor and non-insulated Baker.) My new technique has been to skip the wool liners, as my hands sweat a ton. I just use the "idiot straps," and the moment my hands start to sweat, I take them out and let the mittens dangle; when I get cold, I stick my hands back in. That way, I don't have to stop to change out my liners.

We do use handwarmers as backups, but keep in mind they are not 100 percent reliable. They often expire and don't work, so by all means bring them but activate them in the car (keep DRY in a pocket). They last a long time, but make sure you have extra mittens.

Backup Mittens

I like Outdoor Research flurry mittens, as they are small but quite warm. Norrøna also makes some great mittens.

Backup to My Backup Mittens

Outdoor Research Alti-mitts are a warm mitten inside an even warmer mitten. I always have these as my backup in winter. Hard to find a warmer mitten. Your hands are super important for survival, and even a few pairs of mittens don't add much weight—so don't skimp!

Hats

My saving grace (since I sweat a lot) has been a thin Icebreaker wool hat liner/beanie I wear so I don't over-sweat. When it's windy or very cold, I'll flip my hood on and off over the liner to keep my head protected. If I wear a heavier hat, I over-sweat and then my hair is soaked, which can lead to hypothermia. As always, once we are done with the major part of the ascent, I will put on a heavier layer—either a hat that pulls down over my ears or my Norrøna vest's hood over my wool liner—or, if it's especially cold, my balaclava over both the hood and the liner with my jacket hood for wind protection. That combo has kept me warm and toasty even with ridiculously low windchills.

Snowshoes

Don't posthole! Wear snowshoes instead of punching through the snow and ruining the trail. The key is the right snowshoes. For the Northeast technical hikes, there are mainly three choices: Tubbs Flex Alps, MSR Evo Ascent, or MSR Lightening Ascent snowshoes. That's because they all have very aggressive front crampons for grip, curved side rails to prevent backward slipping, and the best invention since sliced bread, televators, which you can flip up under your heel to lessen the incline of a hill and take some of the tension off your calf muscles. I can't tell you how much I love my ascenders for long/steep ascents. They also help with grip; the snowshoe crampons have a much better angle to bite into the snow. For years I used the Tubbs Flex Alps, but after I broke my last pair, I ordered the MSR Lightening Ascents with the new paragon binding and I love them. They are slightly lighter than the Tubbs and are now my go-to.

Mandatory Pack Items

Dean always repeats the advice he heard from an old friend: "Better to have and not need than need and not have." Our packs consist of things I have never used and may never use, and I'm okay with that. If I can't carry the equipment on a hike that I feel will keep me alive (and with all fingers and toes intact) if something goes wrong, then maybe I should go on shorter hikes or pick a different sport altogether. Each hike is a bit different, and the amount we carry depends on several factors: time of year, length of the hike, number of people on the hike, weather conditions during the hike, remoteness, and terrain (above tree line for hours or not).

There are certain items that, between the two of us, we always have.

All Seasons:
- Two headlamps (with spare batteries)
- Waterproof jacket
- Compass
- Map of the area we are hiking (Hard copy! Don't rely on your phone—batteries die!)
- GPS unit (mostly for track logs to download later into mapping software to see where we have been)
- Ways to make fire (waterproof matches, flint and steel, lighter, tinder, tealight candles)
- First-aid kit consisting of:
  - SAM splint
  - Band-Aids
  - Whistle
  - Moleskin
  - Waterproof tape
  - Ace bandages (3)
  - Triangle bandages (4)
  - Aspirin
- Multi-tool
- Change of socks
- Thermal bivy sack
- Watch

Extra for Winter Only:
- Foam pad (to sit on in case of injury)
- Extra-long underwear top
- Extra pair of wool socks

- SPOT device or my ACR/SAR emergency personal locater beacon
- Thermos with hot bouillon
- Chemical hand warmers
- Outdoor Research Alti-mitts and a few extra mittens
- Facemask and/or balaclava
- Feathered Friends down parka

Hike Index

THE TEN ESSENTIALS OF HIKING

American
Hiking
Society

American Hiking Society recommends you pack the "Ten Essentials" every time you head out for a hike. Whether you plan to be gone for a couple of hours or several months, make sure to pack these items. Become familiar with these items and know how to use them.

1. Appropriate Footwear
Happy feet make for pleasant hiking. Think about traction, support, and protection when selecting well-fitting shoes or boots.

2. Navigation
While phones and GPS units are handy, they aren't always reliable in the backcountry; consider carrying a paper map and compass as a backup and know how to use them.

3. Water (and a way to purify it)
As a guideline, plan for half a liter of water per hour in moderate temperatures/terrain. Carry enough water for your trip and know where and how to treat water while you're out on the trail.

4. Food
Pack calorie-dense foods to help fuel your hike, and carry an extra portion in case you are out longer than expected.

5. Rain Gear & Dry-Fast Layers
The weatherman is not always right. Dress in layers to adjust to changing weather and activity levels. Wear moisture-wicking cloths and carry a warm hat.

6. Safety Items (light, fire, and a whistle)
Have means to start an emergency fire, signal for help, and see the trail and your map in the dark.

7. First Aid Kit

Supplies to treat illness or injury are only as helpful as your knowledge of how to use them. Take a class to gain the skills needed to administer first aid and CPR.

8. Knife or Multi-Tool

With countless uses, a multi-tool can help with gear repair and first aid.

9. Sun Protection

Sunscreen, sunglasses, and sun-protective clothing should be used in every season regardless of temperature or cloud cover.

10. Shelter

Protection from the elements in the event you are injured or stranded is necessary. A lightweight, inexpensive space blanket is a great option.

Find other helpful resources at AmericanHiking.org/hiking-resources